A God in the House

THE TUPELO PRESS LINEAGE SERIES

Kazim Ali,
     Fasting for Ramadan: Notes from a Spiritual Practice

Paisley Rekdal,
     Intimate: An American Family Photo Album

Ilya Kaminsky and Katherine Towler, editors,
     A God in the House: Poets Talk About Faith

A GOD in
the HOUSE

poets talk about faith

Edited by
Ilya Kaminsky
Katherine Towler

TUPELO PRESS

North Adams, Massachusetts

Library of Congress Cataloging-in-Publication Data
A God in the house : poets talk about faith / Ilya Kaminsky and
Katherine Towler, editors. — 1 st ed.
        p. cm. — (The Tupelo Press lineage series)
    ISBN 978-1-932195-19-4 (pbk. : alk. paper) — ISBN 978-1-932195-
30-9 (hardcover : alk. paper)
1. Religion and literature. 2. Reliion in literature. 3. Poets. I.
Kaminsky, Ilya, 1977– II. Towler, Katherine, 1956–
    PN1077.G63 2012
    811'.609382 — dc23
                    2011048206

Cover and text designed by Ann Aspell.
Cover photograph: "A Lone Chair" by Lowell Snowdon Klock
(http://klockworksphotography.com/). Used with permission of the artist.

First edition: March 2012.

Tupelo Press
P.O. Box 1767
243 Union Street, Eclipse Mill, Loft 305
North Adams, Massachusetts 01247
Telephone: (413) 664–9611 / Fax: (413) 664–9711
editor@tupelopress.org / www.tupelopress.org

Tupelo Press is an award-winning independent literary press that publishes fine fiction, nonfiction,
and poetry in books that are a joy to hold as well as read. Tupelo Press is a registered 501(c)3 non-
profit organization, and we rely on public support to carry out our mission of publishing extraordinary work that may be outside the realm of large commercial publishers. Financial donations are
welcome and are tax deductible.

 Supported in part by an award from the National Endowment for the Arts

For Katie Farris,

I haven't lived, died, not enough,
to scratch this ecstasy into vowels

—I.K.

In Memory of David Hadas,

who taught me to embrace
conversations about God

—K.T.

CONTENTS

Introduction: *Ilya Kaminsky and Katherine Towler*   ix
Editors' Note   xii

Infinite Obligation to the Other: *Carolyn Forché*   2

The Devotion of a Mourner: *Gerald Stern*   20

Doubt and Seeking: *Kazim Ali*   32

The Circular Path: *Jane Hirshfield*   46

What Remains Unseen: *Jean Valentine*   66

The Possibility of God: *Jericho Brown*   80

Inches of Progress: *Grace Paley*   94

Footsteps Over Ground: *Fanny Howe*   106

The Subject Is Silence: *Li-Young Lee*   120

God the Mother: *Alicia Ostriker*   134

To Be of Service: *Marilyn Nelson*   150

Incantation: *Annie Finch*   164

Not a Butler to the Soul: *G. C. Waldrep*   180

Beyond Time and Place: *Joy Harjo*   202

Natives of the Earth: *Eleanor Wilner*   214

A Convert's Story: *Julius Lester*   228

Nimble Believing: *Christian Wiman*   242

Homelands: *Dunya Mikhail*   256

The Given: *Gregory Orr*   272

Acknowledgments   289

Less and Less Human, O Savage Spirit

If there must be a god in the house, must be,
Saying things in the room and on the stair,

Let him move as the sunlight moves on the floor,
Or moonlight, silently, as Plato's ghost

Or Aristotle's skeleton. Let him hang out
His stars on the wall. He must dwell quietly.

He must be incapable of speaking, closed,
As those are: as light, for all its motion, is;

As color, even the closest to us, is;
As shapes, though they portend us, are.

It is the human that is the alien,
The human that has no cousin in the moon.

It is the human that demands his speech
From beasts or from the incommunicable mass.

If there must be a god in the house, let him be one
That will not hear us when we speak: a coolness,

A vermilioned nothingness, any stick of the mass
Of which we are too distantly a part.

— *Wallace Stevens*

INTRODUCTION

This book had its beginning over lunch in New Hampshire, where we came together as fellow writers, one a Russian Jewish poet in his early twenties, the other an American novelist and daughter of an Episcopal priest in her early forties. To our surprise, we talked about God that day. This wasn't the sort of exchange we were used to having with other writers. We touched on belief, and time spent in the church and the synagogue, and experiences not easy to articulate or even identify. This book is the result of our desire to extend our conversation to other writers. We conducted these interviews seeking kindred souls who were willing to chart the landscapes of belief in the context of their lives as writers.

Gerald Stern observes, in the interview included in these pages, "Poets — maybe all artists — get away from their own religious upbringing in order to *arrive* at a condition of faith." The condition of faith, one could argue, is essential to any artistic endeavor. What emerges most strikingly from this collection is the attempt by these writers to locate meaning in their lives, an attempt that, though a number of them might not make such a claim, may reflect their arrival at this place.

Questions about one's spiritual life are inherently difficult to answer. Our conversations with the poets gathered here often felt like a joint effort to grab hold of the eels Li-Young Lee so vividly recalls in his account of his childhood. The political climate in the United States and the influence of religious fundamentalism in the politics of this country, and elsewhere, further complicate the conversation. In America in the twenty-first century, irony holds sway over much of our public intellectual life, and a dialogue about faith asks us to set aside irony for a direct engagement with beauty, hope, doubt, and fear. We hope this book will help to chart new directions for discussions of faith outside of the polarized, and polarizing, influences of ideological religious politics.

The poets we spoke with took on this difficult topic with remarkable frankness and honesty. Some writers are included in this volume because their poems touch directly on belief, and others because we simply admired their work. Some, the late Grace Paley among them, had to be persuaded that they had anything to say on the subject. They may locate a larger meaning in God, or in the cows grazing at the side of the road; they may be comfortable defining themselves as Buddhist or Muslim, or may shrug off definitions of any kind. They come together in their interest in exploring what sustains us most, as human beings and as writers.

Some speak of religion as a way of making a communal, cultural, and personal journey. Others find themselves in awe not before a Creator, but rather before creation itself, so the maker is in the made. Many in this book have drifted away from the idea of speaking to God ritually, though not all: Kazim Ali speaks about fasting during Ramadan; G. C. Waldrep discusses his choice to live in an Amish community; and Joy Harjo addresses the daily practice of making a ritual observance to the sun. In the end, what poetry and faith share, perhaps more than anything else, is a sense of awe. In awe is the beginning of a life of wonder. Or, as the poet Jack Spicer put it, in an American idiom: "Poets think they are pitchers, when they are really catchers."

Decades ago, in Zurich, the poets Paul Celan and Nelly Sachs met. We don't know the details of their conversation, but on his return to Paris, Celan wrote these lines:

Of your God was our talk, I spoke
against him, I
let the heart that I had
hope:
for his highest, death-rattled, his
quarrelling word —
Your eye looked on, looked away,
your mouth
spoke its way to the eye, and I heard:
We don't know, you know,
we
don't know, do we?,
what counts.

"We . . . / don't know, do we?, / what counts." In the end, however personal our encounters with mystery may be, we measure them by what we hear from others, who care enough to share their own experiences. For that generosity of spirit, we are grateful.

— Ilya Kaminsky and Katherine Towler

EDITORS' NOTE

The interviews collected in this book were conducted in person or through written correspondence. Our meetings with writers took us from a hilltop in Vermont to the lobby of a Cleveland hotel to a house in California not far from the Pacific Ocean. For the purposes of this volume, we have removed the question and answer format to allow the continuity of less formal responses in a single voice for each chapter. These pieces are meant to be conversational — intuitive, candid, exploratory — rather than crafted essays. They represent a true collaboration, as the writers entertained our questions, in some cases over a period of months, and then reviewed the edited text.

A God in the House

CAROLYN FORCHÉ'S writings combine poetry, documentary reportage, and human rights advocacy. Her work has taken her to conflict zones around the world, including El Salvador during the 1980s, South Africa in the last days of the apartheid regime, and Lebanon under siege. Her first book, Gathering the Tribes, *won the Yale Younger Poets Award.* The Country Between Us *received the Poetry Society of America's Alice Fay di Castagnola Award and was chosen as the Lamont Selection of the Academy of American Poets. Her third collection of poetry,* The Angel of History, *received the Los Angeles Times Book Prize, and her fourth,* Blue Hour, *was a finalist for the National Book Critics Circle Award. She has translated* Flowers from the Volcano *and* Sorrow *by Claribel Alegria, and has co-translated* The Selected Poems of Robert Desnos *(with William Kulik), and Mahmoud Darwish's* Unfortunately, It Was Paradise *(with Munir Akash, Sinan Antoon, and Amira El-Zein). Forché is also the editor of* Against Forgetting: Twentieth Century Poetry of Witness. *In 1998, she was presented the Edita and Ira Morris Hiroshima Foundation Award for Peace and Culture for her work on behalf of human rights and the preservation of memory and culture. She teaches writing and literature at Georgetown University. We interviewed her at her home in Bethesda, Maryland.*

Carolyn Forché

Infinite Obligation to the Other

The world is at once fallen and holy, both at the same time.

As a child, I lived the liturgical year. It was not November, it was Advent. It was not spring, it was Lent, which began with Ash Wednesday. Of course I understand now that these were all taken from different rituals from time immemorial. That was my childhood. It was special and enclosed, and quite sheltered. The area where we lived outside Detroit was largely Catholic and everyone belonged to the same parish.

I am the eldest of seven children. My father is a retired tool and die maker. My mother wrote poetry and painted before she was married, but when she proceeded to have her family, she mostly gave up those things. I was enrolled as of first grade in Our Lady of Sorrows and attended there for twelve years. I was taught by the Sisters of Saint Dominic, Order of Preachers. They were very strict, and brutal, and interesting. My mother would read Teresa de Avila's confessions aloud to us over the breakfast table, so we had these visions of cesspools with snakes crawling through them in hell and so on. I walked to school, a mile there and back, and on those walks I felt that I was somehow directly communicating with God. I did not have a sense when I was a little girl that this was not possible or that it was even difficult. It seemed absolutely immediate and wondrous, and I craved to be alone on those walks, which wasn't difficult because I would fall back behind the others.

My grandmother spoke Slovak, Czech, and Hungarian, and English

3

poorly but passably. She was a very strong influence in my childhood. In the church there was the presence of the Latin language, which I had to learn because I was immersed in it. At home there was the presence of Slovak between my father and his mother, which was the secret language in which they communicated, though my mother was Irish. Of course a language that's used for certain purposes in the household becomes intriguing and mysterious. I believe that I did learn to understand it because much later in my life when I went to what was then Czechoslovakia, I could understand a great deal more of Czech and Slovak than I was prepared to understand. The people in Detroit from Polish and Slavic backgrounds call this "kitchen Polish" or "kitchen Slovak," the kind of Polish or Slovak or Czech that one learns at the side of the grandmother baking bread. My grandmother would reprimand us in Slovak.

My grandmother was enchanting and powerful. I went out with her every night when she would make a fire at the end of our property to burn the garbage, the refuse of the day. But it wasn't so as to dispose of this material, it was so she could talk to me and poke at the fire and send these wonderful sparks up into the heavens. She was a devout Catholic, and somewhat influenced by the mysticism of the Eastern church.

•

My years at Our Lady of Sorrows inculcated in me a certain ethos and a certain awareness of the presence of God, an awareness of the light and the presence of God in everything, but I was also terrified by a peculiar brand of pre–Vatican II cosmology. We read Dante not as a great work of literature, but as a portrait of what lay in store for us, *The Inferno* particularly, if we failed in our mission to become saints or, even better, martyrs. Of course I rebelled.

In the twelfth grade, I began reading Protestant theologians. I was interested in Paul Tillich and Hans Kung, and I began to question the foundations of my holy Roman Catholic faith. A priest came to teach us that year who was a brilliant Jesuit. He didn't punish me for reading these theologians who lacked the imprimatur of the church; he encouraged me. When I began to challenge and work through the ontological proof and the first cause itself, he was somewhat bemused, but took me seriously. We had long discussions about my ideas. Then I stopped going to Mass. This was beyond heretical in my school, it was sacrilegious. I was a bit of an outcast. Mind you, I missed Mass, I missed the Eucharist. But I felt that until I had a pure faith restored, the purity of belief, I would not be able to participate in good conscience, because I mis-identified what faith was. During the academic awards at the end of my senior year, the Jesuit priest had the temerity to bestow upon me the religion award. Hushed silence, gasps all over the auditorium — this fallen Catholic had been given the religion award. I was so furious with him, and he was just grinning and chomping on a cold, unlit cigar in the back of the auditorium. I asked him later, "What were you thinking?" He said, "The others weren't as interested in theological issues as you were."

I graduated from high school at a most inopportune moment — 1968 — and went to the largest state university I could find. I went from being part of a class of eighty-seven to being part of a student body of fifty thousand. It was the height of the fierce combat of the Vietnam war. That's another chapter.

My childhood was very different from what followed. I had left a hermetic world. It's not that I didn't pass through a period of questioning, and it's not that I was completely sealed off from other concerns, but I had grown up in an isolated way. I didn't have a social life when I was a child, beyond occasionally playing with dolls with my friends. I read a great deal, and I mostly helped my mother with housework and babies and child-rearing, cleaning and cooking. I didn't have a lot of time between school and that. When I went out into the world, I was thoroughly unprepared.

This is hard now to imagine, I suppose, but the community in which I was raised was like a village. I didn't know anyone who wasn't Catholic, except that I knew one Protestant girl, and that was amazing, and we were friends. I saw one Jewish girl once, walking down the road. I was fascinated, because they told me she was Jewish, and I thought, "I've never seen a Jewish person." I felt intrigue, awe, wonder. Someone from another planet was there — that's how sealed off we were. I see it both ways now, as positive and negative. It was magical to grow up in a world that was whole and that had a certainty about its cosmic position and mission. I don't want to disparage it or characterize it as overly confining. I might have done so when I was in the eleventh grade, but when I look back on it, I see its beauty and value. I would not, perhaps, have developed an intuitive inner life in quite the same way without having lived in that world.

•

I'm not a doctrinaire Catholic, though I do still attend Mass. These days, I am a syncretist, and I don't attempt to resolve contradictions between spheres of faith and belief. I consider all descriptions of divinity or the deity, descriptions in language, to be figurative, metaphorical in some way. The deity is known to the deity. We apprehend God or *en sof* (the infinite, in Cabalistic belief) or Raman in the way that we can. I believe that the divinity is in all things and that it is possible to know God from within. I believe that God, *en sof,* is everywhere, so the holy is everywhere. For me, holiness used to mean that which resides in the exemplary being of Christ or the exemplary beings of the apostles or martyrs. I now have suffered an intense dispersal of this concept, and the world is at once fallen and holy, both at the same time — the world of matter, the world that is manifest around us. So everything is utterly different from what I might have said when I was a young girl, and yet in another way, it isn't.

The immediacy of God was lost when I left childhood. For some years, I really mourned this loss. It's difficult to characterize one's spiritual experience, but I used to have an unquestioned sense of the continuity of presence. After years of spiritual wandering among faiths, and perhaps due to my inconstancy as a practitioner, this sense of presence is elusive.

There is a difference, I hope, between syncretism and dilettantism. I would just play around; I would splash and play in the fields of spiritual thought — read the Zen sutras, and then jump off a cliff into the arms of something about the Dharma, and then go back to reading the Bible, and then have a certain dalliance with Judaic thought. I was always enchanted. I was always in awe of these texts. If I did this as a practice of *lectio divina,* I could experience these different fruits of human experience of God, without feeling there was a contradiction between them. We all get to be many people, because everything is very protean. Spiritual life is protean, too. That's why you can't ever really feel accomplished spiritually, because in a second, you know — you're not. Everything is changing so rapidly.

•

I wrote all the time, from the time I was nine years old. When I was a girl, I felt intensely the suffering in the world. I had nightmares, from a very young age, about horrendous things happening to masses of people, visions in my sleep that amounted to night terrors. My parents were not only worried about them, they were exhausted by them. These dreams had material in them that I had not been exposed to. We did not have a television set. Nobody understood their source. I still can see some of the pictures that would recur in these dreams. I felt in this presence of God that I was supposed to do something, and that I was going to have to go through many things to prepare for whatever it was, and that life was going to be really hard. All of that was all right because (in the dreams) I was in a universe that was something like a school, like Our Lady of Sorrows, only larger. We had to go through these phases of spiritual learning and then what we were supposed to do would be revealed to us. I had no idea what this was. I did know that I had to say yes to everything. Now, saying yes to everything doesn't mean saying yes to sin. I mean, when something presented itself, I would say yes, whether I was afraid or not. God is completely the uncertain. There's no clinging to God for me; it's more a matter of cleaving to God, being with, saying yes to.

There are many ways in which one can say yes. When Leonel Gomez Vides (the cousin of Claribel Alegria, a poet whose work I had translated) visited me and presented me with the possibility of going to El Salvador, there was no war in El Salvador, or none that anyone was aware of. The misery and poverty and oppression that were going to give rise to that eruption had already begun, but it was invisible, or not visible unless one was living it. When he presented the possibility, I had a crisis of conscience. My friends all said, "You have a Guggenheim, you should go to Paris and write poetry, or at least go to New England." I remember praying a great deal: "Why El Salvador?"

I had mentioned to Leonel that I had always wanted to go into the Peace Corps. He said, "Well, this is your opportunity. I have a reverse Peace Corps. I bring Americans to learn things in the third world. I'm not asking you to help me. I'm going to help you." He said, if I wanted I could work in a rural health clinic, or with the social worker in the capitol. He wanted me to learn as much as possible about the country because he believed that when the war came, American public opinion would be germane to the outcome, and also crucially important to any foreign policy decisions the American government would be making. He had the same misconceptions I had at the time — partly a misconception — that there was a relationship between American public opinion and foreign policy decisions. I now believe that when American public opinion reaches a certain critical mass, that's true, but not until then. I believed then, falsely, that the United States wouldn't engage in any kind of interventionary conflict so soon after the collapse of the American war in Indochina.

I knew that a door was being held ajar for me, and that if I didn't walk through it, if I didn't accept this invitation, I could never tell myself again that I would have liked to have gone into the Peace Corps, or that I was willing to do anything for God, or that I was willing to work with the poor, or that I was willing to put myself at risk. I realized that I would never be able to say those things again because I had been given the chance and said no. That is the only reason I went to El Salvador. I was really afraid to go, and none of my friends approved, and certainly my family did not approve.

When I got to El Salvador, the people I became closest to were people who were quite vulnerable at the time. They were vulnerable because in the early days of oppression it was the church, the priests and the nuns, who had organized the base Christian communities and who were therefore most at risk. Everyone I came in contact with was involved with the popular church, or doing social work or medicine or teaching in adjacent communities, or in the beginning of the nascent human rights movement, people who were attempting to document the atrocities and so on. Very early I discovered these priests and nuns, and also Monsignor Oscar Romero, who was isolated as a bishop.

Monsignor Romero had already had his experience with the death of his friend, the Jesuit Father Grande, and he had already suspended construction of the cathedral and given the money to the poor, and he had already begun the process of rapprochement with the so-called radical priests, who were disseminating the theology of liberation. Suddenly I found myself in the first politically active Catholic community I had ever experienced, among a congregation that was actually living its faith in absolute terms. They were willing to die for each other; they were willing to sacrifice anything, to go through arduous deprivations. And they were filled with humor and delight and joy. I had never been surrounded by people like this before. They knew that I hadn't gone to Mass in quite a few years, much less confession. I went to the cathedral, and I didn't want Monsignor Romero to give me communion because I hadn't cleared things up. He insisted. He knew that I was hesitant, because of my failures, in terms of what I still conceptualized as what was required for sacramental participation.

The wonderful experiences I had in El Salvador transformed my thinking and my spiritual life. The time there returned me to something, but without the encumbrance of certain institutional aspects of the church that have to do with its earthly manifestation as an institution. It was very freeing. I didn't want to leave, but not because I wasn't afraid. Whenever I came close to being wounded or hurt or killed in El Salvador, and there were a few occasions, I was terrified. I would immediately be nauseated. I was not good at this. Other people were much better at it. But I didn't want to leave, nevertheless, because I didn't want to leave this community. I had recovered the presence of God, only this time it was in humanity. I was in El Salvador, living in a place very full of horror, but also full of light. That's where I wanted to stay.

•

My first trip to El Salvador was made in January of 1978. At that time, Congressman John Drinan of Massachusetts, who also happened to have been a Catholic priest and a Jesuit, led the first human rights delegation to El Salvador. I had arrived two days earlier, and the man who invited me said that he would like me to follow Drinan and his human rights investigation. My first introduction to the country came through interviews with the peasants of Aguileras who had been attacked and were being "disappeared." It was quite startling. I would go home for a few weeks and then go back to El Salvador. I would carry things back and forth, such as documents and medicine. I had huge ambitions for what one individual person could be capable of doing.

Monsignor Romero had a human rights office of his own. All of my work was volunteer work, ad hoc and as things came up. I was one of many women who worked with him, almost all of whom were on death lists. He knew that he was at risk. At the very end, in March of 1980, I was very close to Monsignor Romero. This was the month when he was assassinated.

I was totally absorbed in this work and completely spiritually connected to the people I was with. When I finally had to leave the country — and I didn't return for a decade — I was told to go to the United States and to speak as much as I could, to make known what was happening in El Salvador. The problem, of course, was that I was not a journalist; I wasn't anything. I didn't know how to fulfill this task, which, because Monsignor Romero had asked me to do it, I felt was a spiritual obligation. And I was going to fail utterly and horribly. I was trying to write journalism. I published some pieces in *The Nation*, and they were dry and horrible and overly detailed, not at all what Americans needed to know. They were filled with arcane facts about the interior structure of the Salvadorian military. It was ridiculous. I was not a good journalist, but I had been writing poems.

In El Salvador, I needed my poetry. I wasn't thinking about publishing a book at the time I was writing these poems. These were just for me. They were to get things out that I needed to have on paper. I had forgotten, sort of, about being a poet. I thought I wanted now to be working in human rights full time. I also didn't tell people there that I was a poet. But when I returned to the United States, I sent the poems I had been writing in El Salvador to a literary publisher, and he said, "I don't think they're for us." And I said, "Why? You always said you wanted to publish my poems." He said, "It's not that they're passionate — they are, but that's all right. It's not that they're intense — they are, but there's nothing wrong with that, either. It's that, well, they're political." I said, "What do you mean?" He said, "El Salvador, this war, these are political poems. Are you sure you want to do this? To publish these political poems?" I said, "But I don't promote any particular political point of view." He said, "Maybe you should write another kind of poem, a shorter poem about something quieter, and then you could intersperse these, to give tonal modulation to the work." I actually attempted to do this, and I completely failed. So I put the manuscript away and continued to make a stab at being a journalist and writing to congressmen and being active with groups here that were beginning to construct an anti-intervention network and a sanctuary movement. I went back to teaching. I felt very displaced.

When the book of poems, *The Country Between Us*, was finally published, I had a way to fulfill my obligation and my promise to Monsignor Romero. I was in front of Americans, speaking. When I was worried about whether I would say the right things or remember the right incidents, I would always ask him. I felt Monsignor Romero with me a lot. I still feel the presence of those who are gone, especially Monsignor Romero. I had his help, and that's how I was able to fulfill that obligation. I didn't think poetry could do this. Suddenly there it was — it was because I was a poet that I was able to speak.

•

Over the years, I read the great Western poets of the twentieth century, Paul Celan and Anna Akhmatova and Edmond Jabès, who were known here as political poets, but they were also, as a matter of fact, spiritual poets. I came to realize that spirituality is as misunderstood as poetry in our culture. It goes unrecognized. It's safer to relegate these poets to the political sphere.

As dangerous as the political is, the spiritual is far more dangerous. These poets don't easily extricate morality, ethics, the sacred, and the political. For them, it's not possible to think of these as isolated categories, but rather as modes of human contemplation and action which are inextricably bound to one another. One of the difficulties with this whole argument about poetry and politics is the notion of isolating the political from the ethical and the aesthetic.

Poetry can pass through history, but poetry is not dependent on history. When I'm thinking about the spiritual, I'm thinking about a capacity to be awake, a consciousness. In the United States, they're always saying that poets write about the self. The self has a deep inwardness. The self is also that which knows God.

But I don't think that many poets write about the self. In contemporary American poetry, what we often encounter is not the self but personality, which is a very different matter. I don't distinguish between that which achieves its compassion because certain injustices have been perpetrated by political or economic structures. Compassion is deeply spiritual, regardless of its source.

Franz Rosenzweig and his book *The Star of Redemption* have been a significant influence for me. It's a very interesting, monumental work that has influenced many thinkers. This is Rosenzweig's concept of self, which I find beautiful:

> The self is what is condemned to silence in man, and yet it is everywhere and at once understood. It can only be rendered visible acted out, in order to awaken the self in every other man as well.

So it's a kind of mysterious awakening of the self that would be the true writing of the soul. But what we're getting is an enacted dramatization of personality and autobiographical material in a lot of the work that's being published today.

In a sense, if poets truly write about the self, their work becomes spiritual poetry, because then that deep essence of selfhood, the inwardness, the light, can be recognized by anyone as his or her own. What is within us is awakened and given voice in the kind of work that is truly about the self. If we're talking about the personality, or a kind of skewed view of autobiographical experience, that's a very different matter. In the Salvador period, the positive side was that I got to speak, and certain people were able to do work, and we were able to help each other. The negative side was the cult of personality. I became imprisoned in the perception of the audience. When I would speak in front of an audience, there was a kind of disempowerment going on. People would think, "I just have my little life." They would feel that they couldn't do anything, or that what they were living was unimportant. In order to get out of that, I had to stop being a public poet for a while, which is one of the other reasons why there were thirteen years between my second and third books. I was writing, and I was putting everything away in boxes. I was trying once again to escape a public role — I was trying deliberately to quiet that. Also I had to do a spiritual practice, a discipline. I had to do battle with myself.

•

In the summer of 1983 I accompanied Congressman Thomas Harkin from Iowa — he's now a Senator — in a delegation to Israel and the West Bank. My role was to write a report on human rights in Israel, particularly in the occupied territories. When I returned from that, I met my husband, Harry. He was working for *Time* magazine and was assigned to Lebanon. He was gone for several months, and after he came back to New York for a break, I returned to Lebanon with him. I went under the auspices of National Public Radio. I was in Beirut during the war. I was unable to write. We were under shell fire that winter and also sniper fire. It was very intense. It was a more conventional war than El Salvador, which when I was there was a guerrilla war and a war against a civilian population. But Beirut was another matter. I think something happened to me there that happens to people in war zones. I kept notebooks and I had a lot of notes, but I didn't have anything that was very coherent. Interestingly enough, I kept a journal but I was working on a kind of paper that didn't hold up, and it faded. I can barely read much of it now. I'm going to try to transcribe it while I can still see it at all. I left with the Sixth Fleet in the spring of 1984 and wound up back in the United States.

A few months later, I was married and became pregnant. When I was five months pregnant, we left for South Africa. It was the last days of the apartheid regime, as it turned out. There I made contact with church people again, this time Methodists. I worked in Soweto for the Parents of the Detainees, which was an organization of parents who were trying to raise global awareness about the plight of their children. There were about 1,600 children between the ages of eleven and fourteen who were being held in detention without charges. We were trying to get them released and to get the charges clarified. They had mostly been rounded up in alternative schools that had been declared illegal by the apartheid government. Again, I was writing only notes, nothing very coherent. In 1985, we were expelled from South Africa. That's the only nice way to put it — deported, evicted, sent away. I wound up in Paris, where my son was born, during the summer of the Paris bombings.

Motherhood was a very important experience for me — it still is. It has transformed my life. That's what holiness is: my son. But I was also depressed. I needed to come to terms with what it meant to write out of extremity. When my son was two years old, a friend of mine who is a poet said, "You have to write. I'll take Sean for two hours every day. I want to see the pages when I come back." He gave me the gift of being able to devote myself to sustained work again. That's when I began the book *Angel of History*. I had been reading Walter Benjamin. I was also interested in the Kabala and early Gnosticism and Mahayana Buddhism, because all of these had their birth in the Axial Age. I was able to work with all of these elements in *Angel of History*.

•

The thing about writing poetry is that the more you're there working, the more you're there writing, the more you realize you are not writing it. The little threads and weavings that come into the poem — one is not consciously aware of these things, because something larger is working in you. This is an experience close to revelation, to the realm of prophetic language.

I'm interested in Martin Buber's concept of the encounter between the "I" and the "Thou," which is not an objectified encounter between self and other. There's no distancing. There's a wakening to consciousness simultaneously, a recognition. With that recognition comes an awareness of one's infinite and inexhaustible obligation to the other. This, for me, is the realm of the sacred. It makes the concept of the distance between self and other that has given rise to relativism in ethics quite beside the point. I thought through this with Buber's help and later through reading Emanuel Levinas, a Jewish philosopher who lived and worked until his recent death in France. He extends the work of Buber. Buber addresses the encounter between the I and the Thou, which does not objectify the other or render it part of an experience to be acquired or to be known — an object of knowledge — but rather that which cannot be known and yet remains entirely available in the face of the other. From this, Emanuel Levinas creates a realm of infinite obligation and ethos. The law becomes derived from this ethics, rather than ethics from the law. I have found Levinas most helpful in resolving some of the difficulties of relativism in the twentieth century.

Here's what Levinas says: "Artistic activity makes the artist aware that he is not the author of his works." Literature is an event, not an expression of thought nor a representation of the world. The literature of witness is non-representational evidence of what has been endured. In other words, it's not trying to recreate what happened, it *is* what happened. It is language that has been impressed in some way by the events. I don't believe that language expresses spiritual wisdom; I believe that language embodies spiritual wisdom. I don't view thought as being so much expressed as being made possible by language. So that is the realm in which language becomes sacred, becomes sacred as a means of apprehension.

At the end of my poem "The Visitor," there is the line "There is nothing one man will not do to another." It's a truth that I recognized in great pain and horror, but once you know this truth, it's possible to also know that there is nothing one man will not give another, too. We are beings in process, in a deep spiritual process that we recognize and intuit and do not understand at all. It gives me great hope and great faith that it's possible to understand this in a single human lifetime. If we live long enough, if we are given enough time on earth, we can live to see the spiritual potential of human beings.

What else do we need? We're in an incredible adventure here with God.

THE GARDEN SHUKKEI-EN

By way of a vanished bridge we cross this river
as a cloud of lifted snow would ascend a mountain.

She has always been afraid to come here.

It is the river she most
remembers, the living
and the dead both crying for help.

A world that allowed neither tears nor lamentation.

The matsu trees brush her hair as she passes
beneath them, as do the shining strands of barbed wire.

Where this lake is, there was a lake,
where these black pine grow, there grew black pine.

Where there is no teahouse I see a wooden teahouse
and the corpses of those who slept in it.

On the opposite bank of the Ota, a weeping willow
etches its memory of their faces into the water.

Where light touches the face, the character for heart is written.

She strokes a burnt trunk wrapped in straw:
I was weak and my skin hung from my fingertips like cloth

Do you think for a moment we were human beings to them?

She comes to the stone angel holding paper cranes.
Not an angel, but a woman where she once had been,
who walks through the garden Shukkei-en
calling the carp to the surface by clapping her hands.

Do Americans think of us?

So she began as we squatted over the toilets:
If you want, I'll tell you, but nothing I say will be enough.

We tried to dress our burns with vegetable oil.

Her hair is the white froth of rice rising up kettlesides, her mind also.
In the postwar years she thought deeply about how to live.

The common greeting *dozo-yiroshku* is please take care of me.
All hibakusha still alive were children then.

A cemetery seen from the air is a child's city.

I don't like this particular red flower because
it reminds me of a woman's brain crushed under a roof.

Perhaps my language is too precise, and therefore too difficult to understand?

We have not, all these years, felt what you call happiness.
But at times, with good fortune, we experience something close.
As our life resembles life, and this garden the garden.
And in the silence surrounding what happened to us

it is the bell to awaken God that we've heard ringing.

— Carolyn Forché

GERALD STERN is the author of fifteen volumes of poetry, including most recently Early Collected Poems: 1965–1992; Save the Last Dance; Everything Is Burning; American Sonnets; *and* Last Blue. *His recently published memoir is* What I Can't Bear Losing. *He was awarded the National Book Award in 1998 for* This Time: New and Selected Poems. *His other honors include the* Paris Review's *Bernard F. Conners Prize, the Bess Hokin Award from* Poetry Magazine, *the Ruth Lilly Poetry Prize, four National Endowment for the Arts grants, the Pennsylvania Governor's Award for Excellence in the Arts, the Jerome J. Shestack Poetry Prize from* American Poetry Review, *and fellowships from the Academy of American Poets, the Guggenheim Foundation, and the Pennsylvania Council on the Arts. In 2005, Stern was selected to receive the Wallace Stevens Award for mastery in the art of poetry, and in 2006 he was elected a Chancellor of the Academy of American Poets. Stern taught at the University of Iowa Writers' Workshop for many years. He lives in Lambertville, New Jersey, and now teaches in the M.F.A. program in poetry at Drew University. We corresponded with Stern, engaging in a lively dialogue about his Jewish heritage and the idiosyncratic nature of his faith.*

Gerald Stern

The Devotion of a Mourner

*Mine was not faith in anything divine unless the salvation
of oppressed peoples can be called divine.*

I am attracted to the prophets Amos, Ezekiel, Isaiah, and
Hosea, among others. I must say that although they were interested in
justice, as I am, and even kindness, their purposes were the worship of
God; they believed that one strayed from justice when he or she was
not godly. Whatever I mean by justice, I think it has little to do with
the existence of God or its worship. Thus my alliance with the prophets
is only a kind of temporary friendship. We leave each other when they
put on the phylacteries and start waving their index fingers, when they
start pushing people back into the fold. I am not the least interested in
this. Yet, when I reduce their vision to its poetry, I am at home.

Poets — maybe all artists — get away from their own religious upbringing in order to *arrive* at a condition of faith. Certainly this is true
in my life. My religious upbringing was lukewarm — in a traditional
assimilative manner of first-generation American Jewish poets whose
parents wanted to become totally "American." I *was* bar mitzvahed, and
I wrapped the tape around my arm and chest for a day or two, and that
was that. If anything, I became a Jew later. What I knew about Judaism I knew from the inside when I was young. It was purely cultural or
cultural/religious from an East European quasi-Orthodox point of view.
I was "learning" more about America then, though when I was beat up
for being a Jew, I was learning about both America and Judaism.

By saying "purely cultural" I am referring to foods, to their preparations, to the significance of the Sabbath, to a kind of general confusion and somewhat diffuse American Judaism. I remember my grandmother picking out her own fish at Benkowitz's fish market and supervising its killing; I remember her making cookies and root beer; I remember her feeding me the undeveloped shell-less yellow yolks imbedded inside the chicken; I remember the clean tablecloth on Friday and the candles. I remember packing the prayer shawl and the prayer book and the yarmulke in its own little bag before I left for *shul* on Saturday morning.

There was extreme suspicion and hatred among all the nationalities in Pittsburgh, where I grew up — Italian, Irish, Slovak, Polish, etc. But when it came to blacks and Jews, it was doubly extreme. In a song called "National Brotherhood Week," folk singer Tom Lehrer says:

Oh, the Protestants hate the Catholics,
And the Catholics hate the Protestants,
And the Hindus hate the Moslems,
And everybody hates the Jews.

The anti-Semitism was extreme on every level, in the universities, in industry, and on the streets. I was a kind of general who led the counterattacks.

Pittsburgh, because of its very physical nature, lends itself to the mythical in the way that, say, Philadelphia or Cincinnati does not. It had burning furnaces, rivers, hills; great tensions, and hatred; and almost epic wars between classes. My memory, I will admit, is obsessed with that city, but it's not love, or not love alone. Pittsburgh is "the mother." Because of its rivers, hills, and valleys, the ethnic groups were isolated from each other, and the European cultural habits, including even accents, remained. Yet because of these hills, there always remained open spaces that could not be built upon, and tunnels, woods, cliffs, and even isolated bodies of water. This made the place something of a mystery. In a city like Philadelphia or New York, you tend to go everywhere, but in Pittsburgh you were more or less confined to a very few places: your neighborhood, the downtown, and the libraries, universities, and other cultural centers.

I don't think that reality exists in memory alone, unless one is playing linguistic games about what memory itself is. Proust is a myth-creator — the events in his life are only a part of a myth that he creates. It is the myth itself, it seems to me, that, for him, is important. For me, reality is a stone wall, and the bumps on your head are real. My life is about the wall and the bumps on the head. It is dreamlike and perhaps, like Proust, devoid of present suffering, but the wet rag is truly there. Which reminds me that when I had a nose bleed as a young boy, my grandmother put a cold silver knife against my neck. This stopped the bleeding.

I come back to Pittsburgh again and again because Pittsburgh contains my first twenty years of memory. What I believe in, what I am angry about, and what I dream about is contained therein.

◆

The connection of faith with poetry is complicated and ambiguous. When I started writing poetry, at age nineteen or twenty, I was more interested in politics than I was in religion, though I was always suspicious of agitprop. I studied philosophy, economics, and politics in college, and when I got into poetry seriously I radically abandoned the political for the aesthetic. It was only later that I found a way to combine the two — aesthetics and politics — or to make one of the two. As far as faith is concerned, mine was not faith in anything divine unless the salvation of an oppressed people or oppressed peoples can be called divine.

I wrote my first poems when I was thirteen or fourteen years old. I remember sitting at a rickety secretary early morning on Mother's Day when I was maybe twelve and writing a poem to my mother as my gift to her. It was about — believe it or not — the silliness of Mother's Day, which caused her to burst into tears. In its own way, this had a great deal to do with faith. My poem was against hypocrisy, dull repetitiveness, and obedience. My faith was in expansion.

It seemed absolutely natural at that age to write poems. I did not know there was such a thing as a "poet." To be truthful, it wasn't until my second year of college that I suddenly realized writing poetry was a separate and special thing. It's when I discovered this that I became secret and "poetic." I wrote for years to entertain myself and my friends. There was no thought at the time of *being* a poet. Probably it was a total absence of any models in my life or in the city where I lived that confused and influenced me. It was as if I were originating a game called basketball but had maybe seen one game in my life. I had notebooks full of early poems, but I never thought of myself as a *poet*. I remember walking up a flight of stairs at college and suddenly realizing I was queer — that is, I was a poet.

I started to write poetry seriously at a much later age than most other poets. This has to do with my personal history, my stubbornness, and my ignorance. Because of my lifestyle, because of my training, or lack thereof, because of my compulsions, because of my false dreams, I didn't click in — with a few exceptions — until I was almost forty. I saw myself absolutely isolated, alone, making my own way according to my own rhythms. I am not necessarily proud of this. Out of my stubbornness I probably wasted a good decade. I saw myself, as I said in an essay I wrote called "Some Secrets," as just about to reach the critical age of forty and having nothing to give to the world, and realizing that there were generations after me and that I might be bypassed. This led to a little bit of depression, which helped cause a second birth or burst of the poetry that I started to write then and am still writing today.

From then on, it's been a straight ride downhill, or up, depending on whether you are talking about Parnassus or not. From that time, in 1965 or '66 until today, until tomorrow, I have never stopped being overwhelmed with five or ten poems waiting to be written. This may, in its way, be actually connected to the issue of faith.

I suspect that the actual writing, the continuous writing, the writing over and over again, the commitment, is a kind of devotion. Maybe it's not the devotion of a priest; it is certainly the devotion of a mourner.

•

I'm in complete agreement with Simone Weil's statement that "absolute unmixed attention is prayer." I am also in complete agreement with Paul Celan's similar statement that "attentiveness is the natural prayer of the human soul." Sometimes I feel that it is a question of concentration — really, I am shocked by interruption — but I feel that attentiveness is absolutely more than that, indeed other than that. I believe that my mind, my heart, my very soul, in its attention to language, ideas, and form, is in that state that Celan and Weil refer to. But I'm a little nervous about false piety and have never used the word "prayer" in this context. I stopped "praying" when I twelve or thirteen. Before then, I used to spend up to a half hour at prayer, before bed (which I've never told anybody, until now).

In the most literal sense, of course, a prayer is an appeal to God and a poem is an aesthetic arrangement. Thus the poem is concerned with beauty, form, and the like, whereas a prayer doesn't necessarily address those things. But if a poem *is* a prayer, as in the Psalms, then there is no distinction. Finally, I make little distinction between the two, though I try not to remind the reader about it. Prayer is certainly addressed to what is mysterious or invisible or beyond reach and control and — for me — at this point in my life, so is a poem.

Most issues of faith in America refer to what we used to call organized religion. In my view, and I realize it's a traditional view, it is difficult to find true faith in those institutions. There are a number of poets in America who reflect on a literal level their religions, and some of them are, in spite of that, excellent poets. But faith — as we describe it, or as I describe it — is something different than that.

I sometimes use, either deliberately or unconsciously, Jewish belief and even Jewish customs as a touchstone or reference point or element of a metaphor, since it is the religion I am most familiar with or comfortable in. A good example of this is a new poem of mine titled "The Name." Among Orthodox Jews, it is customary not only to not say the substitute names for God, such as Adonai, or Yahweh, but, out of reverence, fear, and respect to call him only "The Name," "Ha-Shem."

As far as the question of where I am now — which interests me most — it's really a question of what you call "God." What I call him, her, it, is existence itself. Maybe the word would be Being; maybe the word would be The Name. I have no interest in an old man — or woman — with a beard. I have no objection to a personal God, but I just don't believe it. I don't think anything listens, except psychologically, to our personal prayers. I like the fact that, at Auschwitz I think it was, there was a play in which God was put on trial. My faith is in existence. And I don't care who this makes happy or unhappy.

•

What does it mean, "Behaving Like a Jew," as I titled one of my poems? One "behaves like a Jew" by being moved, by being overwhelmed, by struggling with issues of justice, by showing affection, kindness, and love of the poor and the oppressed, and hatred of swords, in any form, and love of ploughshares in every form. He or she would be devoted to study, would love books, would walk across the street reading *The Nation*, would see Jesus as a great Jewish prophet, would detest whatever oppression the state of Israel shows to Palestinians (either inside or outside of the state of Israel), would love dead opossums — and live ones, would be suspicious of too much wealth, would be a Jain, a Buddhist, and even, at times, a Muslim and a Christian, of sorts. He, she, would make his beliefs and prejudices clear, would still pay attention to the prophets, would always go into old, half-abandoned synagogues when he passes them by. However, he, she, would not write about bar mitzvahs or weddings or bat mitzvahs, and he would not wear any uniform that comes from the Middle Ages. I want to add that a certain rabbi in Lancaster,

Pennsylvania, was furious with me for comparing an opossum to a Jew, which, I might add, I was not doing in the poem "Behaving Like a Jew."

I would be the most surprised person in the world if I opened *The New York Times* or *The Philadelphia Inquirer* and saw a psalm. Sometimes it might squeeze into *The New Yorker* secretly, or *The Nation*, but never in *The New York Review of Books*. I've seen more than one psalm by Philip Levine, by Adrienne Rich, by Jean Valentine, by Alice Notley. A person may actually write a psalm "for our times" without realizing it. Your greatest poems *sneak* in.

To write an American psalm today means to penetrate the horror, the indifference, and the cruelty — call it the shit — to reach the true place of love and affirmation. This true place existed profoundly in the 1930s and '40s in America; it practically disappeared in the '50s, partially reappeared in the '60s, and is supremely underground now. I guess my life's work is to try to revive it, in my personal behavior, my politics, and my writing.

•

I've been asked so much about my connection with Walt Whitman that this question actually exhausts me. I am interested in the differences. Certainly we both use anaphora, we both hugged the world, we both overreacted. However, dear Walt did not know any Jewish jokes, and maybe took Emerson too seriously. Also, his tomb in Camden is too large and ostentatious. I loved going to his last house on Mickle Street in Camden, New Jersey, and lying on his bed upstairs and talking to his imaginary guests, Oscar Wilde and Algernon Swinburne. I think I don't like the sexual evasion in Whitman's work, though he is, ironically, given credit for his sexual outspokenness. I have read him and taught him for fifty years and more. He is, in my eyes — when he's at his best — the supreme poet.

When Whitman says, "Do I contradict myself? Very well then, I contradict myself," I feel utterly relieved. Did you know that when Lincoln died, Whitman walked the entire length, from south to north, of New York City as a personal act of mourning?

I see myself as simultaneously a poet of the city and of the country. Where I was brought up, the woods were in very close proximity to where I lived. Pittsburgh is of such a nature — hills, woods, and empty spaces always within reach — that the two are absolutely difficult to separate. I don't consciously write about "the city" or "the country." Everything is everything else. If I use aspects of nature as tokens or symbols, it's because they are so readily available and so given to such treatment. Quite honestly, when I wrote "Cow Worship" at the end of the 1970s or the beginning of the 1980s, I could just have easily been in New York or St. Petersburg. It didn't matter. It's just that, after supper, my wife and I took a little ride to look at the cows.

When I was going through deep emotional turmoil in the first years of the twenty-first century, I used to drive with my partner Anne Marie into the country to look at and pet a certain group of donkeys. That was my medicine. I recognize that here I am seeing "the country" as a place of relief or redemption, but I must add that sometimes I get that very same feeling when I first see New York City while approaching the Lincoln Tunnel.

I can't separate praise from condemnation. Condemnation is at least attention. When I drive through Camden — I suppose when Phil Levine drives through Detroit — I am, he is, overwhelmed of course by the horror: empty fields where there were once factories and houses, empty streets where there were once people, nonexistent stores, boarded-up schools, broken glass. It would be, probably, false apocalyptic writing and fake redemption to make something positive out of that. I may have, earlier, been more than a little addicted to the heavenly nature of ruins. I am more inclined now to see them for what they are: the consequence of human greed, indifference, and stupidity.

The governor of New Jersey just fired practically the whole police force of Camden. Camden has 70 percent unemployment. It is getting more and more difficult to praise things; more and more difficult to move from the grittiness of daily detail and elevate the reader's attention to something else. I suppose what is left are individual acts of courage, affirmation, and hopefulness. Yet, at the same time, I am supremely happy — mostly — and find joy in life itself. I don't know what goes on here.

•

I am, and used to be even more, attracted to Manichean opposites. I think that one is born this way, but I also think that it's inherent in Judaism and that, in my life, such as it is, I have found deep examples — and illustrations — of this. Duality, dualism — a part of life/death, youth/age — is inherent. I didn't struggle to achieve this view, I don't work at it, it's just there. In my poems I deal with the literal, and the totemic emerges willy-nilly or ineluctably. Sometimes I just start writing and have faith that the meaning in the words will be, so to speak, by themselves realized.

I twist and turn in every way to achieve a modicum of truth. I rage as I must. If I am "outrageous" it is not for the sake of upsetting the bourgeoisie. If the rabbis hate me, they do so for good reason, or they do so out of ignorance. I love biblical phrases, names, maybe for their music as much as for anything else. I am not in the least interested in religious dogma. If I use religious language it is because of a kind of morbid attraction, and because I got into the habit of constructing poems through their usage.

The holy has to do not with an isolated feeling but with an act of involving yourself with other people. I felt holy when I was able to help free a swimming pool or destroy a wall. I wasn't at the Lincoln Memorial when Martin Luther King delivered his speech, but I know I would have felt that I was participating in the holy had I been there. Moses — forgive me for saying so — was just as holy when he struck the overseer as when he contemplated the burning bush; or another way of putting this, the two were one act.

By the way, Moses doesn't get enough credit. He was a great poet, and Miriam was his mother. Certainly she was his mother if Bethlehem Miriam was Yeshua's mom. I'm thinking of starting a conference in Lambertville called The Jewish Mother Conference. (We'll invite Robert Bly.)

I must say that I'm obsessed with Judaism, but more with Judaism as a survival strategy, and with its historic evolution, and as a despised Jew, than with tribal or ethnic identity. I have affection for Jewish food, for customs, for much of the history, but I reject much of what was, and is, seen as "God," and the behavior that this generates.

I guess I would call "God" existence, maybe even persistence; and I would see the worship — either on a hill, in a river, or behind walls — as lovely, but not *it*. By believing in God you believe in *the future,* especially today the future of the planet, unless you are in love with doomsday; and if you must *repent* it is not by returning to the traditional, unless that includes a new way of thinking and feeling. I think in our language it is called *teshuva* but, for me, it has little to do with phylacteries and pork, or with the *Tsaddik* dancing and eating three meals on the Sabbath with his followers, even if he, and they, feel holy by doing so.

One must find a way to see *everything* as holy — that would be a beginning, if "holy" is the right word. We need to grieve over, and change, the separation between the sacred and the profane. We need to grieve over all separations — not distinctions, but separations. We need to re-examine, most of all, the idolatry at the core of our life. Moses talking to a voice was as close as they could get to abolishing idol worship. But now, even personification is idol worship, in my view.

I guess it's not for me to comment on idol worship in the other religions, though I have strong opinions. It may be that even words — these words, for example, are a form of straying. Mankind, womankind, need *things,* don't they? Pieces of wood, pictures, heroes, messiahs, golems, *ganifs,* calves, beards. I have sometimes made my thinking very clear in my poetry. But only sometimes. And, after all, there are other concerns in poetry.

I have faith in this life. I have faith in eternity. I don't know what the "forms" will be.

THE NAME

Having outlived Allen I am the one who
has to suffer New York all by myself and
eat my soup alone in Poland although
sometimes I sit with Linda he met in Berkeley
or San Francisco when he met Jack, the bread
just coarse enough, the noodles soft but not
thin and wasted, and not too salty the way the
Chinese further down sometimes make them, the
name still on my mind whatever the reason for
mystery, or avoidance, though rat Netanyahu
and pig that swings from a needle or lives in some
huge incubator, they do darkness where there
was light, the *name* hates them, the *name*
in hiding, the *name* with a beard, and Linda she
loves the *name* though she invokes her Christ
as Jack her lover and tormentor did and
taught her to do though it is too easy, that,
it troubles me but what can I say, what *should* I
say while we walk north on the right hand side,
past the pork store and the hardware store, me lecturing
on Logos (my God) and what not Hebrews and Greeks
where Allen and I once kissed, Jack in the sun now.

— *Gerald Stern*

KAZIM ALI is the author of two books of poetry, The Far Mosque *and* The Fortieth Day, *and a cross-genre book,* Bright Felon: Autobiography and Cities. *He is also the author of the novels* Quinn's Passage *and* The Disappearance of Seth, *and two books of nonfiction,* Orange Alert: Essays on Poetry, Art, and the Architecture of Silence *and* Fasting for Ramadan: Notes from a Spiritual Practice. *He teaches at Oberlin College and in the University of Southern Maine's Stonecoast M.F.A. program. His work has been featured in* Best American Poetry 2007, American Poetry Review, Boston Review, Barrow Street, jubilat, *and* Massachusetts Review. *He is a founding editor of Nightboat Books. We interviewed Kazim Ali when he was in Cleveland to give a reading, a conversation in which he reflected on his identity as a Muslim and a poet.*

Kazim Ali

Doubt and Seeking

Prayer is a form of panic, because in prayer you don't really think you're going to be answered.

I have written about faith because I want to understand it; I want to be included in it. Are we creatures or creations? There seems to be a difference that etymology cannot protect us from. Are we divided shards of one another or are we individuals? What do we owe and what are we owed? These are not just questions of God and the expelled Adam, but questions of the individual and the polity. How are we supposed to live together at all (except by empire, which means control, which can *only* come from force and the threat of violence) unless we can answer these questions?

To call oneself a spiritual or religious poet seems strange to me, but once my first book came out, and I started doing readings, people would say to me, "You're a religious poet." I decided to consciously explore the topic more in my second book, but I never planned to be a religious poet. I'm moving in different directions now.

Part of my reticence is that I feel very fluid about what I believe. I'm not certain about too many things. Fanny Howe writes in an essay titled "Doubt" that doubt can be a really fruitful, powerful, spiritual place, and it's a place of active seeking.

You can search alongside others, but I don't think others can help you understand your own nature, or if they can, that would be much further along a spiritual journey than I am. I've always been on my own, a single person in the field of physical matter, on his back looking up into oblivion. There have been times when teachers appeared to me, but they were always single individuals, too, someone I had to be smart enough to follow and not a wise old man with a beard (though there was one, once! — dear Jonji Provenzano, a construction worker by day, yoga instructor by night). My teachers have been teachers of various sorts, sometimes children, sometimes people who were trying to hurt me, figures of substance who appeared, trying to get me to look at myself, to see something.

But to join with others in a gesture of similitude — I can't draw anything from that, or at least at the moment have not been able to do so. I'd rather be wandering in a trance through the streets of a busy city, peeling an orange and whispering to the universe than sitting in a pew listening to a sermon or kneeling on a rug reciting chapters.

•

I grew up in a religious household and had strong beliefs, but I chafed against the restrictions and traditions, and I had a hard time figuring out how these beliefs could fit into modern life and life in the West.

But for me, growing up in the United States in the 1970s, this was a completely different world. I don't know if most people from traditional backgrounds face the same questions I do, but I have struggled with wondering, Do you turn your back on a liberal out-looking secular life in America, and become very conservative or religious? Or do you completely abandon your spiritual practice and give up trying to integrate the two ways of living? If you turn your back on one side or the other, it's easier. It's harder to try to integrate, to bring your cultural and religious upbringing into terms with your daily life as you live it here. My struggle has been to unpack my own identity not just from the layers of the cultural and religious tradition my parents gave me, but also from the cultural and supposedly secular traditions that are instilled in me by the god of America, which is money — the desire for it and the need to spend it. Money, like every other constructed god, is a jealous god and demands its worship.

If I'm a Muslim, I'm a Muslim in a number of different ways. Spiritually, what I think about God is pretty much in line with the Quranic idea. This asserts the unity of all creation and the absolute lack of distance between the individual and the divine. God isn't up in heaven looking down. This is close to what I think. When I read the stories that appear in the Quran and the Bible (I've read both), such as Adam and Eve, and Joseph in Egypt, and Sodom and Gomorrah, and Moses and the Israelites, it's the Quranic stories that really make sense to me. So, in this way, I'm a Muslim. But if you put me in a room with twenty Muslims, we probably wouldn't agree on much. Though if you put *any* twenty Muslims in a room together, they wouldn't agree on much.

One of the tragedies of the so-called fundamentalist Islam is the attempt to flatten out these differences. The Muslim philosophical tradition, like the Jewish philosophical tradition, has always privileged disagreement and difference, with the idea that the individual seeker has to find a way through. Like Judaism, we don't have an ordained priesthood. We have scholars, and it's the people who are the most learned who become spiritual leaders. There's no ordination. There's no sacred distinction between the scholars and the people around them. That's very important and interesting to me.

In Shia Islam, in which I was raised, you select the teaching lineage you're going to subscribe to. My dad follows one teaching lineage and his older brother follows a different teaching lineage. You're just supposed to select your lineage. I haven't done this because I can't make such a commitment. I can't turn over my restless mind to someone else. I can't suggest that this is the way for everyone — I have had a hard time finding teachers and surrendering my own ego to receive their teaching, but someday, perhaps, this will change. It seems this loneliness is a part of my journey, for the present moment at least.

My parents taught us the scriptures and the stories from the Quran. In the Islamic tradition, when a baby is born, the father will whisper certain verses into the baby's ears. I feel I've been hearing my father's voice my whole life, in my ears, and in my memory. He recited a lot of the Quran when we were younger, and that was my first introduction to poetry. My mother used to sing both Urdu and Arabic poems and lamentations, though mostly Urdu. She has a beautiful, musical voice. Secular poetry is recited, but sacred poetry is always sung or chanted in some way. I remember the music most of all.

When I was young, my dad was an engineer on a hydroelectric project to build a dam in the far north of Canada. We lived in a trailer-park town, a temporary town. I'm not sure if it still exists, actually. I remember fir trees that were monstrously high. Other than those trees, it was barren. When the hydroelectric project was done, when I was about ten, we moved to New York City. So I moved from a town of maybe five hundred people to Staten Island, which was a shock. We stayed there for only a year and then moved to Buffalo. A couple of years ago when I decided that I wanted to write more autobiographi-cally, I realized how much I had moved. I went to college in Albany and stayed there altogether for six years, but after that I lived in a series of places (Washington, D.C., New York City, upstate New York), most of these places for only a couple of years. When I started writing *Bright Felon,* it was with the earnest desire to uncover why I was so afraid, why I was so silenced. I wanted to track back through my life, and as I was doing that, I discovered that *place,* specifically moving from one place to another, had such an effect. I barely had any close friends because every couple of years I was picking up and moving and starting over. Of course this partially caused my feelings of alienation and silence, but my tendency to keep moving was also partially because of those same feelings.

．

I fast during Ramadan every year. Fasting is a visceral experience: it uses the body to sharpen or affect the mind.

You could argue that prayer has the same effect in its ritual forms, but prayer means less for me, though the early morning prayers which you pray alone, and the afternoon prayers which you pray silently, mean more to me than the evening prayers which are usually (at least in my family) prayed with the whole household. I guess I am a loner, or lonely, or the only sum of something. I don't rule out a future in which I do perform these prayers or perhaps am not fasting anymore. Like the fasting month, which with the moon travels backward through the solar year, our spiritual lives shiver and change.

I don't live close to my parents and do not see them as often as I would like. But during Ramadan, when I am up in the early morning hours getting food, I know my mom is awake somewhere, too. There's a closeness that is still there no matter how much time or distance has come between us. Fasting is a practice of restraint and a practice of *action,* both at once. It's the most impossible thing I have ever done and also the most fruitful and intense in experience.

I started writing poems about spirituality and religion as a way to grasp what I believed. Now I've written an entire book about spiritual practice, *Fasting for Ramadan,* which is the culmination of my thinking about religious matters. So it might be time for me to keep quiet about this for a while. If you talk all the time about something, you stop knowing anything about it.

•

The histories of the Christian and Muslim and Jewish faiths are so connected. You have mosques that are also temples. The Hagia Sophia in Istanbul is a mosque that has also been a church and is not either of those, anymore. The Mezquita in Cordoba is a cathedral that used to be a mosque. In Spain it's the other way around, because the Christian people won the war. In Seville the huge cathedral is built on top of where the mosque used to stand. The courtyard of the old mosque with the Moorish waterways cut through it and the minaret are still there, but the bell tower is built right on top of the minaret. All the way up, you see Muslim architecture, and then suddenly there's a Gothic cap with bells inside. The melding of the architecture reflects the ways that the religious traditions themselves are connected. Christianity had its reformation and moved further away, but the deeper you look into Jewish faith and traditions and practices and Islam, the more you see that these are very much the same religion. If you look at Orthodox Christianity, you can see more confluences there.

I suppose there's a connection between the multiplicity I find in the religious traditions and my writing. Everything can be two or three things, and I often find myself doubled back in my writing, writing lines in a poem that can switch meanings by the end, or writing a second poem that goes against the meaning of the first one, or writing a poem that answers an earlier one. I'm drawn to the idea of plural thought and multiplicity, like the convex mirror in the Mogul ceiling, which the late poet Agha Shahid Ali wrote a poem about, where there are reflections in all different directions. You can see two things at once, and both can be true.

There's a story that the Muslim invaders burned down the Library of Alexandria, but it's not true. The library was actually destroyed by one of the Christian bishops who ordered all the Pagan knowledge destroyed. In modern times, with some of the splinter movements, we've seen actual actions like this historical one that have been misattributed to Muslims — the Taliban defacing the Buddha statues, for instance. But a disrespect of other religious traditions is not something historically that has happened in Islam. In fact, it's been precisely the opposite. There's always been respect of other traditions. Historians of Jewish history acknowledge the period of the golden age of Jewish civilization as existing in the western Islamic kingdom of al-Andalus, where there was religious tolerance, and Jewish counselors served in some of the highest levels of the government of the Caliph. This new tradition of Muslim and Jewish people being in opposition to each other is a strategic fabrication that started with the Christian powers in Medieval Europe and continues into the modern age, when they still manage to get these people battling each other.

•

Peacemaking is dangerous when powerful men and their god — money — want the war to continue. I think of the bodies of Rachel Corrie and Layla Al-Attar, two women who lost their lives in the Middle East, fifteen years apart, each putting her body on the line for peace and peacemaking.

Rachel Corrie was attempting an American kind of civil disobedience by standing in front of an Israeli bulldozer that was trying to destroy some Palestinian houses. The driver claims not to have seen her, but no one really believes that. And if you have the stomach to watch the video of her death you will see very clearly what the truth is. Layla Al-Attar, on the other hand, was not an activist in the formal sense. She was a painter and director of the Saddam Arts Center, the national gallery of art in Baghdad. She spent her life creating art, strange and lovely paintings, many of which were destroyed when one of Clinton's "precision" missiles accidentally hit her house while aiming for a military target. In Iraq, her death is widely considered to have been purposeful because she had been a vocal critic of the United States and regularly spoke out against the embargo of Iraq and the continued air raids over Baghdad as against international law. As an artist of some stature, her words had impact both within and outside the country, since she had just recently represented Iraq at the Venice Biennale. Her death is one of the most sordid and shameful episodes of the long (1990–present) shameful episode that is America's involvement in Iraq.

What can a poet do? What can a writer do? What can a citizen do? The answers to these questions are not separate. Rachel Corrie's actions (you know this by reading her published journals) progressed not out of single intellectual moments of discovery but from her entire life of karma and behavior. She couldn't have done other than what she did, which is to stand up for those people on that day in the extreme and dangerous way that she chose. You can hear in her writings her desperation swelling day by day until her final actions seem inevitable. The bulldozer was not the rock on which Rachel Corrie broke, but rather she broke that bulldozer. It is the body of Layla Al-Attar, struck in the earliest morning hours, that destroyed the missile we sent, destroyed every other missile in the world.

•

As a gay person and a Muslim, as both of those at once, as someone who questioned established political, social, and gender norms, I had a long, long way to go before I could ever speak myself.

It is easy to fetishize or romanticize silence when you *are silenced.* I was silenced by myself in this case, but silenced nonetheless. Though in understanding God or death — two of the things we humans really want to know about — you have to come to terms with silence in one way or another.

Some poets want to talk into the silence, sound out its limits, and others want to explore that edge of silence, what happens to the world when you look out at it from the lip of the unknown. Some poets do both of these. I think I am in a third category, though I have traveled there from the second: I could never go into the cave of metaphorical silence, not until I had *learned* myself how to speak. I love that verb "learn" — in Urdu (and in pioneer American vernacular, as evidenced by Mr. Edwards in *Little House on the Prairie* asking his son "What did they learn you at school today, boy?") the word means both "learn" and "teach."

I think we have a long way to go in America toward understanding and respecting "difference" of all kinds, and toward changing our own behaviors (personal but also national) that stem from a lack of understanding or willful misunderstanding of difference.

The people who have accepted me for who I am as a gay person have always been flabbergasted that I want to have anything to do with religion or God. The most religious people I know never had a problem with my sexuality. It's the people who are caught up in the temporality of God and money, the this-worldness of everything, that have a problem, because they want to see things go the way they want them to go. If you're a secular American, you want everyone to love money and not have any problems with oppression or colonialism. This is the American way; if you're against the war in Iraq or if you're against the war in Afghanistan or if you're against the global pan-capitalist structure that not only allows your superfluous overspending but *actually requires it* for sustenance, then you are practically unpatriotic. American military spending has always been strategic, and it's always been about promoting American power abroad. If you're against that, then you're against the idea of the nation of America somehow, and you're a traitor.

Being Muslim, likewise: If you don't do this, this, and this, then you're not Muslim, and you're not a part of us, and we exclude you. It's all the same kind of destructive thinking. It's not about the human being; it's not about the individual spirit.

But I feel that I've found my community in different places, among people who accept me in all of my confusions and misapprehensions — misspellings, errata, like the errata in a book. As humans we just don't make very much sense. Other poets, other religious people, other confused people, other crackpots, rebels, outsiders, these are the people who seem to be my community.

◆

Prayer is speaking to someone you know is not going to be able to speak back, so you're allowed to be the most honest that you can be. In prayer you're allowed to be as purely selfish as you like. You can ask for something completely irrational. I have written that prayer is a form of panic, because in prayer you don't really think you're going to be answered. You'll either get what you want or you won't. It feels to me like a situation where you're under the most duress. Often people who are not religious at all, when suddenly something terrible happens, they know they have to pray. I don't think there's anything wrong with that. We all engage with the spiritual at different counterpoints. Prayer is not a refuge or shelter, so much as it is an opening of arms, an acceptance of whatever storms exist in the world. You don't really pray for your situation to change, you pray to be able to handle your situation. It's not the world you want to change; it's you that you want to change.

My father and I took a trip to Cairo together, which I wrote about in an essay called "Faith and Silence." We visited the Sayeda Zainab shrine and the mosque down the road, where Sayeda Zainab, granddaughter of Prophet Muhammad, brought the remains of her decapitated brother to be buried. These are places of pilgrimage for Muslims. I felt confusion about the different stories, whether she had really come to Cairo and not died in Damascus, as some believe, and whether her brother's remains are really there. For my dad, the question of what actually happened in this place was less interesting. He knew that it was a holy place because thousands of people were there praying. His view was that regardless of what had happened there, it's become a holy place, because it's a repository for all these prayers. People have come there and have made it holy.

If our prayers can make a place holy, then it must mean that there's some divine energy that moves through a human body. In the ancient thinking, that divine energy is the breath of the body. The word in Arabic is *ruh,* which means both breath and spirit. In Latin, *spiritus,* or *spiro,* is for spirit and breath both.

As for pilgrimage to holy places, I *do* believe in the spiritual energy that we ourselves imbue places with, and I think intense actions can make a place holy. I went to Laramie, Wyoming, last year, and I begged my hosts to take me (through feet of snow and onto private property) to the place where Matthew Shepard waited through the night to be saved. I felt that even though the fence is gone, torn down by the property owners, you couldn't change what happened there, the awful witnessing of everything human.

I wonder about what Sohrab Sepehri wrote, "I am a Muslim: the rose is my *qiblah,* the stream is my prayer-rug." For Sepehri, every place in the world was imbued with this spiritual energy and to *choose* a locus for that essence, whether a mosque or church or lonely fence or fenceless field, would be to miss the energy completely, the real energy, the feeling in the air around your body in every minute.

Later on in this poem, he says, "My Ka'aba drifts on the wind from orchard to orchard and town to town." There could be no more fixed place than the Ka'aba, site of the mosque in Mecca that Muslims face when they pray. What a wonderful loosening of the divine, from a fixed place to a drifting attention over the landscape of the countryside.

SLEEP DOOR

a light knocking on the sleep door
like the sound of a rope striking the side of a boat

heard underwater
boats pulling up alongside each other

beneath the surface we rub up against each other
will we capsize in

the surge and silence
of waking from sleep

you are a lost canoe, navigating by me
I am the star map tonight

all the failed echoes
don't matter

the painted-over murals
don't matter

you can find your way to me
by the faint star-lamp

we are a fleet now
our prows zeroing in

praying in the wind
to spin like haywire compasses

toward whichever direction
will have us

— *Kazim Ali*

JANE HIRSHFIELD is the author of seven books of poetry, most recently Come, Thief. *Her collection* After *was shortlisted for England's T. S. Eliot Prize and named a "best book of 2006" by* The Washington Post, The San Francisco Chronicle, *and England's* Financial Times, *and her previous collection* Given Sugar, Given Salt *was a finalist for the National Book Critics Circle Award and winner of the Bay Area Book Reviewers Award. Her work also includes a now-classic book of essays,* Nine Gates: Entering the Mind of Poetry, *and she has edited and co-translated four books presenting work of writers from the past:* The Ink Dark Moon: Poems by Ono no Komachi and Izumi Shikibu, Women of the Ancient Court of Japan; Mirabai: Ecstatic Poems *(with Robert Bly);* The Heart of Haiku; *and* Women in Praise of the Sacred: Forty-Three Centuries of Spiritual Poetry by Women. *In 2004, she was awarded the Academy of American Poets' 70th Academy Fellowship for distinguished poetic achievement. She has taught at the University of California–Berkeley, the University of San Francisco, Bennington College, and in many festivals and conferences. We interviewed her at her home near Mount Tamalpais, across the bay from San Francisco.*

Jane Hirshfield

The Circular Path

*Zen is not about belief, but about what happens when belief
is unfastened.*

I came to California in 1974 in a red Dodge van with yellow
tied-dyed curtains, looking for a place to live and for what I thought
might be a waitressing job that could support me while I wrote. But
on the way, I took a detour. I was curious about Zen Buddhism and
knew there was a monastery, Tassajara Zen Mountain Center, in the
Ventana Wilderness inland from Big Sur. Because it was the summer
season rather than the stricter winter practice-period time, I was able
to drive the fourteen precipitous miles of mountain dirt road and stay
for a week as a "guest student." I went on to spend similar weeks at
two related practice places in the same Zen community, one in San
Francisco and the other in Muir Beach. I decided I would stay a few
months, until I understood what Buddhism was all about. After a few
months, what you understand is that you know nothing about what
Buddhism is all about. I became a full-time Zen student for the next
eight years, most of my twenties, with three of those years spent in
year-round monastic practice at Tassajara. That time is the diamond at
the center of my life. Whoever I now am came out of it.

In Buddhism, unlike Catholicism, leaving a monastery is neither
failure nor a rejection. A monastery is a training place, and one of the
traditional models for Zen practice is to take that training back into the
ordinary world of ordinary life. A famous series of images, "The Ten
Ox-Herding Pictures," depicts this process. It shows the practitioner's

47

passage through confusion, difficulty, impossibility, and the extraordinary, until at the end of the series we return to the ordinary marketplace, with the person and the enormous, muscular ox walking easily, without drama, side by side. This model of intensive training and return to regular life, its fidelity to the ordinary, is something that I appreciated in Zen from the start. I liked that the "spiritual" isn't something allocated to specialists, but is regarded as a thing more like water — something plain, free-flowing, available, already ubiquitous. Another central teaching of Buddhism, of course, is that nothing lasts. Not monasteries, not situations or objects, not life itself. In any case, no one enters a Zen monastery for life, not even those who choose to become priests. It's a training situation, a time to practice intensely and without distraction, to learn the flavor of undisturbed concentration. Going back to regular life was what I always thought I would do. As it turned out, poetry was still waiting for me when I emerged.

During the years I was at Tassajara, though, I wasn't writing. Everything was very strict and very simple. We were told, "Do nothing but practice Zen," and I wrote one haiku during those three years' time. When I returned to poetry, a rather different person in many ways, I brought with me two things I now can see would be useful to any young aspiring writer: the monastic model of non-distraction and silence, and the experience of calling oneself into complete attention. The ability to stay in the moment, to investigate immediate existence through my own body and mind, was what I most needed to learn at that point in my life, and to learn to stay more fearlessly within my own experience. I never considered going to graduate school. I did this instead. It wasn't necessarily a conscious weighing of one course of study against the other, but something in me did know: You cannot write until you can first inhabit your own life and mind and heart.

To live as I did at Tassajara, so fundamentally, so close to the way human beings have lived through most of our development as a species, was transformational and restorative. It grounded me in ways that staying inside our ordinary culture could not have done. The practice of *zazen* — Zen meditation — teaches you to be all right with whatever arises inside you, to not be afraid of it or run from it. Sitting through many hours of meditation, you discover that it's possible to stay with whatever you feel, with whatever experience is going on within you, and that all feelings shift, shimmer, change, arise, and then vanish. You are just feeling, that's all, and whatever you feel, while you are on the meditation cushion, there will be no repercussions. And so it is safe to feel things completely, and also to feel that there is a larger space in which emotions and thoughts and sensations come and go, and in which, like some enormous boat, they can perhaps be turned by the smallest shift of awareness's tiller. These are skills useful as well for someone who might want to write poems. They allow awareness and they allow wildness. *Zazen* may look orderly from the outside, but it's about freedom, it's not about domestication or suppression.

•

Daily life in a Zen monastery is highly structured. The wake-up bell rings at 3:30 in the morning. The regular daily schedule in those years was two forty-minute periods of *zazen* meditation, with ten minutes of walking meditation in between; morning service; breakfast in the *zendo* (the meditation hall); study hall; another period of meditation or sometimes a lecture; a brief work period; and then lunch, again in the *zendo*. Meals in a Zen monastery are taken in silence, in a stylized form of eating (not unlike tea ceremony) called *oryoki,* in which each gesture is mindfully made and has its choreographed form. The purpose of monastic life, in any spiritual tradition, is to make every moment equally part of the central intention — even formally unscheduled time is not "time off." Where could you go off to, when your life is the field of practice? In the afternoon there was another work period; bath time; and then evening service; dinner in the meditation hall; two more periods of meditation;

and bed. If you fell asleep instantly, you might get six hours of sleep. But I never did.

At times during each three-month training period, we would instead get up at 2:30 in the morning and stay in the *zendo* virtually continually, until 10:30 or 11 PM or midnight. *Sesshin,* as this intensive retreat period is called, goes on for a week. But even during the regular schedule, you spend a great deal of time in silence. During the work periods, you aren't supposed to talk beyond what is absolutely necessary, just pay attention to your work. Whatever you are doing, that activity is where your consciousness resides. If you are meditating, you are meditating; if you are digging in the garden, you just dig. Of course, this is a very idealized description. Everybody gets distracted, and everybody brings into a monastery whatever person they were the moment before they stepped through the gate. But everything about the schedule and the practice and the other forty or fifty people who are there remind you why you decided to enter that gate, so that when you forget, you are called back to this moment: reminded to notice, to pay attention. Is there a feeling of separation of self, or one of inhabitance and intimacy between you and your thoughts and your actions, between you and all that surrounds and is continuous with you and your life?

Dogen Zenji, a thirteenth-century Japanese Zen master, said: "To study the way is to study the self, to study the self is to forget the self, to forget the self is to awaken into the ten thousand things." This reminds you, in part, that you can't find intimacy with others, whether other people or wicker chairs, by jumping outside your own skin. Intimacy arises by a permeability found inside your own life. We're here, we're in these bodies, we're in these minds, we're in these hearts, we're in these spirits. Zen practice is not about annihilating the self, or about transcending it, but about seeing it as it is — or, as Suzuki-roshi, the Japanese Zen teacher who founded Tassajara, once said, with deliberately incorrect grammar, "seeing things as it is." You walk through the world on your own two feet, tasting with your own tongue and seeing through your own eyes, and intimacy comes to us through this ordinary life that we are given.

In the end, there's no divergence between going deeply into the study of the self, in monastic silence, and finding your continuity with an old pear tree outside the window or a woman sitting across from you on a bus. The only way we can know anything is with our own eyes and our own looking. Anything else is some Platonic idea, and that is not for me a path that holds much interest.

•

I began to write poems as soon as I learned to write. When I was twenty-nine, my first book was published, and my mother pulled out of a bottom dresser drawer a big piece of paper, probably from second grade or so, on which I had written: "I want to be a writer when I grow up." I have no idea where that idea came from — certainly not from my family. But from earliest childhood, writing was a way for me to craft a self. I could unfold myself to myself unobserved, in private. I could find a life that was mine, one that didn't belong to others.

The paths of poetry and Zen have intertwined for me from the beginning — the first book of poetry I bought, from a stationery store on East 20th Street, was a one-dollar Peter Pauper Press book of Japanese haiku. I was perhaps eight years old. I don't know what drew me so strongly to those poems or what I could have understood of their meaning at that age, but I recognized something that I knew I wanted to have in my life. The path has also been circular. Poetry brought me to Zen, and Zen returned me to poetry. In 1985, I took on the co-translation that became *The Ink Dark Moon*, a collection of poems by Ono no Komachi and Izumi Shikibu, the two great women poets of classical-era Japan, whose work I had first read in a handful of English translations when I was seventeen. Reading their poetry in college, those poems steeped in both eros and Buddhist views, was part of what turned me toward Zen as well as part of what shaped my sense of lyric poetry — how poems move, what work they do in our lives. I had no idea back then that I would work further on these women's poems; if anything, I thought that was a path not taken. I did know that I wanted the book to exist, and I waited fifteen years for someone else to translate this body of work before suddenly finding the chance to do it myself after all, thanks to a Guggenheim fellowship for my own poetry and an almost accidental introduction to my co-translator, Mariko Aratani. So you see, each mode of investigation and expression — poetry, Zen — has always returned me to the other. Thus far, they have been the left foot and the right foot of my life.

No one undertakes something as difficult as Zen practice because they already feel the perfection of "things as it is." We humans turn toward a spiritual practice in part to restore ourselves from some felt form of separation or exile. We feel something is wrong, or missing. This is not my usual vocabulary, but one of my poems, "Salt Heart," has a passage that may be relevant here: "I begin to believe the only sin is distance, refusal. / All others stemming from this." Separation from others, separation from self, are close to the root of suffering. Christians might say "separation from God," Sufis might say, "separation from the Beloved." Jung might call it a failure to recognize all parts of the psyche as parts of one self; that shadow-self, refused, grows perilous. Buddhism proposes that the separation of self-hood is a mistake of the mind, an attitude in some way reflected in our English use of the word "selfish." While Zen is the particular practice that drew me, I certainly don't believe there's only one "right" spiritual path — if something is true, it will be findable anywhere, and there are as many spiritual paths as there are people, and probably sparrows and frogs and pebbles as well. Still, for me, this not uncommon sense of being exiled from full presence in the world brought me to both Zen and poetry. Perhaps urban, contemporary life is already an exile of a kind. There is a Taoist poet in *Women in Praise of the Sacred*, Yu Xuanji, who said at the end of one poem, "Everywhere the wind carries me is home." That was not something I felt as a child.

I've been thinking about Yu Xuanji's description of being at home in exile, as I travel more and more in my work as poet. What is it to be home, what is it to be not-home? Exile is not only a matter of physical location. In one sense it is simply the human condition: the expulsion from paradise. We're born into exile. There you were, having a fine and entirely protected time in the womb, and suddenly you are out in the world, where there's cold and hunger and the loneliness of abandonment. One great question we're given as human beings is, What do you do when you find yourself alone, in a condition of exile? Can you make friends with this condition of suffering, or are you going to exhaust your life trying to avoid it? The poet Czeslaw Milosz experienced exile of all kinds: the universal, and also the historical and outward. A large part of his poetry is engaged with exile from a childhood paradise, with exile from his mother-tongue's country. My own exiles have been, thus far at least, only the ordinary, American and human ones.

•

Rilke wrote of being defeated by ever-greater angels — such strengthening angels, I suspect, must be different, one from the other, not the same angel over and over. There are universal questions that cause a person to enter a life of practice, and I think for most of us, these are the inevitabilities of suffering, and of time, of loss and desire, of old age, sickness, and death. These come to us in infinite varieties. Suffering is inescapable. The psyche's work is in no small part to discover what you will do in your life with the suffering that is given you.

Any given poem is, for me, an attempt to know more largely and intimately whatever condition of being I am in at that moment. Each poem is an act of grappled-with comprehension and the entirely provisional resolution of a particular question. We find ourselves off-balance, and the poem attempts to recapture balance, or more truthfully, to spring forward into some new balance that will itself remain momentary and soon start to lean. We each have things we are especially prone to notice.

Some poets notice love. Some poets notice time. Some poets notice the New York City subways or dogs or the circumstances of a particular era of their personal lives.

One thing I would like to do — not in a willed or driven way, but in the way of a request thrown to the Muse — is to broaden the reach of what my poems are able to notice. Novalis proposed in one of his aphorisms that a person spends the first half of life looking inward and the second half looking outward. Once you've come to some kind of comprehension of your own condition, the world becomes ever more interesting. I do think that anyone who claims that his or her poems aren't in some way personal is self-deceptive. That old saying "the personal is political" can also be reversed: life happens in us, and not in some abstract collective. But poetry exists in part to enlarge us, to deliver us into the not yet known. Writing is an act that generates and expands attention. And if I'm lucky, I may write something that helps expand the life and attention of others as well.

There is also the matter of empathy and compassion, two movements of the psyche that I think are indelibly a part of good poems. Metaphor is made by mixing the experiencing self with what is outside it. Simone Weil said, "Absolutely unmixed attention is prayer." The path of Zen is about attention, about a full inhabitance of your own life, and it's also about the lives of others, and about noticing and alleviating suffering. Your suffering is not discontinuous from the suffering of the world. Attentiveness, when freed from the intentions of self-promotion, is a practice that inevitably leads to compassion. And compassion initiates the ability to do anything useful, to think anything original and ungrasping, to work with the actualities of a situation with some breadth of being and some hope of hope.

•

It's in my nature to question, to look at the opposite side of a story, a theory, a leaf. Whatever is present, its opposite is almost always present as well. I believe that good writing also does this. Great literature does not take sides. It is not partisan, small minded, or narrow. Art tells us that where there is sorrow, there will be joy, and where there is joy, there will be sorrow. A uni-dimensional poem would be unbelievably dull and boring. Sometimes the other side is so deeply buried, you really have to part the grasses of the poem to find it, but in good poetry, that second dimension is always there. The poems we remember hold in themselves something startling and unexpected, some undertow, some magnetic pull toward a fuller, subtler truth.

This offered entranceway into a more complex and vertiginous scope of being is why good art thrills. I keep coming back to this idea: acknowledging the 360-degree fullness of things and ourselves is the task of art, and of the spiritual in our lives as well. We're the part of existence that is able to do this: to stop, to look around, to ask "What else?" It's what we're good at — seeing the multiple facets, and feeling and holding the contradictory dimensions of lived experience. A deer or a turtle might walk through the world at times in a kind of mystical ecstasy, knowing its life acutely and without division. We can't really know if that happens or if it does not. But even if it does, it will be experienced wholly from the inside. Because we are human, and have the awareness of exile-consciousness in us, we also look from the perimeter and from the imagined ends, and we consider what comes before and after our individual fates. We see, at least some of the time, from what isn't necessarily our own first point of view. This ability to question ourselves doesn't need to be self-dividing or coldly objective. It can lead just as easily into the warmth of intimacy and the shelter of felt connection: "To forget the self is to awaken into the ten thousand things."

Horace memorably said that the purpose of poetry is to *delight* and *instruct,* and if there isn't joy, why bother? If a work of art were not beautiful to us — though at times this might mean the most recalcitrant kinds of beauty — we wouldn't stop to offer it our attention. The nourishment of Cezanne's awkward apples is in the tenderness and alertness they awaken inside us. Art wants to seduce. It wants to entrance. And because art is also entrancing, its second purpose, Horace's *instruction* (an idea, to be sure, rather out of fashion these days), is forestalled from bullying didacticism. We are meaning-making animals, and meaning, to me, can itself be a resonant beauty. It may well be that beauty, at base, always holds also some measure of meaning, however unparaphrasable. A mathematician can be moved to tears by a proof.

I think of the power of Issa's haiku: "On a branch floating downriver, a cricket singing." The poem is entirely image, without comment. But for anyone who hears it, even if you never make this fully conscious, it is also a portrait of the condition of our life. We're always on some branch, being carried precariously in the current. And what are we doing? We are singing. You can see this as a bitterness or you can see it as gallantry, but you cannot detach the image from larger meaning. That is what a good image does. A different association or world might be evoked in some other person's mind by Issa's cricket, but the image is solid enough to hold all readings. None is wrong. Every image in a poem is a portrait of a state of soul. If you say, "door handle" to me in the context of Zen, I stay just there; if you say "door handle" to me in a poem, some part of me leaps also to cross a pine threshold, to pass between the painted verticals of a sturdy wooden frame. I see the handle, I see the door, I see the house, I see what each of these things exists to make possible and what each makes possible also to say.

A central task of any life is to affirm what comes — to step through the world's offered door. What I hope may also be felt in my own poems is that this agreement is not a simplistic or passive acceptance but is hard won.

Sometime during my second year of monastic life, I looked at the poems I had written in college. What I saw was that every poem yearned toward vanishing; every poem ended with a little trail of ellipses, or some conceptual or imagistic drift into fog. I was horrified. "My poems are suicidal," I thought, "they want not to exist." And I knew that I didn't want to be the woman who wrote them, who yearned so strongly to disappear. Such a realization is a turning point in a life. I must have already started to make this turn, of course, or I could not have seen what I saw. Westerners who don't know much about it often think Buddhism is nihilistic, a refusal of full participation in the world. But the experience of Zen is really quite the opposite of nihilism. If anything, it is one path toward being more deeply inside this world, a practice of inhabitance and presence without separation. And so I vowed, in that moment of shocked self-recognition, to taste, to see, to hear, to touch, and to be tasted, to be willing to be seen and heard...

Life will vanish on its own in any case. We don't have to worry about that, we will die. But what do we do in this moment, while we live? Whatever people find in my poems of radiance or grace comes out of this struggle to turn away from disappearance and toward presence.

For us, honey is a gift; for the bee, it is labor.

•

Zen is not about belief. It's more about what happens when belief is unfastened. One traditional description of Zen is that it is a teaching outside of words, outside of teachings. The teaching of Zen is: Drink your tea. Find the taste of this moment on your own tongue. There are, of course, many words and many teachings in Zen, but they are words that welcome questioning, and that are grounded, as electricity is grounded, in the arc of the real. The teachings of Zen are meant to be tested against what can be known from inside your own life. Most people, for instance, know that Buddhism has an unusual relationship to the concept of self. But this isn't a question of doctrine, it's simply the experience that emerges if you pay close attention. If you sit down quietly and only look at what is there, you find yourself continuous with the rest of existence, and permeable to it. "Self," then, is only one impermanent point of view, among many others.

Zen is often described as a practice but not a "religion." In the Western tradition, Deism, which says that the body of God is distributed equally through all existence, comes closest, perhaps. Take the god-ness out of it, and you're close to Zen: What is is enough. You don't have to add anything to reality to feel awe, or to feel respect, or to see the radiance of existence. Radiance simply is. No one needs to do a conceptual somersault in order to place radiance inside a specific entity. This may seem simplistic, but I truly believe that if you put a person in a prison cell with nothing but the chance and the desire to pay attention, everything they need to know about the radiance of the world is there, available, as well as everything they need to know about suffering, loneliness, longing. I also believe that if you brought a group of mystics, from every possible tradition, into a room, they would understand one another pretty well. At the most profound level of mystical experience, there is, I suspect, no difference in what people feel.

I remember walking with my mother when I was very young. I was holding her hand, and I looked up at her and said, "It's really too bad we aren't Catholic, and I can't be a nun when I grow up." That must have horrified her, or I wouldn't remember the conversation. But obviously there was something about monasticism that I was drawn toward and recognized even then. Something about the idea of a single-minded, dedicated, and undistracted life that I must have sensed mattered. I'm quite sure that it wasn't Christianity per se that made me say that. The magnet was not the belief, it was the mode of being. Perhaps I had some premonition of the shape my life would take. And when, years later, I did find myself living that life, I felt a deep consonance. Monastic life, deep in a wilderness, felt to me the way human beings were meant to live.

My associations to the word "religion" are not particularly happy. I do realize that such associations are always idiosyncratic, but even in childhood a divine being never made much sense to me. The Judeo-Christian belief system I saw around me didn't hold much appeal. Something of that tradition is surely there in the background, of course — habits of mind and temperament from the culture at large, and also from my family's Jewish tradition and culture. One grandfather was something of a mystic, and briefly joined the Rosicrucians; one great-great-grandfather, from Philadelphia, was a rabbi in the Civil War. Still, I received virtually no religious instruction. My family did have a Passover seder each year, and I liked the horseradish, the bitter herbs, and the salted, hard-boiled egg, but the story didn't really take root as "mine" any more strongly than, say, the Thanksgiving story of Pilgrims and Indians or the Christmas carols we sang at school. I suppose I feel that at this point in the world's history, all these stories might be better felt to belong to us all, as our great, common, human heritage. Their use as devices of division grieves me. Identity politics isn't something I find congenial, even as, on the other hand, I would not like to see the world made homogenous and single. For me, this is perhaps the most deeply troubling kōan of our cultural age — how to preserve difference without fortifying the sense of combative separation.

•

Human beings fall rather easily into the consciousness of purposeful action: "I want this, so I will go get it." " I need this." "I have to do that." "If I don't do this, something bad will happen and I will die." Such is the basic murmur of mammalian consciousness. Spiritual practices (along with other basic lineaments of human culture, of course) are in part a set of techniques to free a person from unquestioning enslavement to that imperative mind. They allow us to look around, to step back and see things as they are, to apprehend thoughts, impulses, concepts as part of the larger whole. Art does this as well, and art plays a role in a human life that is probably not unrelated to spiritual ritual. Both stop you in your mammalian tracks and let you see and know your life through larger eyes and ears.

For instance, we think of animals as not able to know they will die. This may be wrong; perhaps some of them do. But we do know that all human beings, at some point in our species' history, developed the capacity to comprehend mortality, and it seems very likely that this happened at around the same time that art-making and ritual also enter the archeological story. "Death is the mother of beauty," as Stevens wrote.

A work of art offers a paradoxical liberation: it is something that changes everything while being perfectly useless in any ordinary sense. I suppose some people collect paintings because they think their value will increase in ten years or a hundred years, or because owning a certain object conveys social status. Thorstein Veblen's "conspicuous consumption" is patently real. But I think poetry, as an art form, proves that this cannot be the whole story — no one gains social status from knowing or "owning" a poem. Art's role in the contemporary world may well be precisely to be *un-useful,* to reveal the importance of uselessness in our lives. You can't eat a painting. You can't do anything except stand before it, know the world differently, and walk away changed. That's what a painting can do, what a poem can do. Art halts the mind's unthinking plummet and lets you see the experience as a new whole.

Many words describing written and expressive form — "stanza," for instance, and "statement" — have in their etymological root some connection to stopping, or turning, or pausing. Almost anything you really want to take in, you stop to take in. This is true even of music listened to while dancing: Your body may be moving, but your whole being is given over to the music. You aren't doing anything else, and you aren't skimming past. I think we desperately want for time to slow down in the ways it does when we are inside a fully given attention. All my life, I have loved the condition of being where things are so deeply themselves that they and I fall into each other, and everything seems to stop. In such moments, nothing is longed for, nothing left out.

Inaction, and pure experience, are not much valued in contemporary American culture. The more usual attitude is to want to be engaged and purposeful, to change things, to prove or transmit some belief system or to attain measurable achievement, to support, to serve. And these things will be needed, if we want to avoid destroying ourselves and much of the planet with us, even though of course it is action, not non-action, that created the problems to begin with. But it seems to me that too often an untempered desire to change things means changing them for the worse. This is the lesson of Voltaire's *Candide*, and the lesson of many of the most disastrous events of the past century. The current war in Iraq is only the most recent example of a devastating consequence when people believe they know, with certainty, how to change something for the better. But if you can start by letting things be themselves, and feel yourself part of things as they are, then perhaps, like some eighty-year-old man with an eighty-year-old bonsai tree, you can look around and say, "Maybe if I trim this particular set of small needles, the bonsai tree and I will be more completely both ourselves and in harmony with the true nature of everything else." Does this change everything, or nothing, such a subtle action? We can't know. But the bonsai master trims the tree knowing that it will outlive him, shaping it toward its next eighty, or eight hundred, years.

It's worth recalling that non-doing is part of every spiritual tradition. What actually happens in a moment of prayer, at a baptism or a funeral, at a ceremony of blessing the boats? In these moments, outer action is stopped, so that when doing resumes, it will, ideally at least, be altered, taken up in a different spirit and broadened intention. These rites can be used to narrow us, but ideally, they will lead instead to enlargement, non-self-attachment, and compassion.

What I am trying to say doesn't mean that you don't give a hungry person food if you can. It doesn't mean you don't register to vote, or, if it's your nature to do so, enter the halls of power yourself. It means, though, that you aren't trying to change things for reasons of ego or personal power. Rather, it's so the tree and you can live completely. Maybe a bonsai is a bad choice of example. A bonsai, after all, is stunted, captive, "unnatural." But a bonsai is art — made by us in collaboration with the actual energies of life. A bonsai's only reason for being is to bring those energies into view inside slowed time, and so to bring our own beauty and fate and energies into clearer view.

·

All my writing life, I have travelled through long swaths of silence. I wrote in solitude as a child and mostly hid the writing under my mattress, never showing it to anyone. In the summers, my parents would send me to camp, and so every summer I stopped writing, and every fall I started again. I became used to the sense of poetry-writing as something that has its seasons and rhythms. Then, again, when I was practicing full time at Tassajara, I wrote no poems for three years. When I left there, and was no longer under the monastic prohibition against doing any practice other than *zazen*, the intention of poetry came back. It was still something I did only for myself. Finding words to hold experience was simply my way.

When I stop writing now for a time, as does still happen, it's not in general something I experience as a struggle, more that inspiration does not come. Still, I recognize this as a sign of some wrongness in my life, in my relationship to my life. After I finished *The Lives of the Heart*, I fell silent for almost a year. There were circumstantial reasons for that, but I worried enough about it that I finally started a dream notebook, wanting to keep some conduit open to my inner life. For many years afterward, even after poetry returned, I continued recording my dreams, and then one day I stopped. This wasn't a decision; I simply stopped.

Whenever I've started to write again after a long pause, I've found that the poems as well as the self have changed. It's as if the abandonment of the forms and music of the person I was before allows an evolution into something new. Silence can be a protective liminal space, gestational, and as gravitational as sleep for the creative mind. When the old forms, images, and sentences don't perpetuate themselves by repetition, the mind, eye, and ear drop their old patterns and can fish in new seas. Think of a field lying fallow or of a well that has some chance to refill, simply by going undrawn. The non-doing of meditation also renews. Mostly I trust these times. What choice do I have? But I also realize that some day poetry may simply not come back. If that happens, I'll have to think of something else to do with this life, to repay the gift of existence. The world certainly doesn't need any more poems. One shouldn't force the Muse. The world will have its full harvest of poems whether I myself am trying to write them or not.

It Was Like This: You Were Happy

It was like this:
you were happy, then you were sad,
then happy again, then not.

It went on.
You were innocent or you were guilty.
Actions were taken, or not.

At times you spoke, at other times you were silent.
Mostly, it seems you were silent — what could you say?

Now it is almost over.

Like a lover, your life bends down and kisses your life.

It does this not in forgiveness —
between you, there is nothing to forgive —
but with the simple nod of a baker at the moment
he sees the bread is finished with transformation.

Eating, too, is a thing now only for others.

It doesn't matter what they will make of you
or your days: they will be wrong,
they will miss the wrong woman, miss the wrong man,
all the stories they tell will be tales of their own invention.

Your story was this: you were happy, then you were sad,
you slept, you awakened.
Sometimes you ate roasted chestnuts, sometimes persimmons.

— Jane Hirshfield

JEAN VALENTINE was born in Chicago, earned her B.A. from Radcliffe College, and has lived most of her life in New York City. She won the Yale Younger Poets Award for her first book, Dream Barker, *in 1965. Her eleventh book of poetry is* Break the Glass, *just out from Copper Canyon Press.* Door in the Mountain: New and Collected Poems 1965–2003 *was the winner of the 2004 National Book Award for Poetry. Valentine was the State Poet of New York from 2008 to 2010. She received the 2009 Wallace Stevens Award from the Academy of American Poets, and she has received a Guggenheim fellowship and awards from the National Endowment for the Arts, the Bunting Institute, the Rockefeller Foundation, the New York Council for the Arts, and the New York Foundation for the Arts, as well as the Maurice English Prize, the Teasdale Poetry Prize, and the Poetry Society of America's Shelley Memorial Prize. She has taught at Sarah Lawrence College, the graduate writing program of New York University, Columbia University, and the 92nd Street Y in Manhattan. In our conversation with Valentine, which took place through a written correspondence, she reflected on those moments when matters of the spirit become manifest in the physical world, and the attempt of poetry to capture such moments.*

Jean Valentine

What Remains Unseen

We live between suffering and the ultimate reality of love.

I was born into a Christian social setting, but not a belief or practice. From the age of five I lived in the country/suburbs, and saw the spirit life in the world of nature, and in what I called the fairies (little lights, shapes of moving light). One of my liveliest memories, from when I was about five, is the weeping mulberry tree, its animated branches and leaves, and its embracing shelter, like an outdoor "room of our own" — my sister and I used to play there. Though it was close to the family house, this was a secret home, a green and magical space that could have come out of a fairy tale. It had no square lines, but a round, earthy floor inside the circle of its branches, which came right down to the ground. I felt there both the beauty of the tree, and its protection. It was in the branches of the tree that the fairy lights often came and went. The place inside the branches was always opening, not closing. It held the universe beyond our lives. Being in this "room" was like lying on the ground and looking up at the stars: they were protective, although trillions of miles away.

As a child, by and by I picked up that everyone around me didn't feel this way!... and I learned I had to keep my reality to myself. I got the same "secret" feeling about spirituality as I got, later, about sexuality: they both seemed to arouse a sort of punitive alarm. So I learned about their outside, as well as their inside, power.

The Christian image of faith I like is the mother and child. Both the mother-figure and the world of nature (which appeared animated, like in Disney films, and was always benevolent) were a faith-life to me: the mother as here, nature as here, in the same entire affectionate world as animals and us. In those days I saw everything as an animate reality. For instance, the claw-footed bathtub had actual clawed feet, not imitation claw feet; and the leaves moved, as I did, because they wanted to. And that is where I am now, with some important differences.

The most important difference is that the reality of mother-love, and the sense of belonging in nature and human nature — that reality which I had sensed under the tree, under the stars, at the stable, in the human warmth that was to be trusted — that reality broke up; and I began to understand, as I do now, what the Buddhists call impermanence. I have come to understand that earthly love is real, but lasting only in the un-seen. Though, as it turns out, that is plenty.

•

Our mother seemed to me preoccupied during my childhood, and we had a warm but mostly absent father. A loving mother-figure took care of us until I was four; her name was Clara, and I remember her love for us and for her handsome little son, Raymond. He visited us once in a while, but I see him in my mind's eye, in a picture frame, which Clara must have kept in our house. (Who took care of Raymond all the time, while Clara took care of us?)

When we moved to the country, when I was five, I was "adopted," emotionally, by my babysitter Eileen, and her mother and father, and her boyfriend, Eugene. The family ran a riding-stable right next to our house. They let me "exercise" the horses — ride around the near fields on their big, slow backs — and "groom" them — brush them, with a stool to stand on. And when the blacksmith came, I got to watch him hammer the red-hot iron shoes and tack them into the patient horses' feet; he always made me a horseshoe-nail ring. Faith, at that time, took the form of being found dear, as the cats were, and the dogs, and the horses; and of finding the human world, and oneself as part of it, good.

That way of seeing broke up, I think partly because I was eleven and twelve years old, and partly because our father came home from the Pacific in 1945 not physically wounded, but — like so many — with post-traumatic stress disorder, unnamed then, and untreated. It's hard for me to tell what was natural in that change in myself, and what was related to the war. Damages came to our family, like billions of families, during World War II, and there was no healing to turn to, for my family; although among the damaged, we were, on the face of it, some of the least touched by that time. For us, the wounds were inner: a traumatized veteran, an exhausted wife, and three emotionally ragged kids. Now there was alcohol, verbal violence, and much inexplicable (to me) intensity and meanness in the air. Looking back, I'd say it was desperation.

So the faith that I have now is importantly different, in that much of it is no longer shown in anything present; but I think that this faith is in some ways sturdier, because of the years of "failing better" (as Samuel Beckett urged), of being healed (held) through longing, brought into knowledge of God who is closer than a tree, or a stable, or a mother — "closer than consciousness itself," as Father Thomas Keating put it.

Now I feel that spiritual reality is entire, and is ultimately love, and that we live between suffering and the ultimate reality of love. This is where I am now.

•

When I was nine (this was 1943), somehow I got ahold of one of those American poetry anthologies. I remember vividly that it had oval pictures of the poets on the cover, so for a while I thought poets' pictures were always oval. I was also reading Edgar Allen Poe's stories. It was a thrilling time for me. School was a blank, though not a malevolent one; home was very tense, but I had a room of my own and could read there at night, and I could be outside most of the daylight hours. My favorite poem (like many people's) was "The Highwayman." I started trying to write things that rhymed, but I couldn't get into much narrative (still true to this day). Here's an example that I remember of my efforts in those days: "I think I am a sniffing mole / sniffing and sniffing in my hole." Not much of a storyline! But before the war we had lived in a place that had a lawn, and moles, and mole-traps with long spikes, so that would attract anyone's imagination. (Poe's, anyway.) What drew me to poetry was partly privacy, I think; if I had painted or played an instrument, it would have been much more out in the open in the family. And loneliness. Poetry became my invisible friend.

I came up against over-rational thought in my high school and college education in the 1950s: memorizing Greek metrics, diagramming sentences. It was a very repressed, right-angled culture, which I felt alienated from, and then *bang!* A poet friend handed me Ginsburg's *Howl,* and there they were, the Beats, and California, and the Sixties! Poets I already loved were also opened up, in those decades — Lowell, and Bishop, and Berryman. Others, like Lorine Niedecker, I found only later.

I wasn't *in* the 1960s, for a few reasons, so I remember them. But I found them a great relief, and a homecoming. For all the heartbreaking violence, the culture felt like you could breathe in it again, with the Civil Rights and peace movements. But through this time, I personally only felt "found" in my own still fairly unconscious poetry and dream life — as Anne Sexton expressed it, "rowing toward God," or toward something or someone not rational or material. I already had one foot in God (God forgive me the phrase!), but it was as if God also opened: John the 23rd, Vatican II, French movies.

.

Although Galway Kinnell has said that he thinks Emily Dickinson was not a believer, and I don't disagree, I know that for me she has been a lightning rod of belief in love of the invisible. She often uses Christian stories and symbols, which may just work for her as metaphors, but this doesn't interfere with lightning rods. Sometimes doubt can enforce belief, because it takes the situation so seriously. I think of Osip Mandelstam's lines: "Flowers are deathless, Heaven is round, / and everything to be is only talk."

I am drawn to poets whose work allows the Other its existence. Not in accepted spiritual terms, perhaps. But that would sometimes be part of the Other's quality, I suppose. Frank O'Hara's "The Harbormaster," for instance, and John Berryman's "Dream Song 29," and Elizabeth Bishop's "Sonnet." Gerard Manley Hopkins, George Herbert, and (strangely, maybe) W. B. Yeats. But most of all, Paul Celan and Anton Chekhov — can we count him as a poet for a minute? I think of his story "Easter Eve." One of the literary works that speak strongly (to me) of faith is not a poem, but the movie of Tony Kushner's *Angels in America*. And in art, I think of the shift in seeing ordinary light that the artist James Turrell has brought about — it is sacred when you see it.

Celan wrote, "The poem wants to reach an Other, it needs this Other, it needs an Over-against." Maybe this need is faith.

•

For me, there's a likeness between poetry and prayer that is not so much an aspect of thanks or supplication or other conscious activity, but the more unconscious activity of meditation or dreaming. The likeness lies in poetry, meditative prayer, and dreaming all being (potentially, anyhow) healing, and somewhat out of our hands. For me, poetry is mostly silence. The deeper, the better. There's much to be said for consciousness and the rational mind, but it wouldn't be said in support of the kind of art that I feel most touched by. For me, the unconscious life, and beauty, (so, *truth and beauty*...!) feel closer to the whole world we live in, which to me is God, than other consciousnesses in my life. It goes without saying that you can be close to these two states of mind in suffering, as well as in certain physical places. When I say that the poetry I like best is mostly silence, I mean that it seems to have come out of silence, to exist in the midst of silence, and to go toward silence. This seems to be true in some music as well, and in some art of the most right-brain or intuitive kind, art that is less conceptual and/or narrative (speaking roughly).

In the early 1980s things fell apart in my life, in a way that turned out to be blessed: I started meditating during this time, which I kept up for about a year. But for five years, writing left me. The first poem I wrote after that is called "Trust Me." In that poem, I felt a little difference in my writing in terms of silence, and in terms of not knowing, hesitation, uncertainty. Wonder rather than statement.

Some poems by others, which I would in no way compare my own poems to, but from which I get a sense of silence, include Emily Dickinson's "The Difference":

The difference between Despair
And Fear — is like the One
Between the instant of a Wreck —
And when the Wreck has been —

The Mind is smooth — no motion —
Contented as the Eye
Upon the Forehead of a Bust —
That knows — it cannot see —

She is describing a sort of silence, almost silently: everything has been accomplished, only the chill, "smooth," untroubled iambic blind witness is left.

And here is a haiku of Basho's:

Darkening waves —
cry of wild ducks,
faintly white.

Other poets I love, who seem to write out of silence and back toward silence, are Paul Celan and Tomas Tranströmer.

I do think that most of us do what we can, and it's as simple as that. Life happens. To take a great example, Walt Whitman visited and nursed the wounded of the Civil War. Elizabeth Bishop lived in Brazil for fifteen years. Both these experiences the poets were active in choosing, but they also just "happened." Dickinson was in a position of wealth and education to be Dickinson. Those circumstances might not have been good for anybody else, maybe, but they were good for poetry. These are examples of greatness, but most of us do what we can. Like watching the Northern Lights or something.

Seeing huge animals, such as whales, gives us a sense of the sacred. Bishop's poem "The Moose" captures this. I remember seeing a camel walk down the aisle of the Cathedral of Saint John the Divine (on the day of the blessing of the animals) and feeling this same awe. The jars and bottles in the paintings of Giorgio Morandi point to this sense of awe. Or a simple act: A writing student came to her teacher, Grace Paley, and said, "I have nothing to say," and Grace said, "Yes you do, you just don't have anybody to say it to. Say it to me."

In the 1950s, Flannery O'Connor, and I think Robert Fitzgerald, and some other literary people were discussing Holy Communion, and someone said that the wine and bread were symbolic. Flannery is reported to have said, "Well if it's symbolic, I say to hell with it!"

•

I want to speak about the poet Eleanor Ross Taylor (whose ninety-first birthday is June 30, 2011). And Marie Ponsot just had her ninetieth! I wish there was something we could do, like set off rockets: We didn't get our independence, but we have certainly gotten some wonderful poets.

Eleanor's being a woman — and being the kind of poet she is — was hugely important to me in 1960 when I read her first book, *A Wilderness of Ladies*. And remained so, for a long time. She was married to Peter

Taylor, a famous and very much respected fiction writer, so it seemed to me that it might be possible.... Not to "get ahead": Eleanor wasn't much known, in spite of Randall Jarrell writing a brilliant introduction to that first book. But I thought it might be possible to write a quiet (emphasis on quiet) outsider kind of poetry, even with all these big guys around. I remember asking Eleanor, about forty years later, "Do you think we often fall in love with the person who recognizes our poetry first?" and she said, with her beautiful smile, "Oh, I think it's obligatory."

I felt that Eleanor was drenched by what I could maybe call the after-effects of being raised in a *believing*— or recently believing — community and family. Probably many Americans of her generation (and later generations) are in this kind of echo. But except for Lowell in his kind of out-there Christian phase, and Berryman, I don't think many poets I knew were believers. I felt that Eleanor was especially strong in allowing faith into her persona poems, for instance the poem about Florence Nightingale, and one of my favorites, "Rachel Plummer's Dream."

It was important to me then, and is now, that though she might not say so socially, Eleanor was a believer in irrational experiences. I was comforted by that, because I am, too. This was a strong bond, though I don't remember ever talking to her about it. (It probably would have embarrassed me, if not both of us.) But it made me feel more accompanied. And I always thought Bishop also had a sort of unexpressed faith, which I loved in her work.

Over the years I didn't align myself with any school or current fashion. I didn't know of any, though they were around — the Poetry Project at St. Marks Church, the Beats, and the feminists, at least. Well, everyone knew the feminists, and that movement did affect me, of course. I admire Grace Paley and Adrienne Rich, among others. They did so much with the women's movement, and the anti-war movements, their writing affecting things and being affected by things. I couldn't do much in that way. I've always been pretty out of it, and in those days, I was more so; I'm not happy about that, but it's the case. Yet the wonderful thing about living in New York City is that there are so many groups, or schools of thought or art, that you can't feel too out of it. You might feel out of this or that, but it didn't mean you were being excluded. For a while the women were being excluded, but then that was a big population of writers and artists! People of color! Gays! The walls of the little castle were cracking long before I was born.

What I find myself admiring is how generous many of those poets were, across schools and groups, in their commitments, their teaching, their endless support of other poets. Just the name Robert Creeley brings tears to people's eyes, and many other names, too, such as Muriel Rukeyser. I hope that we, now, are being half as generous.

◆

Some poems come as complete gifts. Once, when I was in my twenties, a poem, "First Love," was a gift like this. I don't think these experiences are perhaps so uncommon to poets. Once, I asked Marie Ponsot, "Where did you get that Hopkins poem, 'Why Vow'?" And she said something like, "I was sitting there for a few days, writing an essay on Hopkins, and he came right in the window!"

Much later in my life, I had seen a museum photograph of Lucy, a skeleton of a woman from Ethiopia, whose age is about 3.2 million years. The photo I saw in a magazine was the kind where they reconstruct a face from bones, and I remember liking her face and reading, without any particularly avid interest, the short paragraph about her. Then I went to sleep. When I woke up, I felt slightly hypnotized, and went to the desk, and wrote for most of the day, without will or thought, but with happiness and excitement. About four or five in the afternoon, I went outside and called my friend the poet Anne Marie Macari, and told her what was happening, and said I was a little alarmed. I had experienced depression in my life, but never mania; should I be worried? (I felt like I was walking about a foot off the ground, by this point.) Anne Marie laughed gently, and said, "Isn't it strange how when good things happen, sometimes we feel like we're doing something wrong?" She advised me to not operate any heavy machinery, and to go back and write. She said that she thought there would be more of this poem coming.

So I went back to my studio (I was at an artists' colony, MacDowell) and wrote some more, slept, and wrote some more in the morning, till about noon. Then I just put down my pen. I knew it was done.

This makes me think, as part of the discussion of faith and the spirit, that there is, at certain times and places, a clear, unwilled porousness between us and not only other beings, but what they have to say, or to give. This didn't surprise me, because I had had similar experiences before, of a smaller kind; but this experience was so "far out," and lasted so long, that it left me much less lonely, and almost completely without doubt that we are not only not alone, but are accompanied and loved. I don't mean just by poets or other artists: by everyone, probably by every thing. I have wondered if the writing of this poem left Lucy feeling less lonely. I wonder, too, does that state of porousness exist all the time, and do we only tune into it now and then?

Maybe some day I will meet a shaman.

Because if we are speaking of belief in God — well, if Lucy was so good as to come in the window — it isn't that much of a leap, for me, to think that we are living in a porous universe; and that sounds to me like a universe who wants, if I can put it in a child-like way, to love us.

•

For me, the difference between the vision and poetry, or between the sort of "otherness" you can feel about a dream and words from a dream, is the same difference between the sacred and the ordinary sense of reticence, or even withholding, in daily speech. The poem is just what you can somehow bring back, but you yourself know it's only a shred of a memory. Like beautiful wet stones from the beach, which dry.

This is where I come back to the point in this conversation that is most interesting for me: the relationship between silence and language, which I think is awkward. Sometimes there is too much noise — but social life, and friendship require it — and sometimes there is too much isolation socially, and lonesomeness, but… "the bliss of solitude…" (thinking of Wordsworth's daffodils). I have been very fortunate to have as much solitude as I have had, and I have been lucky to often have a silent workroom.

Over the years, I find that I am more and more compressed in my own work, as I go along — emotional compression, not necessarily in short lines, or short stanzas, or short poems, though I do write this way mostly. I think poetry, at its best, is a kind of enacting of the emotion or the thought in its excitement. For instance, Dickinson's intensity of thought and feeling, the mortal and immortal longings that she feels over a lifetime: her swiftness. I find some poetry boring, and what it seems to lack is not wisdom, necessarily, or descriptive powers, but intensity — maybe in a very particular sense this intensity is love, if love includes intelligence. I guess my mind only feels interesting to me when I write at my most intense, swift, and compressed. I feel this more as I go along. My friends tease me that I will end up with nothing at all on the page. It would probably be hard to find a publisher for that, on this planet anyhow.

•

I used to go to healing services — in the worst years of the AIDS epidemic here — and the priest would ask anyone who wanted to do so to just come up to him after Mass, and he would pray for you and touch your forehead with a drop of blessed oil. When people were touched by this oil, they often fell backward onto the floor. So often, that they always had people standing behind you to catch you. The priest would say beforehand, "Sometimes people do have this experience of falling over. Don't think it's some special grace. God just needs to get your attention!"

Mircea Eliade said, "We become aware of the sacred because it manifests itself, shows itself, as something wholly different from the profane… *something sacred shows itself to us*… something of a wholly different order, a reality that does not belong to our world, in objects that are an integral part of our natural 'profane' world."

For instance, the fairies I saw as a child.

A loved one, dead, who appears, speaks to you — as a tender example: Jesus, dead, looking like a gardener, saying Mary's name.

A Joseph Cornell box.

Ordinary speech can seem reticent, then. Even the most loving. Then comes the longing for art. The art falls short, but the space of the longing in making art can be visited sometimes by the sacred.

Trust Me

Who did I write last night? leaning
over this yellow pad, here, inside,
making blue chicken tracks: two
sets of blue footprints, tracking out
on a yellow ground,
child's colors.

Who am I?
who want so much to move
like a fish through water,
through life ...
        Fish *like* to be
underwater.

Fish move through fish! Who
are you?

And Trust Me said, There's another way to go,
we'll go by the river which is frozen under the snow;

my shining, your shining life draws close, draws closer,
God fills us as a woman fills a pitcher.

                      — *Jean Valentine*

JERICHO BROWN worked as a speechwriter for the Mayor of New Orleans before receiving his Ph.D. in creative writing and literature from the University of Houston. He also holds an M.F.A. from the University of New Orleans and a B.A. from Dillard University. He is the author of Please, *which won the American Book Award. The recipient of a Whiting Writers' Award and fellowships from the National Endowment for the Arts and the Radcliffe Institute at Harvard University, Brown is an assistant professor at the University of San Diego. His poems have appeared in such journals and anthologies as* American Poetry Review, jubilat, Oxford American, Ploughshares, A Public Space, *and* 100 Best African American Poems. *We met with him in the La Mesa hills in San Diego, California.*

Jericho Brown

The Possibility of God

Poetry is so different from prose, because it's infused with doubt.

Other than passages from the Bible itself, there are phrases that have been touted in the African American church throughout its history, and ways of speaking these phrases, that were quite attractive to me when I was young. I loved being a part of a community that had a shared lexicon, a lexicon that, for us, somehow pointed to our very survival. Something about that language made me feel protected and favored, if not by Christ, then by those who professed Him. I imagine that all parents are interested in their children having some sense of importance, and this is where my parents thought their children should get theirs. I was too young not to believe that God was on my side.

The Mount Canaan Missionary Baptist Church that I attended as a child is in the largely African American Allendale neighborhood of Shreveport, Louisiana. The Reverend Harry Blake has been pastor there for more than fifty years. He was on Martin Luther King Jr.'s staff and is still thought of as a leader who helped to end segregation in northern Louisiana. He kept our church at the forefront of political movements in the 1960s and continued to do so in the 1980s and '90s when I was a kid.

The black church is a very theatrical place, full of pageantry and prone to pomp and circumstance. I always think of the order of service itself as being a lot like a poem. I knew what was going to happen, but I didn't know how it was going to happen. I knew my pastor would be preaching in a robe, but I didn't know whether or not it would have a train. I knew someone would shout in ecstasy at some point, but we never know the exact point or how loudly or whether it would be a man or a woman. Would it include running or simply a flailing of the arms? This is the way I think of form and surprise and suspense in poetry. Hearing sermons gave me my first ideas about how a spoken thing is an artful thing, a piece of work with highs and lows and, yes, a moment of climax.

I was raised in a church where part of growing up was getting in front of people and doing what we saw our pastor doing every Sunday. You could show just how free you were individually. You had to be vulnerable to an audience for them to see that you believed. I think that's ingrained in me, no matter what I'm doing.

Here are the words to a song I learned in the pews at New Canaan:

Lift every voice and sing
Till earth and heaven ring,
Ring with the harmonies of Liberty;
Let our rejoicing rise high as the listening skies,
Let it resound loud as the rolling sea.
Sing a song full of the faith that the dark past
has taught us,
Sing a song full of the hope that the present has
brought us,
Facing the rising sun of our new day begun,
Let us march on till victory is won.

These words are, of course, the lyrics to the Negro National Anthem. I have a hard time answering questions about faith because my people insisted that belief in God could be the only explanation for their survival on this planet. You remember. We learned the words to our national anthem in the same churches where we prayed and shouted and preached and sang and fell to the floor crying. Belief and freedom are inextricably tied.

I will never understand the spirit of my ancestors, but I know it.

I know it lives in me. And though fear insists on itself, I intend to acknowledge this spirit as one that overcomes us. I write because my writing mind is the only chance I have of becoming the manifestation of their hope. I write because my writing mind is the only chance I have of becoming what the living dead are for me. I exist because I was impossible for someone else to be, before me.

I love the church now, and it scares me. I still listen to recordings of the preacher Carlton Pearson. I am a lover of gospel music until the day I die. But to be honest, when friends invite me to church, I usually find an excuse not to go because I'm afraid that someone behind the pulpit will at any moment attempt to erase or degrade my existence as a gay man. It's not a comfortable feeling, not a feeling with which to enter a house of worship.

•

I remember the music of my childhood most. Not just gospel. My parents played a lot of R&B and jazz in the house. In Shreveport at the time, the radio stations didn't make much of a distinction between old and new music. This was before the advent of hip-hop or just at its beginning. My older cousins were impressed by my ability to memorize the words to songs, and they insisted that I sing them when we played together. I took things so seriously as a young child, maybe because my parents' love for one another was so violent. When Minnie Riperton came on the radio singing "Loving You," I believed her when she got to the lyrics, "No one else can make me feel the colors that you bring." I understood that to be what love was like — synesthesia. Where I grew up, R&B and pop singers had a kind of superhuman status. When I was a child, it was fine if I overheard gossip about a murder that had occurred two blocks away, but the fact that Marvin Gaye's father had shot him was only discussed if adults thought I could not hear.

Like many places affected by the loveliness of Reaganomics, Shreveport was crime ridden in the 1980s with gangs who helped to dismantle African American neighborhoods by distributing crack. I wasn't at all aware of this because I thought of it as home. I don't know that anyone thinks of home as dangerous until they move to a place as homogenous as San Diego.

I came of age in a situation where I was never allowed to speak. And since my father was too violent a man for me to dream of expressing myself through the kinds of trouble for which my cousins and other young men in my neighborhood have been imprisoned, I turned to the page. Because I am a human, I have to speak: I only do that with any kind of success when I am writing poems.

Lyrics in popular music often refer to a man or woman in love with one word: Fool. I remember once asking my father why he and my mother didn't just call it quits. I was ten years old at the time, and he was crying in front of me, complaining that she shouldn't have made him cry in front of one of his children. He answered, "Because I love her," and then he slapped me across the face for having the gall to ask him something like that.

None of the reviews or essays about my book *Please* give a real examination of how the father and the Father are collapsed in the book, or of how the speaker means to please him and/or Him and keeps failing at every turn. They do notice that my father was capable of loving me in a tender storybook way and also of slapping the shit out of me quite often. Well, this is the God that was illustrated for me as the one and only God when I was growing up. And that's why I don't believe in that God any more. As an adult, I have to believe in a God who is a lot better than my dad. I get along with this God better, and He helps me get along with the father I still can't seem to please.

At some point, I stopped thinking that desire is evil.

We say "make love" when we talk about sex, and this can be real — real for two people who are genuinely "in love." Maybe this is too Allen Ginsberg of me, but I can think of nothing more powerful than a kiss. What would happen if our world leaders kissed when they had their big, important meetings? Not war, I assure you. If we think of a kiss this way, is a kiss not the same as a prayer?

•

As a child, I fancied myself a writer, first of songs, then of poems. I kept poems in journals that I thought of as the places to keep and code obvious tragedies that weren't to be discussed openly where I grew up. I always thought I'd have what adults termed some kind of a "real job" and then retire from it in time to do what I wanted to do in earnest. As my relationships with my family became more and more strained in my late teens, I began to understand that I didn't have to wait to have, do, or be anything I wanted. An example of this was my choosing English as a major while an undergraduate. I convinced my father that the major was best for those planning to attend law school, but I knew I just wanted a major that would allow me to read and think about poetry and fiction.

For most of my writing life, I've worked with the certainty of something I had in mind since age six or seven. (Maybe eight, but the thought was definitely in its firm place by the time I was ten.) One of my problems to this day is that I have to remind myself that my parents love me, and in our culture, that means I owe them something. There is also the fact that because of them making love, I was born. Still, I grew up thinking that the goal was to get out of my parents' house so as not to be a burden on them anymore.

My parents are very "religious" people, and my father and I have had literal fistfights over my sinful life. By the time I began writing, I had completely convinced myself that I didn't have anything to lose in the realm of family because I didn't have a family that really wanted anything to do with me anyway.

I see that this all sounds very dreary (true or not), but that revelation was really quite a gold mine for me as a poet, because I could write without any particular hate or love for my friends or family. I just needed to get the poems right for the sake of what liberty I felt I had in the midst of writing.

I began thinking of myself as a poet the year after graduating from Dillard University in New Orleans. That year, Gloria Wade Gayles,

Terrance Hayes, Major Jackson, and Toi Derricotte moved to the city, and we all participated in the NOMMO Literary Society, a community workshop run in conjunction with Runagate Press editor and poet Kalamu ya Salaam. Around that same time, I also had the opportunity to come in close contact with Charles Rowell, Brenda Marie Osbey, and Natasha Trethewey. As I think back on such a confluence of influences taking root in the mind of a twenty-two-year-old, it seems that poetry picked me before I had any chance to pick poetry.

•

I'm a fool for the best of our literary clichés. I really do believe that the personal represents the public, that the private is the political. The elegies, the persona poems, and the portraits in my book allow me to write what I hope connects to something larger than myself. Maybe the word for this is "humanity." I don't know. I do know that I'm a believer in the soul. I don't know if we each have one or if one courses through all of us. The books I love most attempt a soul conversation by summoning all the people a poet can write onto a few pages and putting them in contact with one another.

A man I had a huge crush on, a man who didn't pay me any serious attention really, once said, "Performance is not at odds with essence." Since that was the only smart thing I heard him say before he made it clear that he wasn't interested in me, I've always thought that it was meant for me to hear. Performance pushes the performer into a space where he is much more real and honest and vulnerable than he is at any other point in his life. This is also the feeling we get when we read really good poems, when we hear them read aloud. Jessica Savitch used to say that she felt more herself when she was in front of the camera reporting the news, and Esther Hicks told Oprah Winfrey that the experience of tapping into "infinite intelligence" is one in which she becomes and sees herself. I feel at once whole and permeable when I am writing, and I feel this all the more when I take on other voices.

For me, writing in the voices of others intensifies the experience of composition. Poems pierce the self, lay us flat before powers unseen, make poets and readers relational beings. I believe that all I can do is confront and represent every inch of my loves and my hates, my ability to do good and evil, my lust after the flesh and my respect for it. When I am doing that, I am writing well.

•

I think of writing, first, as a process of listening to some series of sounds that enter my mind (is this the opposite of prayer? simply listening?) and, second, as a process of embodying those sounds. I try and leave as much as I can to instinct, intuition, and reflex — even in the final stages of revision. Because I'm so interested in both music and voice, I find myself trying to figure the personality of the sounds as I am composing. At some point in the writing of a first draft, I start to take on the characteristics of the voice asking to be channeled through words that convey a mixture of the sacred and the profane, the ironic and the ecstatic.

God is the very best of us, and he is manifested when we visualize, build, and acknowledge the best. But the God in my poems is often referred to by speakers who don't know this about him, or who have him mixed up with a being that could inhabit, know, or possess anything but the best, so they are afraid of him.

I have to admit that I don't know what the issues are if they are not spirituality, sexual identity, and race. I'm of the impression that that's what my poems address, and that's what they'll always address. Dealing with masculinity and femininity, identity and gender, sexuality and race, and what the soul has to do with all of this seems to me to be my calling as a poet. Confronting these things and their complexity is my job. (Though I don't actually "identify" these as my topics. For me, that would be like trying to identify the color of my breath.)

My poem "Herman Finley Is Dead" is an example of a speaker trying to understand death and trying to understand his own fear of it. He is as demanding of God after the death of a loved one as anyone is, I imagine. I'm always writing with a hostile reader in mind, a reader who would say that my poems are too black or too gay or too sincere or too ironic. I wanted to confront this reader with all the might I had in this poem, and I only had a few words for that might.

•

I served the City of New Orleans for four years working for Mayor Morial, who is now president and CEO of the National Urban League. He's an amazing leader who made his love for that city absolutely contagious. He is also a major role model for me as my fraternity brother and the man willing to take a chance on me and give me my first job right out of college. (The word "give" is supremely important here, considering the desperate shape I was in.)

I enjoyed writing speeches when I was employed doing this, but there is nothing as exhilarating as being overtaken by a poem. A speechwriter goes into each speech knowing the message and figuring the best way to communicate the message as he goes. A poet figures ways of communicating and wonders if he has a message. I prefer the latter, because it gives me a chance to question beliefs that I myself hold dear.

There is no room for such questions when working to drive a message home. I was always aware of my point when I was writing speeches. The joy of writing poems is not knowing the point, following the sounds of words wherever they may take me. I weep my way through the making of most of my poems and hardly feel that I have any control or power over the content that begins to emerge from them. I do my best writing when I am the most vulnerable to the writing, when I allow for the construction of images and lines that, in the midst of composing, frighten me.

I've always said that you know you're a poet when you type an em dash and you hit the delete button, and you type a colon and you hit the delete button, and you type an em dash and you hit the delete button, and you type a colon and you hit the delete button. If you can do that for about three hours straight, trying to figure out which one is the best one, if you can do that for three hours and call that a good time, then you're probably a poet.

When I write and revise, I imagine myself in the middle of a conversation, often a disagreement, with someone I love. I mean for the experience of writing to be like the experience of saying, "I love you" or "I'm sorry" or "Baby, please don't" to a person I need in my life. The only difference is that, because those phrases are so trite, I have to find the language and pacing necessary to let that someone know I really mean it.

The poet must be free of thought in the drafting process and heavy with it while revising. But then again, maybe that's not it at all. The important thing for me is following whatever is tugging at my mind. The poem is the place where it's okay to be consumed with a single set of ideas. Or maybe that's wrong, too ...

I'll go a step further and say that poems ask us *not to understand* in the same way that we often find ourselves *not* comprehending the possibility of a God in this world.

One of the first poets I loved was Essex Hemphill. There's a young man with whom I had a short affair, who is a jazz pianist studying at the Berklee College of Music, and once I was showing him some poems by Hemphill. He read one poem and said, "I don't get it," and I said, "You don't get it because you're trying to get it. Stop doing that."

I said, "The first time you heard Thelonious Monk you didn't get it, but you liked it. It felt good, and you were okay with that and you moved on. Then the next time you heard it, you were like, 'Oh, and there's this.' Then the next time you heard it you were like, 'Oh my God, there's this too!'" I said, "Just read the poem. Just enjoy the poem." So he sat there and he read the same poem and he said, "Oh wow, that is a lot better!"

Is this our problem with perceiving God? Poems do carry meaning, but that doesn't mean their meaning has to be what first attracts us to them. If that were the case, we wouldn't know who the hell Wallace Stevens was.

I've never believed that what attracts us to poems is immediately understanding what's going on in them. As a matter of fact, I think just the opposite. I do want poems to have meaning, but I also think that having meaning isn't the end of the conversation about poetry or about faith.

•

Shortly after leaving New Orleans, I had reason to see several doctors, and I became very afraid that I was going to die. This had never crossed my mind before. It's that feeling you have when you almost hit a car, that shaking inside, and I was having that feeling all day, every day. I hate to use the cliché of poetry as therapy, but I really did feel like I could deal with the coming of death if I wrote about it.

Today, I'm writing about war, disease, the destruction of the natural world, and brotherhood through a rewriting of Bible scriptures. I see the Bible as a text to go back to just like "The Love Song of J. Alfred Prufrock" is a text to go back to.

Because my newest work is exploring masculinity, brotherhood, and sibling rivalry, I am presently most attracted to any biblical story that includes two or more brothers, or two or more sisters: Cain and Abel, Lot's daughters, Isaac and Ishmael, Jacob and Esau, Rachel and Leah, Joseph and his brothers, Mary and Elizabeth, and so on. I think of these stories as myths...I want to write poems that last as long as these kinds of myths have and that mean as much to those who read them.

A great achievement of countless black American poets has been making plain what the world they desire is like, and allowing readers to contrast that world to the dangers of the one in which we actually live. I've always thought of writing as participating in a conversation, the method by which I am able to respond to the many questions that I think Gwendolyn Bennett and Gwendolyn Brooks and others ask me when I read their work. Putting poems in print gives me the chance to ask them — and hopefully a few of the unborn — questions that I have, too.

The poem mirrors the life of the believer, and mirrors the process of prayer — of having a conversation with the supernatural. For instance, line breaks have everything to do with doubt. That's why poetry is so different from prose, because it's infused with doubt. At the moment of a line break, even if it's for a millisecond, you're thrust into doubt; you're thrust into a place where you're not certain what just happened or what's going to happen. Only faith that the next line will land us on solid ground is what keeps us breathing.

The artist's answer to any question is always, "Risk." My goal is to write poems that take risks in their form and their content. Because of my evangelical past, I have always been attracted to work that manages to say what may be thought unsayable, poems that make clear the vulnerability of the poet to his or her work. I am not interested in poems that fear what I think of as a necessary mixture of the sacred and the profane. My dedication to risk allows me to write work that, I hope, fuses an imitation of modernist fragments with fairy tale, fable, and sermon.

I am an elegiac poet...so far. Maybe the joy I feel every day hasn't gotten into my writing just yet. But it will.

Hope is the opposite of desperation, it's not as comfortable as certainty, and it's much more certain than longing. Hope is always accompanied by the imagination, the will to see what our physical environment seems to deem impossible. Only the creative mind can make use of hope. Only a creative people can wield it.

Today, I believe that anything one visualizes consistently becomes reality. Isn't that what prayer is? Maybe that means my beliefs have not changed at all: Lift every voice and sing *till* earth and heaven ring.

I am a believer. True believers see their way as the way. That doesn't mean I can't stand someone else's way. It means that I am capable of joyfully getting lost in my own. Spirituality is important to me, because I think there is something among us greater than the physical, something that we know exists and can address directly.

I love God. I love liberty. I shame one if I lose the other. I think of God now as way more patient than I could ever be. I have to believe that God is better than me and better than all of us. That's the only thing that could make God God.

HERMAN FINLEY IS DEAD

1947–2005

The birds know a day
Made for defeat.
Not one of them sings.
Instead, they make a toilet
Of your newly washed car.
Don't cry over it. Listen
To the birds — you, too,
Should shut up. But first,
Tell every alto you know
To hold her muddy breath.
Bid every obese soprano
A forty-day fast.
Get any man who ever sang
In a choir, head bowed,
None praying. Summon
Both the interpreter
And the speaker of tongues.
Pinch their burning lips.
Contact the necessary
Limp-wristed whose every suit
Is an Easter suit, bright
And loud enough to flame
In hell. I want them all
Wearing their worst black.
Call Nelson Demery
And Shanetta Brown.
Tell them to turn off the radio

Whether the station plays
Gospel or blues. Tell them
Herman Finley is dead. Then,
Tell them what God loves,
The truth: the disease
Your mother's mouth won't mention
Got bored with nibbling away
At the insides of his body
And, today, decided
To swallow Herman Finley
Whole. Tell them they must
Chop and torch each piano
Before helping me bolt the doors
Of all the Baptist Churches
From Shreveport to Monroe.
I don't want a single hum.
We will not worship
Save for silence. Watch
The birds shit in peace.
When the choir director's arms
Fall, the choir must not sing.

—*Jericho Brown*

GRACE PALEY was a celebrated fiction writer and poet, a life-long activist and pacifist, and a crucial figure in the women's rights movement from the 1960s on. She was born in the Bronx on December 11, 1922, the daughter of Russian Jewish immigrants. She published three volumes of short stories that established her as a master of the form: The Little Disturbances of Man, Enormous Changes at the Last Minute, *and* Later the Same Day. *Her book* The Collected Stories *was a finalist for both the Pulitzer Prize and the National Book Award. She is also the author of a collection of essays,* Just As I Thought, *and a number of volumes of poetry, including* Leaning Forward *and* Begin Again: Collected Poems. *Paley lived in Manhattan, where most of her stories were set, and Thetford Hill, Vermont. She taught at Sarah Lawrence College and the City College of New York. From 1986 to 1988, she was New York's first State Author and from 2003 to 2007 served as the Poet Laureate of Vermont. We spoke with Paley at her home in Vermont, a year before her death in August of 2007 at the age of eighty-four.*

Grace Paley

Inches of Progress

This world is simply great and mysterious. I don't have to find a god or not find a god.

When I was young, I believed improving the world was part of what it meant to be Jewish. I did not know the Hebrew phrase *tikkun olam* — repairing the world — until a few years ago. I just believed it was up to us Jews to improve the world. Not that we did. By the time I got older I saw we were not improving the world, but still, to me being socially active was a natural way to be Jewish. I'd have a hard time defining *tikkun olam* if someone asked me to. I would say *we have a responsibility in the world.* That would explain it the best way. It's not so much that we should improve the world; you know, that's kind of snotty, to claim to improve. But we have a responsibility to maintain the honor of the world and human decency and goodness to one another.

I didn't find this in the Jewish religion, though. I found it in the people on the street. We had no religion at home. My father still knew his Hebrew, and on Passover he still read the whole Haggadah at top speed. We always had a Passover, but the other holidays just seemed to go by. It was not a religion to us because my father wasn't religious.

My parents were atheists and socialists, but my grandmother lived with us, and I used to take her to *shul*. She was not an atheist, though she was not very religious.

The way my parents were seemed normal to me. I grew up in the Bronx. My childhood memories are from the Depression, the late 1930s.

The people on my street didn't work then. The men had no work, but my father was the neighborhood doctor. So I was a rich person relative to all my friends. I had a very happy childhood because the streets of New York are wonderful for children. You're free on the street as a child. In summertime, you could play on the street till 10:00 at night. Your mother would look out the window, or someone else's mother would, and say, "Come on, come back up to the house." Sometimes a kid would go and sometimes another half hour would pass. There was always somebody there on the street. There were always children to play with.

My family talked politics at the table. This was the normal conversation. My father would read the paper and say, "Goddamn." They talked Russian to my grandmother, who might answer in Yiddish or Russian, but mostly by the time I was growing up they spoke English at home, though they read Russian. My father got a Russian Socialist newspaper of some kind.

I would take my grandmother to *shul*. On the High Holidays, Yom Kippur or Rosh Hashanah, she would go. She stopped going on Saturday. It was too much, because my parents were really not helpful, and I was a kid. The synagogue was two doors away from our house, so she could go herself if she wanted, but I don't remember that she did. That *shul* was small, in a two-story brick house, like the house we lived in. Ours was the house with the doctor's office and that was the house with the *shul*, pretty much the same kind of building, except it was a little excavated inside, you know. They had to make a big hole, and they had to place the women in the balcony so they would practically die of breathlessness. The old men would come by on a holiday. They would blow their nose in the street, and then they'd go in the *shul*. If my grandmother wanted to go to services on the High Holiday, she didn't like going to that little *shul*. It really was oppressive. I would take her to a better one, a bigger one, a few blocks away.

Today that *shul* is the Iglesia Pentecostal, just like the Roman temples used to be Greek, so the Puerto Ricans go to the Iglesia that used to be a little *shul*. On the Lower East Side now, it's the same.

•

At suppertime when I was a kid there would be, if everybody was there, my father and my mother, who were social democrats and very upset about the Soviet Union. Then there would be my aunt who was a communist, and my other aunt who was a Zionist. There were big differences of opinion. They would talk and talk, and life went on no matter what. As my character Zagrowsky says in one of my stories, "I tell you what life is going on, you have an opinion, I have an opinion, life don't have no opinion." That was true for my family.

I still remember my mother reading the newspaper at the table when I was a kid. Apparently the Nazi party has just gotten itself together, and Hitler is in power. It must be around 1939, maybe a little earlier. My mother says to my father, "Look, Zenia, it's beginning again." Those words — "it's beginning again" — have reverberated in my ears all my life. *It's beginning again.* The fear you hear in those words. As a person who has never really suffered any prejudice, I remember those words.

I have letters from 1912, 1914, in Russian, from a woman writing to my aunt. The woman writes, "I don't know what to do about the boys. I don't know what to do with the two of them. They've gotten some foolishness in their head. They are going to some farm and taking classes to learn how to be farmers. They want to go to Palestine. I tell them they can't, they mustn't do it, and they say, 'But what have we here? We have nothing here.' They're right," she says, "they have nothing here. There's nothing here for them, and so," she says, "I have to let them do what they want. But why do they want to be farmers?" She's horrified. "What's wrong with these children? They want to be farmers? In Palestine of all places?"

My mother used to say she still remembered standing at the boat in 1905. The pogroms in Russia were terrible in 1904 and 1905. They started in the 1890s, and they were terrible. *The Jewish Forward* had a piece about this a couple of years ago, looking back to 1905. They quoted from the accounts back in 1905, saying, "In the towns and in the villages, the slaughter has been immense." So my parents came to this country. My father went to school immediately and learned Italian and English and became a doctor, and late in life became a painter, when he retired from being a doctor. My son says, "My grandfather is an artist retired from a doctor." They did well. Not all immigrants have done equally well, but if you talk to Italians or Irish or Serbo-Croatians, the country welcomed them. Now we are unwelcoming to immigrants because they are a poor and undereducated class. The bad thing is these old-time immigrants are not standing up enough for the newer immigrants — the Latino people who have been coming across the Mexican border, and others. There are many different cultures in this country, which makes it a very interesting country.

I'm an American. I don't feel national pride or anything like that, but on the other hand I'm very interested in this country. I'm very interested in the history of it, and I feel that it does have some valuable ideas that really have transformed many people. Certainly this is true when I think of my own parents coming here and all the other immigrants who have come here. They came for a reason, and they were satisfied, one way or the other.

◆

The word "spiritual" makes me nervous, so I just make a joke out of it. When people talk about their spirituality, I don't know what the hell they really mean. Does it mean the mush in their head? Does it mean they just don't know what to think? Our friend Michael Lerner has a big Jewish spiritual organization, and I think that's nice for him, but I don't need the word and I don't entirely understand it.

I think there is really a problem with the use of the word "spirituality" right now: It's too loose. People who don't want to talk about religion use this word. They want you to know that they are spiritual people, even though they are not religious; that they have souls, so to speak. I am wary of that kind of conversation. I prefer for people to talk about the reality of what's happening, and about what they feel for one another, what men feel for women, women for men. How we feel about our children.

Is this spiritual?

•

As a young person, I read a lot. In poetry, I liked W. H. Auden more than anyone. I loved British writers and the novels I grew up with, Twain, Dickens, and so on. I was not influenced by, say, Walt Whitman or anyone like that. His freedom was not my freedom, and so it didn't affect me. But Saul Bellow had begun to write already. He freed the Jewish voice in some ways that I didn't even recognize, but his work was all about men. Still, for Jews who were crazy about the English language, he was the one.

My father must have told us Bible stories, because I had biblical stories bred in me from early on, and I don't know from where. It wasn't my grandmother so much. I am very interested in the Bible. It's the King James version that I know, which is also great English literature. I think it had an effect on me because I've read the Bible a lot. I love the style of the King James Bible more than anything else. I was always a big reader, and I read good literature. I keep telling students, "You've got to read." We have a great tradition in English literature. We're very lucky. We have this big English language, which is so receptive of other languages. English takes everything in. The French have laws that you can't say this, you can't say that, but in English you can say any goddamned thing you want.

I started out as a poet, and then when I was older, I thought I'd like to try to write stories. It turned out that I had a lot of subject matter, which I didn't realize at first. At first I just had the first story I wrote. I was amazed when I finished it. I couldn't believe it. I suddenly had this large subject matter of the lives of women. I found this subject matter because I'd been spending much of my days with women and children in a way that I hadn't before, in Washington Square Park mostly.

Nothing happens without political movement. It just so happens that when I started writing prose, the women's movement was coming together. I didn't know this. What happens is that you're part of something without knowing it. The black power movement had a literature that lived with it, that supported it. So the women's movement began to develop. Tillie Olson and I didn't know it, but we were part of a movement. I became more and more interested in the lives of women, and I didn't know how to write about this material in poetry. I can now, but I couldn't do it then. So I had these stories, and I began to write them. I wrote them slowly over fifteen, twenty years. Really not much, but that was the basic voice that I had, and it was a normal voice to be writing in at that time, but I didn't know this. I mean, I was not doing it on purpose. I tried writing from men's points of view. I have a few stories from men's points of view, from people of different color, different races, but basically, my material was women's lives, and I was a part of what was happening at that time, that's all.

I was very surprised by how well I was received. My experience was that men's writing was interesting, and I really thought that for most people the lives of women would be very narrow in their appeal. But I couldn't help the fact that I had not gone to war, and I had not done the male things. I had lived a woman's life and that's what I wrote about.

•

Some of the poetry I was writing before I began to write stories was very literary. I was a big reader. I was a big imitator, too. I sounded like I was a little bit British in my poetry. The fact that I came from the Bronx was irrelevant. When I began to write stories, I had the luck of having written poetry so that I had the language in my mouth. On the other hand, fiction was much looser since it was prose. That had a great effect on me when I continued to write poetry. The poetry improved my prose, but the prose was equally good for my poetry. It loosened it up and made me more relevant to myself.

I struggle to be truthful to myself. I think that's what literature is about; it's the struggle for truth. It's the struggle for what you don't understand. So as long as I don't understand things I will be able to write, but once I understand everything, I won't be able to write anymore.

What kept me going, writing stories, is that all of a sudden I found the form I could use to try to understand in dialogue the people I'd been living with, the women I knew, and to try to make some history out of it somehow.

In prose I get the world to speak to me so I can understand it better, but it's the same in poetry — speaking out to the world but also getting the world to speak to you. In prose, you get these people to talk and figure things out for you, but in poetry you are on your own. So in poetry you're really speaking more to yourself, addressing yourself and trying to understand something. But both voices, prose and poetry, are mysterious.

You have to be a very good listener to be a writer. I talk a lot, but I'm a good listener with people. I'm interested in people, but I also like them. I'm very lucky in that because there are a lot of embittered people, grouchy people, writing books.

Writing does allow you to have those moments of understanding, if you're writing very often. You don't know that you understand, but sometimes you have characters talking to each other and the purpose of their conversation is for you to understand something about them, which could happen without your knowing it. In a way, you keep writing to understand more. You don't do it, and then say, "Oh, now I understand, the story's over." You're left pretty much still wondering, so there is that wonder and mystery.

I tell young writers, you should have a low overhead. Don't live with anybody who doesn't support your work. Very important. And read a lot. Don't be afraid to read or of being influenced by what you read. You're more influenced by the voice of childhood than you are by some poet you're reading. The last piece of advice is to keep a paper and pencil in your pocket at all times, especially if you're a poet. But even if you're a prose writer, you have to write things down when they come to you, or you lose them, and they're gone forever. Of course, most of them are stupid, so it doesn't matter. But in case they're the thing that solves the problem for the story or the poem or whatever, you'd better keep a pencil and paper in your pocket.

I gave this big advice in a talk, and then about three hours later I told a student that I really liked his work and asked how I could get in touch with him. He said he would give me his name and address. I looked in my pocket, and I didn't have any pencil or paper.

•

I have spent my life protesting and being socially active, but I never expected I would really change the world. I do a lot less protesting now, because I'm not that well. The world today is worse, but the people are better. I think this has to do with the revolutions of the 1960s and '70s and the work we all did in that period. The important thing to remember about the Iraq war is that the whole world protested against it. For the first time in history, the whole world, not just me and my husband Bob, but the whole world came together to try to stop a war before it started. That had never happened before. I have a book with pictures of those protests from all over the world, from Africa, from Asia, from all over Europe. In every country people said, "No, no, don't do it, don't do it." Whatever happens now, this fact is in the world. It's in the history of the world. I think that with those protests, we made maybe a couple of inches of progress. Some light flared there for a minute and that minute may be carried on.

That's why I say the world right now is a little worse, mostly because of what our country is doing, but the people are better because almost everywhere in the world there are people who are really thinking that they have some responsibility to make a peaceful world and to live decently. We'll see what the next generation can do.

Everyone should be socially active. I advocate that plumbers should do something — everybody should do something. Writers and artists don't have a special responsibility.

When the Iraq war started, Sam Hamill from Copper Canyon Press got all these poets together. Before anybody said a word, he had ten thousand poets writing letters to the White House saying, "Don't go into Iraq, don't go in." The writers were on top of it. I have no complaint about the writers.

During the Vietnam War we had something called Angry Arts, which Bob and several other artists organized. For a whole week all the artists performing in concerts at Town Hall and Lincoln Center stopped and got up and turned their backs. Everybody was quiet for several minutes to make the statement that we were against this war. Artists were making murals all over the city, and the poets were in trucks driving around reading poems. The artists were present.

But everybody should be involved, not just the artists. Carpenters, teachers, everybody.

Because of that one moment when the whole world came out against the Iraq war, I'm optimistic. That has made me optimistic, but apart from that, I have a lot of anxiety about the state of the world. When you think of the things that have happened in Rwanda and Darfur, that are still happening in Darfur, it's very discouraging. The degree of just plain murder is incredible. What's happening in Iraq, where they're all killing each other, is just terrifying. I'm neither optimistic nor pessimistic; I'm just on my knees hoping that things change somehow.

Looking out at the countryside here, I find it so amazing. If you look out the window, it's so amazing, and the countryside is being murdered. People don't understand what is being done to the countryside. In some parts of the world, they seem to understand it better than here. Here we don't seem to get it that the fields are being wrecked by poisons and the air is close to the end of breathable. There is a great effort in America to stay happy and not worry and not understand and not do anything about it.

I want people to look at the world and see what's happening to it and take some action. This planet is so lovable. It is so various and so lovable, including all sorts of parts of the world that I've never seen, and I've seen more than most people. Just in what your eyes see, and how people live on the earth, it's amazing, but it's going to end if we don't get our leaders to pay attention.

Human beings come from some little amoeba or paramecium someplace. That's what I learned in biology. Human beings come from several million years of development, which is quite wonderful. I have a lot of regard for what human beings have become. It took us a million years to learn how to speak to each other, and we did it. It took us another million years to work with each other, and we did it. I think the human race is remarkable. If we could only be nice to other animals, it would be even better.

Meanwhile, a human is just like any other animal. It's abusive and consumes the other species. That implies that we should all be vegetarian. Well, in a sense, I am saying that. Until we live in a world where we stop abusing each other and the other creatures, we will not have reached our perfection.

◆

I don't think in terms of being an atheist or not. I would just say that we live in mystery, and the making of this world is simply great and mysterious. Just this morning, I was listening to a man talking about finding rocks that were four billion years old. So we live in mystery. I'm not unsatisfied with that. I don't have to find a god or not find a god. There's a quote — I don't remember who said it — "Find me a god because I am full of prayers." I think my husband could be described this way. He's an old Episcopalian boy. He has lost his God, but I think he's full of prayers.

I'm not full of prayers. I'm full of language.

HERE

Here I am in the garden laughing
an old woman with sagging breasts
and a nicely mapped face

how did this happen
well that's who I wanted to be

at last a woman
in the old style sitting
stout thighs apart under
a big skirt grandchild sliding
on off my lap a pleasant
summer perspiration

that's my old man across the yard
he's talking to the meter reader
he's telling him the world's sad story
how electricity is oil or uranium
and so forth I tell my grandson
run over to your grandpa ask him
to sit beside me for a minute I
am suddenly exhausted by my desire
to kiss his sweet explaining lips.

— *Grace Paley*

FANNY HOWE has taught at Tufts University, Emerson College, Columbia University, Yale University, and the Massachusetts Institute of Technology. She is professor emerita of writing and literature at the University of California – San Diego. A prolific novelist and short story writer, and author of more than twenty works of poetry and prose, Howe has become one of the most widely read of American experimental poets. Her recent collections of poetry include On the Ground; Gone; Selected Poems, *winner of the 2001 Lenore Marshall Poetry Prize; and* Forged. *Her volumes of prose include* Lives of the Spirit / Glasstown: Where Something Got Broken; The Wedding Dress: Meditations on Word and Life, *a collection of essays; and the memoir* The Winter Sun: Notes on a Vocation. *She has received awards from the National Endowment for the Arts, the National Poetry Foundation, and the California Council for the Arts as well as a fellowship from the Bunting Institute. In 2008 she won an Award in Literature from the American Academy and Institute of Arts and Letters. In 2009, she received the Ruth Lilly Poetry Prize, given annually by the Poetry Foundation to a living U.S. poet whose lifetime of accomplishments warrants extraordinary recognition. We interviewed Fanny Howe in writing, a correspondence that led to a candid and lively back-and-forth about what aspects of a faith experience can be articulated.*

Fanny Howe

Footsteps Over Ground

The Mass is an account of the cooperation of transcendence with the ordinary.

I was never, as a child, taught respect for religious faith. My parents were skeptics, born in the first years of the twentieth century, the terrible century. Events confirmed their opinions on enlightenment and moral governance, so I absorbed their feelings and acted accordingly, hating (fearing) school, grown-ups, authority, and my own inheritance. I preferred animals and strangers to my forefathers.

In 1961, I dropped out of college and married. In 1963 I left the marriage, and I fell apart. In 1968, I married again and had three children in four years, and that marriage fell apart. In 1980, I married for the third time, with determination to fulfill my vow. You see, I married the Catholic church this time, which meant that I could make no more casual but momentous mistakes.

This marriage has been like any other: loving, boring at times, disappointing, occasionally joyful, in the end a matter of habit and perseverance. Unlike a human marriage, it bears no fruits and gives no physical warmth. The Catholic church turns a person into a Protestant, mentally. You find yourself constantly arguing with texts, testing them, and feeling indignation against dogma, dull vocabulary, hierarchies, moralizing, and patronizing vocabulary. You are not "spiritual" when you are Catholic. You are critical. You have a strong sense of structural evil in the world and your own compliance with that evil. Your intellectual muscles are tested again and again by Papal opinions.

Faith is not the issue. Worship, as a word, is not applicable. So why not just *be* a Protestant? Because then you could not argue yourself to the abyss of understanding, slip over edges, grasp onto the Gospel teachings for dear life, and hear the same words over and over and over — morning, noon, and Sunday — in every city in the world. All Catholics are Protestants already, although not all Protestants are Catholic.

It is irrationality worked to a perfection of logic that is the greatest offering of Catholicism. It is not sensible, and inevitably it asks people to pretend that they are obedient even when they are not. This contribution to hypocritical behavior is disagreeable, but when you are arguing with a fixed position, you have to argue with yourself, too. You have to continuously re-examine your place in social and ethical structures. Your thinking gets stronger rather than weaker. You are put on the spot, and at the same time you are subtly led to the last station in life, given a shove, and pulled back at the last minute.

As it is in the liturgy, so it is in the world: Truth is as fleeting as a sunbeam, and each time you go to Mass you see truth drop in a place it hadn't before. A word here, a phrase there, and each time a different one is as potent as the little sip of wine at the end. The truth exists, but it surrounds rather than informs people's acts, which are constructed around evasion and resistance.

You don't need to have faith to continue the habit of going to Mass. The daily Mass is faster and more to the point than a drawn-out Sunday liturgy with its dull homilies and platitudinal music. Yet we are told that it is an obligation to appear on Sunday, and so soon this is a habit: the habit of losing your productive laborer's mind, and simply accepting what comes. And then, of course, you have made a solemn vow and you don't ever want to break another one again.

◆

We live half-stunned by emptiness and the effort to stay on a horizontal plane in a circular situation. However, it may not be mad to hope that there is meaning in the end. I would call my faith this kind of hope.

The word "faith" is not an attractive one to me. I can only think of faith as footsteps over ground. But then there is coincidence, and a slowly developing sense of a structured future reality that is puzzling, and it increases with work, experience, and age. How people stay in your life. How memories are so strong and books passed along through decades, and at the same time there is no evidence of yesterday as a place. Dreams. Predictions. And a sense, when there is a ghastly tragedy of exploding earthquakes and tsunamis, that the you who is expelled from this belt of reality into paradise might be the person who was standing at the sink half an hour before it happened, or ten years before it happened. In this way, time is a secret, and your fulfillment in time is unknown.

I started going to Mass on brief experimental forays when I was a teenager and I had a close friend who went to church. Then I took instruction from an Episcopal priest when I was nineteen in California, between trips to North Beach to listen to jazz and poetry. I wanted the world to be both magical and full of meaning. I was always in a state of shock or awe at existing. It was inevitable I would end up Catholic, and a lover of all religious literature and acts from around the world. Simone Weil said Catholicism is a religion for slaves. She meant it as a great compliment. And I understand why. I have always imagined that the great religions came from those who had seen very little justice in this life. It's not really a paradox.

If I can only be horrified by reality, then I will have to kill myself. If I find it recognizable, I will be okay. The liturgy helps me to recognize the world and time. While the Eucharist is totally mad in terms of human reason, the ritual has another kind of intelligence, one that manages to be both earthy and cosmological. *Metaxu* — Simone Weil's "Every separation is a link" — a bridge that you rarely cross outside of reality.

The calendar year for daily working life is the same for all of us, but there is a second calendar: the church calendar that refers to the birth, murder, and resurrection of Jesus, which is an absolutely archetypal story, a poetic rendition of any human life. The Mass, with its readings from the Gospel stories, and then the Eucharistic rite, repeated for centuries, is an account of the cooperation of transcendence with the ordinary. If it is an opiate, all the better!

•

To get up in the morning and go out the door and put your feet on the ground and walk: This is all the faith I know. I cannot have a spiritual moment without remembering the evils of war, poverty, and illness. So I am trapped with my one eccentric action, going to Mass to think about people I care for or who are gone. If I think very hard about them, I call it prayer. I am safe in the building where I and other people can hide and concentrate on the possibility of change.

So-called spirituality is not the point of the Mass. There is as much of that in a pub on a rainy day, or on an underground train. Most of us know what is meant by suffering, pain, poverty, disease, oppression, betrayal by friends and politicians, illegitimate birth, imprisonment, and the insignificance/vulnerability of a powerless person. These are contained and contemplated in the readings at Mass, and then comes the Eucharist, and of that: the less said the better.

I would be lying if I didn't say that I wonder sometimes if I can stand another day of this marriage, which can be lonely and ugly. Its presiding culture (what is left of it) is often repulsive. The caps and capes and gowns and silken shoes are ludicrous. The vile sexual molestation of children has made many of us look at every priest with hostility and suspicion, no matter how well we know him. The religious women live in wretched buildings, compared to the monks, and only the truly poor of spirit, those living at a Gospel level, have our trust.

•

In the 1970s, when Liberation Theology was developing and we were receiving its early writings, I believed that this was the most profound analysis of social imbalance I had ever encountered. I had not yet married the Catholic church, but I was counting my steps on the way around the streets of Jamaica Plain, pushing babies in prams. At that time Jews were the only people I knew who would talk to me seriously on the mystery of God. Reading Simone Weil and Gustavo Gutierrez was certainly part of my passage. As did lots of people, I also read texts from the Gnostic tradition, Kabbalah, Christian mysticism, Rumi, the Bhagavad Gītā and Buddhism. The visions of these texts suffused my readings of Saint Paul and Hildegarde von Bingen. These are robust and poetic visions that give heft and depth to my experience of the Mass and ideally will eventually come to find their way into the Mass itself.

The specter of justice appears at every stage of human experience. It is in every syllable, transaction, sentence, bar of music, tone of voice, painting, and portion of the natural world — the desire for justice, the loss of it, the anger at its absence, and revenge in order to restore it.

When I went down to the bottom of the social well and had to get food stamps for myself and my young children to live on, and stood in unemployment lines, with no one to help me get out of the murk of living in economic fear (this lasted about four years), I realized that most rituals in the world are about standing in line and waiting for a change to come. In the urban Catholic churches in America, the ones I know, at least — like the Franciscan Church near Penn Station in New York — there is generally a crowd composed of everyone. There are no "others," and there is art, poetry, and music.

My father was a teacher of civil rights and the Constitution. He also was an activist in these areas. He was interested in law and justice all the time. He was very fair, very judicious in fact. He was fully conscious of complexities in human relations but remained undistracted in his attention to individual rights. He was against capital punishment because of the possibility of error, not because he believed in salvation of the soul.

My ability to keep fiddling with words and poems was fostered in the eye of such scrutiny, at the level of sound and excess: what is fair and what isn't.

•

My novels tell stories that are not autobiographical, but are studies of people I *almost* was myself, in reality. I had gone to the West Coast at age seventeen from a sheltered Boston childhood. It was the tail end of the Beat movement, and some of my friends were believers in Marxist ideals and poetry. But women at that time, as beautifully depicted in the movie *Let's Get Lost,* sat on the backs of motorcycles and in the back seats of cars and competed for the attention of bad boys.

We were white women. Around campuses, it was a white world, but not necessarily in the cafés and bars in San Francisco where the poetry readings took place. All this movement and expressiveness was an opening to the 1960s to come.

If I was representative of my generation and culture — rebellious, ignorant, and idealistic to a fault — these faults were displayed in my early novels *First Marriage* and *Bronte Wilde.*

Later I lived on the Lower East Side of New York City, on the Bowery, which was just about hell. It was the day and the time. Warhol and assassinations. Poverty and poetry were one and the same. My friends were zoned out. I had a guide dog named Woofer who was my only link to the animal real. Trees helped, too.

I left New York and went south with a boyfriend, where I took notes for CORE (Congress of Racial Equality), and then I worked on housing violations in Boston's Roxbury neighborhood, after my New York adventure had ended with no hope. My novel *The Deep North* tells the story of this seepage.

A few years ago, Nightboat Books published five of my novels under the title *Radical Love,* and I am grateful to have them out in the world. I have to say that these were poems to me, even with the problems of plot. I didn't write poems when I was working on those novels, and I worked just as hard on them, and their language, as I would work on poems. I feel sorry for the novels now, as if they are forgotten living people. I care about them a lot, though they are hardly ever mentioned or read. Some day I will try to understand why not, given the context of my generation, the timing, and their subject matter.

◆

When not with children, I have lived most of my life alone, for better or worse. I am overly attached to freedom, you could say. I like to do what I want. I like being alone at the window or on the streets.

Even as a child I preferred invisibility to being noticed. We had a very ethical and artistic childhood, my sisters and I. None of us graduated from college. We all married very young. Our parents were permissive, liberal, but not reckless. They would have no problem with writers or any kind of artist being one of their own, but hoped for us to be financially safe. They lived on an academic salary; there was no trust fund or anything like that.

When my children were young, I woke up at five and scribbled, or wrote while one was nursing and the other two were in day care. Usually, I have had to go to work at a job. In recent decades, I have worked from early in the morning until about two. I like to write outside of my household, to sit on a bench or platform, or in a café or office, and each day's work is a bit like practicing for a better day. I think, actually, I should have been a musician because I work with such a routine goal.

I have been lucky with friendships and have worked at keeping them alive, but my friends have done that, too, so this has not been real work but reciprocity. I have no idea what to do with men, although I have been close to a few. I prefer old-fashioned friendships with men because I like having a man around, but then it's great going home alone. Only one man was kind and loving and acted like a grown-up, and he had four children and I had three, so it was too difficult in the end. Many of my closest friends are women who have no interest in poetry and never read my books. They like to look around with me, go to a movie or out for tea or wine.

It would be impossible for me to have no one to call or see. But I am known for disappearing and moving around a lot. My mother called me "a tinker who makes a little mess and moves on."

My story is a story of failure. Failure at schools and failure in domestic relationships. What kept me going? The faces of people I pass, people who are still laughing, and folk music, popular music, classical music, and my love of the arts generally. In my most recent book of poems, *Come and See,* Russian movies and novels are all around me. Something primitive is trying to come forth, something raw and hard, as I have felt very strongly the dread of *fatelessness* rising from the masses of people passing. My aspiration for meaning is, paradoxically, energized by Catholic mysticism.

.

True prayer seems to belong to extreme situations. And prayer is addressed to the silence of the night. Across the Muslim world, the people at prayer on Fridays, and in the middle of the street, have given us a great image of humility before the unknowable. Right in the middle of war.

I never think of a possible God reading my poems, although the gods used to love the arts. Poetry could be spoken into a well, of course, and drop like a penny into the black water. Sometimes I think that there is a heaven for poems and novels and music and dance and paintings, but they might only be hard-worked sparks off a great mill, which may add up to a whole-cloth in the infinite.

I spend a lot of time working at the words — the way a plumber might fumble around for ridges in pipes — and daydreaming. I think I was drawn to writing because I couldn't express myself verbally, aloud; I still find this to be hard. I tend to be quiet and prefer to listen than to speak, but I am practicing scales in my mind all the time. Most commitments are reactions to failures, let's face it. You join the disabled when you are old and become invisible, dispensable.

It was learning other languages — Latin and French — that brought poetry into my own hands and heart. It was always intriguing to misunderstand a text and follow the misunderstanding to a new logical conclusion. Not lost but found, in a fog. Whatever it is that happens in the translated version of a poem is something that is always happening in ordinary discourse, but in translations these qualities are restrained, at a distance, with a touch of formality, and we should pay attention to them while we can.

•

Recently I had a sudden emergency surgery and then for eight weeks found myself in my apartment alone for twenty-three hours a day. For one hour each day a friend would visit, bring something nice to me, have tea and cookies, and then leave. It was new to me to "receive" in this way and to rediscover books that had been put away some time ago.

I returned to Baudelaire and read his poems aloud in the original, maybe two or three each day, and this helped with the aphasia that followed the anesthesia. If I read the French out loud, my early love of the poem re-awoke. I recognized the sounds and images from years before, and I found my whole mind beginning to find language, if very incompletely. Henry James was too difficult for me. Even Thomas Hardy, my great love, seemed impenetrable. But poetry, especially poetry in translation, was open, as were certain philosophers like Walter Benjamin, Simone Weil, and Giorgio Agamben. I read Friedrich Hölderlin's poems in several translations. And I had Paul Auster's wonderful anthology of French poetry.

In my time alone, recovering, I was increasingly contented. The sunspots on the walls and floors, the view from my window, the sounds of children in the park, and then snow floating past... reflections of glory or of "truth." I realized that we can almost but not quite see ahead and into another reality, through misty membranes like leaves of a book. But the figure must hide in the folds (time vertical), though sometimes it plays tricks, so you glimpse it in a dream or a coincidence...

Of course I wasn't out there shoveling or grinding my tires in slush, so it was simple for me there on the fifth floor to have visions.

·

Surely the new world will be born somewhere unnoticed by the West right now. We have to leave behind the dreadful twentieth-century cemetery and face the effects of that era on the earth and on our imaginations.

All our thoughts and gestures take place in a historical context. I can see myself as having been at the end, rather than the beginning, of a historical period. This is not to say that the old questions and answers will disappear, but that there will be a radically new vocabulary, mostly thanks to scientific inquiry and translations. Maybe we will learn what time is, finally, but be unable to absorb it for several generations. I wish that I would be here to know what they understand about time.

It would be good if we in America could learn new languages to express feelings and ideas from other cultures, if we could be multilingual and nuanced, if we could put consciousness and self-criticism to good use. I can't submit to the idea that all cultures tend toward capitalism, or that all children must lose their wonder. I think that scientists and artists share a sense of the possible as a great wonder. So I can only hope that our new technology will shed light on the margins, and hope that there are roaming minds in young and faraway youths who will figure out a way to interrupt destructive patterns.

In my most serene moments, I feel that there is a God behind God, and I feel that the God we discuss is the one that contains time and all the galaxies, universes and tricks of light and leaping planets. This recognizable God receives and judges our lives according to some measurement we can only imagine through readings in religious texts, and by observing love in action. Only a few can go free to the far God — probably the last, the weakest, and the most good-natured.

(But when I say "God," this is a last resort of language and the origin of a nausea that follows the failures of other words, including all of the above.)

VETERAN

I don't believe in ashes; some of the others do.
I don't believe in better or best; some of the others do.
I don't believe in a thousand flowers or the first robin
of the year or statues made of dust. Some of the others do

I don't believe in seeking sheet music
by Boston Common on a snowy day, don't believe
in the lighting of malls seasonably
When I'm sleeping I don't believe in time
as we own it, though some of the others might

Sad lace on green. Veterans stamping the leafy snow
I don't believe in holidays
long-lasting and artificial. Some of the others do
I don't believe in starlings of crenellated wings
I don't believe in berries, red & orange, hanging on
threadlike twigs. Some of the others do

I don't believe in the light on the river
moving with it or the green bulbs hanging on the elms
Outdoors, indoors, I don't believe in a gridlock of ripples
or the deep walls people live inside

Some of the others believe in food & drink & perfume
I don't. And I don't believe in shut-in time
for those who committed a crime

of passion. Like a sweetheart
of the iceberg or wings lost at sea

the wind is what I believe in,
the One that moves around each form

—*Fanny Howe*

LI-YOUNG LEE was born in 1957 in Jakarta, Indonesia.
His mother was a descendant of Chinese royalty and his father
was a personal physician to Mao Tse-tung. Disillusioned with
Communism, Lee's parents left China only to experience persecu-
tion in Indonesia, where his father was imprisoned by Sukarno.
From Indonesia, the family traveled throughout Asia, eventually
coming to the United States in 1964. Li-Young Lee attended the
Universities of Pittsburgh and Arizona, and the State University
of New York–Brockport. He is the author of Rose, *winner of the*
Delmore Schwartz Memorial Poetry Award; The City in Which
I Love You, *a Lamont Poetry Selection;* Book of My Nights; *and*
most recently, Behind My Eyes. *His memoir,* The Winged Seed,
received an American Book Award from the Before Columbus
Foundation. His other honors include a Lannan Foundation liter-
ary award, a Whiting Writers' Award, a Guggenheim Foundation
fellowship, and a grant from the National Endowment for the Arts.
We interviewed Li-Young Lee when he was in residence teaching in
the M.F.A. program at New England College.

Li-Young Lee

The Subject Is Silence

I realize that it's my own mystery I'm looking at.

English is not my first language, though it is the language in which I write. I feel the real medium for me is silence, so I could be writing in any language. To inflect the inner silence, to give it body, that's all we're doing. You use the voice to make the silence present. The real subject in poetry isn't the voice. The real subject is silence. It's like in architecture, where the medium is not really stone or metal, but space. We use materials — brick, glass, whatever — to inflect the immaterial, space. I would say that the real medium of poetry is inner space, the silence of our deepest interior. It just happens that as time has gone by I get better and better with English. As I use it every day, English grows less alien to me. But I'm still using it for this one thing, to inflect the inner space as I feel it.

The early years of my childhood were spent moving from country to country with my family, from Indonesia to Hong Kong, Macau, and Japan. The other day I opened the back porch door and got a blast of winter air. Suddenly I was reliving the newness and strangeness of our first winter in America. It was an almost overwhelming visitation from childhood. I do have such memories, and they're very vivid, but they're not surrounded by any narrative. Maybe I don't have a narrative because that's the way my mind works. Or maybe it's because my parents were inundating me with narratives of their own, so I couldn't make one up as we went along.

My father was very involved with the books of the Old Testament, studying them and translating them, so he was reading to us all the time from them and telling us his versions of those stories. A lot of the narratives he gave us were biblical. I guess, looking back now, it was his own form of *midrash*. The way he told those stories, the way he interpreted them for us, led us to believe that we were the children of Israel, and the Indonesian dictator Sukarno was Pharaoh. And, of course, my father saw our plight as a version of surviving the flood. The ark was the family, along with the stories, songs, and photo albums we would need to start over again once we had found shore. On the other hand, my mother, who came from the ruling family that was displaced when the Communists took over China, was filling us with the stories from her childhood — haunted mansions, heroic uncles, ignoble ancestors, concubines, and so on. My parents' stories probably helped us. They gave a kind of mythic content or background to our experience, which saved it from being just late-twentieth-century exile.

My earliest memory in Indonesia is of the servant bringing in a basket full of eels and pouring them into the yard, and chasing them around chopping the heads off, because we were going to eat eel that night. For a child seeing that — the eels being beheaded — it's both violent and vivid and sexual. When we moved to the United States, I remember the little house where we lived in Seattle. I remember a hill and the woods in the back. I remember that it was sad. I remember my mother crying a lot. One of my father's first jobs was in the China exhibit at the World's Fair. He was "the Chinese man," the token Chinese. He was unhappy about that.

•

My father was imprisoned in Indonesia. Sukarno said that my father and the CIA were planning to bomb Indonesia. It was ridiculous, and the charges were made up. Sukarno was just locking up Chinese out of Sinophobia. My father had a conversion experience in jail. While in jail, he was supposedly dying. They asked him, "Do you want to be buried in a brown suit or a blue suit?" He said, "Blue." They pronounced him dead. His cellmate washed his body, and the state gave him a blue suit. They were going to bury him, and I don't know whether he wasn't dead, or he came back to life. He told me, "I died. I saw things." But he didn't die. He said this was God, giving him back his life. He gave his life to the ministry after this.

My father was not a Christian before this conversion, but afterward there were things we experienced that he saw as divine intervention. For instance, we were being taken from Indonesia to a prison colony, and on the way the ship stopped outside Hong Kong. We were there to let some people off, but we weren't allowed to leave because we were under arrest. A chartered boat came along. A man got on our ship and said that he was looking for someone. The captain of the ship said, "That person isn't here." The man said, "He chartered this boat. It's paid for. I'm supposed to take him in to the harbor." The captain said, "I'll look around, but he's not on our list." My father happened to be walking around and saw this man, and they knew each other. He was an ex-student of my father's. They started talking, and the man said, "I'm here to pick somebody up, but he's not here. I've got this boat." My father said, "Why don't we get on it?" But of course we couldn't get on the boat because they had to give us our passports to let us leave.

I remember my father and mother whispering back and forth very excitedly. It was Christmas. We looked out the portholes and saw the green Christmas trees on Hong Kong island all lit up. My parents approached the soldiers and asked if we could get off. The soldiers looked at our passports, looked at their lists, and said sure, we could get off. The list should have told them we were under arrest, but it didn't. They gave us our passports. In fact, they looked at me and my brother and said, "These two, when they grow up, you must bring back to Indonesia, because that's their home." They knew who we were, so why did they let us go? I don't know. My father said that was God. It was like in the Odyssey when the gods cloud somebody's vision.

•

I've taken that personal, historical — I'll call it a horizontal — phenomenon of my childhood, traveling from one country to another, and seen it as a metaphysical phenomenon. I feel as if I've been exiled not from any one country but from a state of identity with the world. When I was little, there was an identity between me and the world. I was the world, the world was me. There was no difference. Then suddenly I began to feel so apart from that connection. I've been exiled from Eden, I guess you would say, exiled from the Garden.

What I have gone through on the horizontal plane of history just happens to coincide with what we all go through in our psychic lives. For me that coincidence of the personal history and the psychic history is something I see as lucky. It's clearer for me.

But I would like to be known as a poet of reconciliation, a poet who made it back from exile. You see, I have children, so everything's at stake. My final report to them can't be that our true human condition is homelessness and exile, though if that's what I ultimately discover, that's what I'll report. At this point in my life maybe there's a lot of homesickness and exile in my work because this is what is true for me. But my hope is that someday I will be a poet of blessing and praise. Still I know I need to get there authentically. I need to find my real way home.

If you tell yourself that the whole world depends on everything you do, suddenly when you have children, you feel that it's concretely true. I met a man, a professor, who was telling his class, "There's no meaning in the world. It's all fabricated by language. Language doesn't refer to anything." I asked him, "Do you tell your children that? You profess that to other people's children. Do you profess that to your children?" He said, "Of course not. Why would I do that?" It would get dangerous if his kids walked around saying, "Your words don't mean anything. They don't refer to anything. When you talk about love or safe sex or whatever, it doesn't refer to anything." So why is he professing this to other people's children?

Whatever you profess, whatever you write in a poem, is a self that you are making, and this is the self that you give your children. Yeats said that we make the self in the poem. My children don't get what I say, they get who I am, and who I am is in large part the self I uncover in my poems, whether that's a homeless wanderer or a man rooted in a deeper repose.

•

When my family came to America, we were poor. My mother sold her wedding ring at one point so we could get by, but my father's work as a minister brought him in touch with people who had even less. He saw suffering that was astonishing, destitution rivaling the worst slums of Jakarta or Hong Kong, except that it was in a rural setting. In the area where we lived in Pennsylvania, the people were coalminers and steelworkers, but most of the mines had closed down and the mills were beginning to fold, so many people were out of work. There was a great deal of alcoholism, and there were those who didn't even have money for alcohol. It was baffling to find people in the twentieth century living in the hills in unheated shacks. I remember being dumbfounded, thinking, "That guy lives in a shack and survives on squirrels and dandelion leaves. What the hell is this? Where am I? Aren't we in America?" Traveling with my father to visit shut-ins, I saw many shocking things and inhuman conditions.

There's no need to romanticize poverty, but I think it was good for me. If you're poor, you wear terrible clothes which you got from the neighbor, and when you're done with them, you're going to give them to your brother, and so on. On Christmas, we had nothing. We gave each other presents from our own belongings because we didn't have real presents to give. When you live like this, you ask, "Where is my value in the world?" You can't say, it's because I'm rich, or it's because I'm clean, even. You begin to value people differently. Does this mean that everybody should be poor? I would say that I was fortunate to experience poverty and fortunate to get out of it.

125

All my father's life he was wrestling with visions of God that he found contradictory. On the one hand, there was a God who acted in history and time, and on the other hand, there was a God who was a condition of the pure present. I think this is my obsession, what I wrestle with, too. But I'm beginning to believe that the two visions aren't mutually exclusive, or that the two views are a single view, a fruitful paradox.

The whole idea of a historical God was very interesting to my father when he converted. He started to feel that he had a destiny.

I do believe God unfolds a divine will in history. By history, I mean human phenomena. I think a divine will is unfolded in human phenomena. When we read history, we can read history as either the story of humans or the story of humans and God. For me, if history is read just as human endeavors, it's not interesting. I think a deep sense of order permeates all phenomena. Call this order God, or Tao, or the vast hand of Buddha, or whatever your Jewish mother or Chinese father called it. I believe poetry is grounded in this order.

Ever since I was a kid, I would ask my father, "Is there a God?" and he would say, "Who wants to know?" I would say, "Quit playing games. Is there a God?" He would shake me and say, "Who wants to know?" He would laugh. I never understood. Now that he's been dead twenty years, I'm beginning to understand what he meant. Is it God who wants to know? It isn't me, because where did I get the idea of God? If I've never heard of a mango, don't even know the word mango, have never seen one, never tasted one, I would not out of the blue say, "What is a mango?"

I'm not sure how having a father who was a minister and growing up in the church influenced me. If you take the genetic view of upbringing, you would say it made me obsessed about spiritual matters. If you take the Buddhist or *karmic* view, in another lifetime he and I were both obsessed with this stuff, so I became his son. I don't know whether my obsession with otherworldly matters comes from him or just comes from me.

Growing up in church made for a rich symbolic life. The church itself was a huge symbol, especially when it was empty. I loved sitting in the church by myself when it was empty. It was a very pregnant symbolic life — the loaves and fishes, all the stories of the Bible, and communion.

I don't attend church now because it's not pregnant for me anymore. I see formal religion as taking calcified poetic images and worshipping them for two thousand years, but the poet is making for himself or herself fresh religious images. Emily Dickinson addressed the way people worship. She said, "They worship an eclipse."

I always thought poetry was the opposite. There's eclipse, covering, and there's apocalypse, uncovering. I think poetry provides a very important service. It uncovers our deepest identity. When we read a poem, that's what we get — our deepest identity, who we are fully. Religion is a path to this uncovering, but it's not as immediate. Poetry provides a very deep, immediate service, like a church service. It is proof of contact with God, proof that contact with God is possible, and not through a middleman. Read Emily Dickinson. Through all her quarrels, she affirms this.

•

Now the "I" in a poem is either a very deep "I" embedded in a bigger "I," or it's just this dry "I," tiny little "I," floating around like confetti. I'm afraid this sounds like I'm referring to the ego. I don't mean the ego. I don't mean that we humans are the only thing. But every time we look at a poem or a piece of art, the real subject is the "I." Art can give us a version of the "I" that is manifold, deep, and has divine and human content. But when I say divine and human, it's as if they're separate, and they're not. Divine *in* human content is what I mean. That's what poetry is.

I do think that poetic consciousness is the fullest, most complete consciousness. It gives voice to the fullest of who we are. As I'm walking around in the world, I'm noticing what is around me. I look at the bridge out there and the river, and I think that's so beautiful, that's so mysterious. Then I realize that it's my own mystery I'm looking at. The river is not there saying, "I'm beautiful." So the idea of beauty is something I give to the river or project onto it. The river is embedded in nature, right? It's part of nature. I'm embedded in nature. The river is embedded in God, I would say also, and I am embedded in God. So when I look at the river, it's nature looking at nature. It's God looking at God. Where does the "I" come from? Why do I have a sense that there is a me, something separate? Where does that come from?

What we encounter in art is presence. Every time we encounter a poem, we encounter a version of a self. Sometimes the self we encounter in poetry is vapid and tinny, *jejune*. There are poems where the presence is more complete and poems where the presence is not as complete. What troubles me are the ethical implications of projecting into the world an "I" that is less than the best of who we are, a presence that may even be toxic in one way or another.

Poetry may begin in a conflict, but it ends in marriage. I think praise, as Rilke says, is about an inner marriage. And an outer one — us and the world. Somehow we are harmonizing with the world, even with its worst parts. We are married to it. That's why I am disappointed by poetry that is a kind of mimesis, a copy of what is around us. We look at the culture and it's fractured, so we make a fractured text that's mimetic. If the world is fractured, the work of poetry is to marry everything, to integrate everything. I think it's a nasty trick to leave a reader in a bad place, because we can choose.

You can't say, "I wrote it this way because it's more authentic." No, you chose that ending. You can't say, "The world is a terrible place, so in order to be truthful I want the poem to reveal all the ugliness and mendacity in the world." That's only part of the picture. I want the whole picture. It seems to me poetry gives the whole picture by practicing the whole presence.

•

I love thinking about God. The problem of problems, as Freud put it, is the ethical problem. That's it. Right and wrong. Good and bad. If a poet doesn't tackle this problem, doesn't face it down and come to a conclusion, then he's just making knickknacks; he's decorating. There must be an ethical consciousness that is available.

For me, the only possible ethical consciousness available to human-kind is poetic consciousness, because poetic consciousness accounts for the most of who we are. Any other standard doesn't account for enough. I think I'm in agreement with Blake here. Poetic consciousness equals complete consciousness, accounts for the whole human being. On a social scale, this would be a government, an empire, that accounts for all of its population — the poor, the rich, women, men, children, old people, black, white. Poetry is a way to integrate all of who we are. The beast, the murderer, all of it. I think that's what Rilke was trying to do in the elegies, when he talks about the murderer. I don't mean give the murderer free rein, but we have to account for that psychology and understand it, without pushing it aside. Poetry is a way to integrate all of our consciousness.

Of course, Buber spoke of this question of ethics in *I and Thou*. But I would want to move past Buber to I and I. If we can walk through the world and practice I and I — Christ said this, right? Treat your neighbor as yourself. If I looked at everything as myself, that would be complete enlightenment. You could never hurt another person.

But we're so unenlightened, we do hurt ourselves. There's all these people cutting themselves, people killing themselves, drinking themselves to death. So we haven't even gotten past just loving ourselves. We're not there yet. The practice of poetry can help us move toward this. It can help us be more comfortable with things in ourselves we don't like.

.

I do believe that poetry makes better people. How come we're not al-lowed to say this? Nobody says this. There is a great poet, I won't mention his name, who said, "Poetry isn't therapy." I think it is, and in fact, when I read his poems, I felt that they saved my life. Am I stupid? Am I one of those idiots who goes around saying that poetry saved my life? His poems, I can say this, saved my life. And I bet they saved his life.

My poems are addressed to an "all" — the stars, the trees, the birds, everything. When I'm writing a poem, I feel like the whole future of the universe depends on that poem. Of course I'm laughing, chuckling to myself as I say this. I'm embarrassed that I feel this way, but I do. Someone asked a poet I know after September 11th if he could write a poem for the occasion of September 11th. He said, "I already did. It's all I have ever been doing." In a way, every poem is written at Ground Zero. Yehuda Amichai said, "Every poem I write takes all of human history into consideration, all the atrocities, all the good stuff, and it's the last poem I'm going to write." So you're there — that's Ground Zero. You write at Ground Zero all the time. The audience is everything: birds, trees, stars, women, children, men, old and young, grandmothers, aunts, uncles — everybody is listening.

Sometimes a poem comes out and it's done. Sometimes it takes a long time. I do sense when I'm revising that it's about a balance between fate and destiny, and chance. Somehow the poem has to have a lot of fate in it. The sense that a line, for instance, is destined and could not have been written in any other way. At the same time, a poem has to have all the excitement or danger of chance. How do you negotiate those two things in a poem?

It does feel to me that when we write poems, we're dealing with very basic things in life. We want to fulfill our destiny, which we feel in our belly and in our hearts. At the same time, we want to keep it open to fateful chances, some sort of paradox like that. So revision is for me a lot of fun. It's joyful.

For me the question of what is poetry is very narrow, but then my definition of what is God is very wide. So I would say that God is all through Robert Frost, even though he said he was an atheist. I see him wrestling with God in "West-Running Brook," "Directive," and "The

Most of It." In Frost, the surface subject is the people, but when you read the lines, you see that there is divinity in those lines. There is a will in those lines that is beyond Frost's personal will. God is a mystery, but God is also our deepest identity. If the presence of God is not in a work of art, it's not art to me.

People who read poetry but don't write it are like those who have just heard about the burning bush. They've got to write poetry. They've got to read it also, because then they've heard about the burning bush, but when you write it, you sit inside the burning bush, which is different. I think everybody should write poetry. I do. I have friends who say, "The only people who read poetry are people who write it." I think, "Well, of course. And everybody should be writing poems, right?"

My Father, in Heaven,
Is Reading Out Loud

My father, in heaven, is reading out loud
to himself Psalms or news. Now he ponders what
he's read. No. He is listening for the sound
of children in the yard. Was that laughing
or crying? So much depends upon the
answer, for either he will go on reading,
or he'll run to save a child's day from grief.
As it is in heaven, so it was on earth.

Because my father walked the earth with a grave,
determined rhythm, my shoulders ached
from his gaze. Because my father's shoulders
ached from the pulling of oars, my life now moves
with a powerful back-and-forth rhythm:
nostalgia, speculation. Because he
made me recite a book a month, I forget
everything as soon as I read it. And knowledge
never comes but while I'm mid-stride a flight
of stairs, or lost a moment on some avenue.

A remarkable disappointment to him,
I am like anyone who arrives late
in the millennium and is unable
to stay to the end of days. The world's
beginnings are obscure to me, its outcomes
inaccessible. I don't understand
the source of starlight, or starlight's destinations.

And already another year slides out
of balance. But I don't disparage scholars;
my father was one and I loved him,
who packed his bags once, and all of our belongings,
then sat down to await instruction
from his god, yes, but also from a radio.
At the doorway, I watched, and I suddenly
knew he was one like me, who got my learning
under a lintel; he was one of the powerless,
to whom knowledge came while he sat among
suitcases, boxes, old newspapers, string.

He did not decide peace or war, home or exile,
escape by land or escape by sea.
He waited merely, as always someone
waits, far, near, here, hereafter, to find out:
is it praise or lament hidden in the next moment?

— *Li-Young Lee*

ALICIA OSTRIKER, author of twelve volumes of poetry, has twice been nominated for a National Book Award. Her most recent volume of poetry is The Book of Seventy, *which won the Jewish Book Award for Poetry. Ostriker is also the author of two volumes on women's poetry,* Writing Like a Woman *and* Stealing the Language: The Emergence of Women's Poetry in America; *and three books on the Bible,* Feminist Revision and the Bible, The Nakedness of the Fathers: Biblical Visions and Revisions, *and* For the Love of God: The Bible as an Open Book. *Her most recent book of criticism is* Dancing at the Devil's Party: Essays on Poetry, Politics, and the Erotic. *Ostriker's poems have appeared in* The New Yorker, The Paris Review, Antaeus, The Nation, Poetry, American Poetry Review, The Atlantic, MS, *and* Tikkun, *among other journals. She has received awards from the National Endowment for the Arts, the Poetry Society of America, the Rockefeller Foundation, and the Guggenheim Foundation. She is professor emerita of Rutgers University and a faculty member in the Drew University M.F.A. in poetry program. We corresponded with Alicia Ostriker in writing and appreciated her willingness to reflect on how, despite an upbringing with little religious education, she came to find biblical stories and questions of faith to be powerful sources for her work.*

Alicia Ostriker

God the Mother

When Sarah laughed, I laughed. When Jacob wrestled all night with a stranger, I wept with joy.

Who knows where the sense of the sacred comes from?

I was raised in the 1930s and '40s in an adamantly atheist family of socialist Jews. Neither my parents nor my grandparents were religious. The first Passover seder I ever attended was at the home of a friend in middle school, and I had no idea what it was all about. My religious education consisted of being told that religion was the opiate of the people. My father was an ardent union man, and one of the songs we used to sing around the kitchen table was the famous Joe Hill parody of the Salvation Army hymn "The Sweet By and By":

You will eat by and by
in that glorious land above the sky;
work and pray, live on hay,
You'll get pie in the sky when you die *(it's a lie!)*

So how did it come about that I go through life seeking God, and at the same time questioning all the texts that claim to know what God is?

A good snappy answer would be that you have to rebel against your parents, so as a child of atheists I had to become religious. But that's not the truth. The truth is more mysterious. I suspect that some of us are naturally attuned, or open, to the joy of what Walt Whitman called "original energy," or what William Blake celebrates when he says "Everything that lives is holy," or what H. D. means by "spiritual realism," or what Li-Young Lee means when he says "… The deepest possible silence is the silence of God. I feel a poem ultimately imparts silence. That way it's again disillusioning. It disillusions us of our own small presence in order to reveal the presence of this deeper silence — this pregnant, primal, ancient, contemporary, and imminent silence, which is God."

•

In my case, beginning in early adolescence, I sometimes found myself experiencing the world around me, the universe around me, as holy. I could be crossing the street to go to the subway — which emerged from underground at Dyckman Street where I lived in a housing project in upper Manhattan — and there were the shadows of the elevated train tracks and the two platforms, and the bright blue sky above with some small white clouds, and the brick buildings set in grass plots behind me, and the dirty lively street and the rushing traffic, and suddenly everything in the world was One. I knew that the realities I could see and also the realities I couldn't see were just as they were meant to be, very good. Even the evil things were meant to be as they were; they were good too, were right. Everything fitted and was moving together; everything was filled with holy energy and unity. Or I could be sitting on the grass in Central Park with a book in my lap, smelling the earth and grass, feeling how alive they were; then noticing a bum sitting some distance away from me, I'd see that that the bum was an angel, and I'd gaze and gaze at him.

Art, too, could reveal the holiness. I remember the moment I first laid eyes on Van Gogh's *Starry Night*. I'd been taken to an opening of a show at the Metropolitan Museum by the wealthy parents of a girlfriend. Her father was an art dealer who lived on Fifth Avenue, and I was this rough diamond, this scholarship kid, this object of their charitable benevolence. They were trying to "civilize" me, as Huck Finn would say. I was usually pretty resistant, and resentful of their kind efforts. Remember, I was a Red Diaper baby. Part of the ideology I drank with my mother's milk was that rich people were my enemies. I was *proud* of being poor... But there I was, in a roomful of ladies wearing mink coats, pushing my way past them, when suddenly in front of me appeared this painting! This Revelation! This, at last, was what people meant when they talked about Art with a capital A. At the same time, it was a manifestation of Reality with a capital R. The divine Reality, the divine energy that sweeps through the universe, that is the truth inside everything, that we can't see with our eyes — and there it was in those swirling blues and yellows, and those curves of trees. The energy was there in those brushstrokes.

When eros entered my life, I experienced the sweetness of sex between my boyfriend and myself as holy. When I first read section 5 of "Song of Myself," where Whitman describes his body and his soul making love, I just about swooned:

> I believe in you my soul, the other I am must not abase itself
>   to you,
> And you must not be abased to the other.

> Loafe with me on the grass, loose the stop from your throat,
> Not words, not music or rhyme I want, not custom or lecture,
>   not even the best,
> Only the lull I like, the hum of your valved voice.

> I mind how once we lay such a transparent summer morning,
> How you settled your head athwart my hips and gently turn'd
>   over upon me,
> And parted the shirt from my bosom-bone, and plunged your
>   tongue to my bare-stripp'd heart,
> And reach'd till you felt my beard, and reach'd till you held
>   my feet.

Swiftly arose and spread around me the peace and knowledge
    that pass all the argument of the earth,
And I know that the hand of God is the promise of my own,
And I know that the spirit of God is the brother of my own,
And that all the men ever born are also my brothers, and
    the women my sisters and lovers,
And that a kelson of the creation is love,
And limitless are leaves stiff or drooping in the fields,
And brown ants in the little wells beneath them,
And mossy scabs of the worm fence, heap'd stones, elder, mullein
    and poke-weed.

It didn't matter at all to me if he was masturbating, or having sex with another person, or just imagining it all — he was describing arousal, and orgasm, and the gradual return from ecstasy to normal consciousness — that worm-fence, that poke-weed! Hilarious! And sacred at the same time. I'd never seen anything like that in print. Likewise when I first read Blake, my response was a huge emphatic, "Yes!" They were putting into language what in my deepest self I already knew but had no words for. Here's Blake in a humorous poem called "The Question Answer'd":

What is it Men in Women do require?
The lineaments of Gratified Desire.
What is it Women do in Men require?
The lineaments of Gratified Desire.

Well, sure. Only nobody had the honesty to say so before Blake. I was also drawn to John Donne, George Herbert, Gerard Manley Hopkins — all the poets who deal in one way or another with the sacred seemed to be speaking to me and for me. But especially Whitman and Blake, because they weren't tied to church or dogma. In fact, they were spiritually alive while being *opposed* to church and dogma. I liked that!

138

For me, it's the great heterodox poets who grasp the most powerful spiritual truths. The divine all around us, and the divine within us, and within everything—every atom.

Gerard Manley Hopkins says, "The world is charged with the grandeur of God." Paul Eluard says, "There is another world, but it is inside this one." Blake says, "All deities reside in the human breast." This makes perfect sense to me. These statements are all abstract, but all of them are saying that we find the sacred within the physical world. That's where I find it, too. I've never been a devotee of the God who sits on an exalted throne remote from us, the sex-hating dualistic God Blake cleverly calls "Nobodaddy," who is nothing but an egocentric tyrant demanding to be worshipped. I've never been interested in transcendence, or an afterlife. I'm for immanence. This life, and that's it. If there's sacredness to be found, it's to be found right here.

•

My first real encounter with Judaism was reading the Bible one summer while I was in college. My then-boyfriend—subsequently my husband—had said he thought I'd like it. Ha! That was an understatement. Reading the Bible was a quite different experience from reading poetry, even the poetry of Whitman and Blake. I bonded with that book as if it were a dream of my own. Mine, I kept thinking, this is mine. Of course I was reading the magnificent King James translation, but it was the stories that captured me, first of all. When Sarah laughed, I laughed. When Jacob wrestled all night with a stranger and in the morning said "I will not let thee go except thou bless me," I wept with joy. When David danced before the Lord, I wanted to dance, too. When Job raised his voice in anger and challenged God's goodness, I understood where Jewish anti-authoritarianism—and my own habit of questioning authority—came from. When the prophets demanded in God's name that we feed the hungry and clothe the naked, and imagined a world without war, I was right there with them. They were attacking priests and kings! They were inventing social justice! When the woman in the Song of Songs declared, "My beloved is mine and I am his," calling on her lover to "come into his garden and eat his pleasant fruits," I felt that the men and women in the Bible were *my* mothers and fathers, and the God was *my* God — whether I liked him or not. My reading of the Bible didn't affect my writing until the mid-1980s, though.

By the '80s I had identified myself as an American poet (thank you Walt Whitman, William Carlos Williams, and Allen Ginsberg, all poets who veered away from Englishness in language and tone, and toward democratic inclusiveness). I also saw myself as a feminist poet (thank you Sylvia Plath, Anne Sexton, Adrienne Rich, H. D., Muriel Rukeyser, and hundreds of other beautiful, courage-giving women). As a critic, I had published a set of critical essays entitled *Writing Like a Woman*. Now I was writing *Stealing the Language: the Emergence of Women's Poetry in America* — a far more ambitious task that in fact took me ten years to accomplish. The process involved looking at more than two hundred individual volumes of poetry by post-1960s women, as well as numerous anthologies.

What was happening collectively in women's poetry since the 1960s that had never happened in literature before? Women were trying to define their identities for themselves. They were writing intimately of the body. There was sharp anger and violence in their poetry, which proved incredibly painful for me to write about, because it brought up so much of my own rage around certain relationships — relationships patterned by a world that fears and demeans women. I was able to get through the chapter on anger only because I promised myself I could write about women's new vision of the erotic after that. But my final chapter claimed that women's revisionist mythmaking was the most radical wing of the women's poetry movement. If myths are basic human stories that encapsulate our deepest passions and yearnings, myths also hold the key to the treasuries where our meanings for "male" and "female" are stored. When they are re-told by women, when the fabric is spun by women, everything changes. I was writing about Rukeyser's poem "Myth," a poem both witty and profound that recounts an unrecorded conversation between Oedipus and the Sphinx. Old and blind, Oedipus wants to know where he went wrong, and the Sphinx tells him that he answered her famous question incorrectly.

> "When I asked, What walks on four legs in the morning,
> two at noon, and three in the evening, you answered,
> Man. You didn't say anything about woman."
> "When you say Man," said Oedipus, "you include women
> too. Everyone knows that." She said, "That's what you think."

I was looking at poems written from Penelope's perspective instead of from that of Odysseus, or from Eurydice's rather than from that of Orpheus. And the reimagining, re-defining of war, peace, and the meaning of civilization in H. D.'s triumphal epic poem "Helen in Egypt," her answer to Ezra Pound's "Cantos." Imagine Helen of Troy, the sex-object blamed by poets for three thousand years as the reason for the Trojan War, announcing:

> I am not, nor mean to be
> The Daemon they made of me
>
> and
>
> I will encompass the infinite
> In time, in the crystal
> in my thought here.

I myself had a hand in re-spinning the tale of Eros and Psyche, in a poem sequence called "Message From the Speaker at Hell's Mouth." That Psyche was, of course, *my* psyche, *my* soul. Fairytales, too, could be re-spun, as Anne Sexton devastatingly demonstrated in *Transformations*.

•

When I finished writing *Stealing the Language,* I thought I'd said all I needed to say about women's writing changing the culture. How wrong I was. For while that book was in press, I found myself one rainy evening alone in my home, thinking about the story of the Book of Job. At first my thoughts revolved around the happy ending of that book. It seemed wonderful to me that Job could challenge God's justice, rightfully, and that God ultimately gives him back his health, his wealth, and his reputation in the world as a man of virtue. Wasn't Judaism extraordinary as a religion in which a human being can question the Creator of the Universe, and get away with it? Even be rewarded? But then a new thought occurred to me. How did Job's wife feel about having her ten children, whom God let Satan kill off on a bet at the beginning of the Book of Job, replaced by ten new children? Was that a satisfactory happy ending for *her?* At that moment I felt a scream thousands of years old rising in my own throat. The episode of automatic writing that followed — I was in some kind of trance, my pen did the writing — told me that revising other people's mythology was not enough. Recovering from the trance, I discovered that my pen had written of Job's wife, a silenced woman. My pen had asked what Job's wife would say to God when she got up the courage to demand, like her husband, an answer to her suffering. At that moment I realized that I needed to wrestle with the Old Testament, needed to confront its God, its stories, its charismatic men and its mostly silenced and nameless women, for myself. What did all those stories mean to me? How could I enter them? I began writing *midrash* before I knew what *midrash* was.

The book begun that rainy evening became *The Nakedness of the Fathers: Biblical Visions and Revisions,* in which I combine autobiography with retelling the great, compelling stories of the Bible, from before the Garden till after Job, diving into these stories, spinning them *my* way. Wrestling, or trying to wrestle, a blessing out of this deeply patriarchal yet deeply powerful Book, just like Jacob wrestling the Angel.

Some of my versions of the stories explore their psychological and political significance. The tale of Cain and Abel, for example, is a tale of sibling rivalry turned fratricidal. Noah, the survivor of a world in which virtually all other life is destroyed, suffers survivor guilt and becomes an alcoholic. Hagar is the mother of an *intifada* warrior:

I call him Ishmael. I whisper to him:
Fight to your dying breath.

Rachel is a trickster. Samson is a psychopathic killer. David is a brilliant politician. Solomon makes trade not war, and becomes the lover of Sheba. And so on. But the ultimate thrust of *Nakedness* is theological.

It seems clear to me that the being we in the West call "God the Father" swallowed God the Mother in prehistory. That is to say, the God of male monotheism, who keeps demanding worship, the warrior and judge and tyrant God that Blake calls Nobodaddy, absorbed the powers of goddesses who were worshipped for millennia before He came on the scene. The Sumerian goddess Innanna and other ancient goddesses were in charge of things like childbirth and lawmaking, for example. But remember the wolf who swallowed grandmother in the story of Red Riding Hood? Grandmother doesn't die, and God the Mother doesn't die. She's there inside the belly of the beast. Which is to say, we can see traces of her in the biblical texts. I'm interested in that. But I'm also interested in the return of the repressed. In the final section of *Nakedness*, called "Intensive Care," I imply that God the Father is in pain, just as we are in pain, because he is pregnant... with His repressed female self. That's the argument I make in the essays of *Feminist Revision and the Bible*, as well. What I really believe is that we can all be midwives of the Divine Female; we can help her be born into the world again.

In Kabala, the tradition of Jewish mysticism, the divine Female is called the Shekhinah. God and His Shekhinah have been divided since the catastrophic moment of creation, and the purpose of history is to reunite them. Whenever we perform a good deed, we assist in that reunion. And good sex models that union. This is all part of the midwifery I'm talking about.

But we also — we poets — we also have to *imagine* her. That's our job. That's what I found myself trying to do in *The Volcano Sequence*. That book burst from me with the "thick and magnificent rage" of a volcano, after a block of almost three years. I channeled those poems — let them arrive, became an aperture for them, promised I wouldn't tell them what to say. As they arrived, I could be angry about the image of the Father God we have created, the warrior and judge and tyrant. My psalms were born as anti-psalms:

> I am not lyric any more
> I will not play the harp
> for your pleasure
>
> I will not make a joyful
> noise to you, neither
> will I lament
>
> for I know you drink
> lamentation, too,
> like wine

I could crave the presence of the Shekhinah, the Beloved. I could invoke her and yearn for her. I could realize that she is in exile, mute, amnesiac. I could address her:

> come on, surely by now you remember who you are
> you're my mother my sisters my daughter
> you're me
>
> we will have to struggle so hard

to birth you
this time

the brain like a cervix

Obviously, *Volcano* records a struggle. Obviously, too, this is a collective labor in every sense. Among the many poets I see as part of the birth pangs are H. D., Anne Sexton, Lucille Clifton, Audre Lorde, Ntozake Shange — remember the end of "For Colored Girls Who Have Considered Suicide When the Rainbow is Enuf?" The Lady in Red chants, "I found God in myself / and I loved her / I loved her fiercely." This is not some touchy-feely New Age thing. It happens. It is real. The piece — the small piece — I was able to accomplish in *Volcano* involved recognizing that we need to (I need to) see the Shekhinah in the lives and bodies of our actual biological mothers whom we have rejected ... and I was able to write some psalms that were not just anti-psalms but real ones, psalms of yearning for the Beloved:

my head is uncovered to my naked hair
I am dressed immodestly

my old body lacks teeth, lacks a breast
still cherishes itself

I eat what I want I am
an animal of flesh

as you know for you formed me in the womb
and made my desires what they are

I am waiting for you
in a bed of pleasure

Writing *Volcano* took me as far as I have been able to go, so far, in my spiritual quest. Maybe this is not very far at all. Maybe I can go no further, I don't know. Meanwhile, of course, I've been writing other kinds of Jewish poems. The manuscript I am currently trying to put together gathers these poems from books I've published over the last thirty years. I'm hoping they speak to each other and that the whole is larger than the sum of the parts. Some are family poems, one set tracks the role of women in Judaism, and there's a selection of poems from *Volcano* in it, but there are also poems about the holocaust and poems about Israel. I'm obsessed, of course, by the tragedy and waste of the conflict between Jews and Palestinians. When are we going to beat our swords into ploughshares? When are we going to learn, as we are commanded, to love the stranger as ourselves? When will we recognize that feeding the hungry and clothing the naked is worth more than any ritual? The present title of this manuscript is "The Book of Life," and the long title poem imagines a dear friend and myself:

As if outside the synagogue we stood
On holier ground in a perennial garden
Jews like ourselves have just begun to plant.

◆

Like other poets, I am often asked if I have a spiritual practice. Yes, writing is my spiritual practice. Ultimately, the words come from somewhere beyond myself, though they travel through me in order to reach the page. "Not I, not I, but the wind that blows through me," says D. H. Lawrence. Probably many poets would say the same, especially today. Although it is going on below the radar of the critical establishment, isn't it clear that our culture is in a post-secular age? Poets — and novelists and playwrights (think of *Angels in America*) — everywhere in our country are struggling with matters of the spirit. Matters of spiritual experience, I should say. Struggling outside of churches and synagogues, outside of doctrines and dogmas. This renaissance of spirituality has nothing to do with the right-wing fundamentalisms that play such a destructive part in our political life. From Lucille Clifton to Franz Wright the testimony grows. Jane Mead can begin a poem called "Concerning That Prayer I Cannot Make":

> Jesus, I am cruelly lonely
> and I do not know what I have done
> nor do I suspect you will answer me

The poem can articulate a despair utterly unanswerable, yet it can end

> all you bare trees
> burrs
> brambles
> pile of twigs
> red and green lights flashing
> muddy bottle shards
> shoe half buried — listen
> listen, I am holy.

Something is happening here, but we don't know what it is, do we? There is a book to be written about this. I hope somebody writes it soon. I hope this present collection helps.

I do believe in the future. I believe that a future can grow organically out of the past, and I believe that when women's multiple and layered spiritual experiences and revelations, and the poetry born from them, contribute as much as men's spiritual experiences and revelations have, everything will perhaps look different, on our speck of a planet. God, and the soul, good and evil, will have new meanings. Maybe we'll have a better world.

A better world is what my mother and father believed in. We can't overcome six thousand years of worshipping a god made in man's image overnight, and we can't stop the wars and violence committed with the help of that image tomorrow. But there is a saying in Talmud: "It is not incumbent on you to finish the task. Neither are you free to give it up."

The Blessing of the Old Woman, the Tulip, and the Dog

To be blessed
said the old woman
is to live and work
so hard
God's love
washes right through you
like milk through a cow

To be blessed
said the dark red tulip
is to knock their eyes out
with the slug of lust
implied by
your up-ended
skirt

To be blessed
said the dog
is to have a pinch
of God
inside you
and all the other dogs
can smell it

—Alicia Ostriker

*MARILYN NELSON was born in Cleveland, Ohio. Daughter
of a career U.S. Air Force officer, she grew up on air bases all over
the U.S. She is the author of eleven volumes of poetry, including* The Cachoeira Tales and Other Poems, *winner of the L. E.
Phillabaum Poetry Award;* The Fields of Praise: New and Selected Poems; *and* The Homeplace, *which won the 1992 Anisfield-
Wolf Award, given for a book that widens understanding of
racism and diversity. She has also published collections of verse for
children and young adults, including* Sweethearts of Rhythm:
The Story of the Greatest All-Girl Swing Band in the World
and Halfdan Rasmussen's Hundreds of Hens and Other Poems for Children, *which she translated (with Pamela Espeland)
from Danish. She is a three-time National Book Award finalist
and has received the Poets' Prize, the Boston Globe – Horn Book
Award, a Newbery Honor Award, and a Coretta Scott King Honor
Award. From 1978 to 2002 she taught English at the University
of Connecticut – Storrs. She has also served as the Poet Laureate of
Connecticut. We interviewed Nelson in writing, engaging in a conversation about many subjects, including her long, close friendship
with a Catholic monk who left the monastery to travel around
the world leading meditation retreats. Nelson's poetry collection*
Magnificat *describes the spiritual influence of the man she calls
in print "Abba Jacob," who is also portrayed in her most recent
children's book,* Snook Alone.

Marilyn Nelson

To Be of Service

Surely everyone has a spiritual journey, even if it is never recognized as such.

Not long ago I heard a sermon that began with the priest's instructing the congregation: "Go back to a place in your childhood, where you felt secure, happy, and loved." The sermon went on to describe the place that the priest had returned to: his grandparents' idyllic summer cottage on a Carolina lake. It sounded like a wonderful place to be, the rightful source of a childhood's spirituality. I realized that I have no such place to go back to. I went back to the back seat of a car, the green Kaiser (which everyone in the family called the "geen" Kaiser in imitation of my younger sister, Jennifer) of my early childhood. Since Daddy was in the military and was often transferred from one Air Force base to another, our homes were temporary apartments in officers' quarters furnished with military-issue furniture and bedding.

My most vivid childhood memories are of the back of Daddy's head. He's driving, dressed in uniform, because there were some discounts given to uniformed military personnel in the 1950s, as well as the benefits of comradeship when military personnel met each other at rest stops and restaurants and asked, "Where are you off to?" "Where are you stationed?" "Do you know my friend X?" And there was also the safety factor for an African American military man driving with his family. Daddy was the navigator in a B-52 crew. Once, a policeman who had stopped our car for speeding ran up to the driver's window. Seeing that the driver was black, he yelled, "What do you think you're flying, boy?"

Daddy replied, "B-52s." The policeman, recognizing the uniform, said, "Well, I guess you know what you're doing. But be careful." He did not give Daddy a ticket.

Because Daddy was an officer, our car was always saluted when we drove into or out of the security gate of any military installation. In the 1950s, when the United States was still in the throes of waking up to and casting aside its centuries-old racism, our "geen Kaiser" felt like a capsule of safety and respect. Jennifer and I had quiet disputes and played games in the back seat; Mama passed out sandwiches and fruit from the front seat; there was singing, storytelling. The world flew by.

•

I've often read the admonition to parents that they should give their children "roots and wings." My parents certainly did that. Mama was devoted to family history and African American history. The pride she drew from her roots was essential to her character. Though it was clear that my sister and I would grow up in a milieu very different from hers — Mama grew up in one of the few all-black towns in the country, while her daughters lived in integrated neighborhoods and went to integrated schools — she made a point of teaching us about black history and black culture. Daddy was literally a flyer, part of the first generation of black men to fly airplanes. Though he had a relatively successful military career, he had dreamed of medical school but was unable to become a doctor because he couldn't afford it. He had been driving a taxi and going to law school part time when he was recalled by the military during the Korean crisis. Late in life he wrote poems and plays, and he acted. Mama was a gifted and successful teacher — and one of the rare African American teachers to teach all-white classes in the early 1950s — but she had dreamed of being a concert pianist, a composer. Both of them had had doors closed in their faces because of their poverty or their race. Their experiences of frustration, as well as the successful work they did accomplish, influenced the direction of my own life.

•

Surely everyone has a spiritual journey, even if it is never recognized as such. Mine began with wonderment. I remember wondering about other people's lives; where were the cars we met and passed on a street or highway going? What were the people in them thinking? What were their lives like? Though both of my parents had been raised in A.M.E. churches — African Methodist Episcopal — we usually attended Sunday services at non-denominational Protestant base chapels, where I went to Sunday School and Vacation Bible School. I remember being moved every night, at the age of eight or nine, by the magic brightening of the glow-in-the-dark plastic cross I kept in the headboard of my twin bed.

Since we moved so often, there was very little consistency in my religious instruction. My parents seldom spoke about religion, per se, except to reinforce our belief in the Golden Rule. One of our aunts gave us annual subscriptions to the Unity publications, *The Daily Word* for adults and *Wee Wisdom* for children. Unity describes itself as a positive, practical, progressive approach to Christianity, honoring the universal truths in all religions and respecting each individual's right to choose a spiritual path. These little publications became an appropriate contribution to my parents' laissez-faire attitude to religious education.

When I was about twelve I started reading the Bible, ambitiously intending to read it from cover to cover. Then I saw Audrey Hepburn in "The Nun's Story" and discovered Dr. Albert Schweitzer in the pages of *Life* magazine. I began to live a secret life of prayer and promises, asking God to let me be a doctor in Africa when I grew up, promising God that if I became a poet I would be true to the message God gave me for humanity. I read the lives of saints and the sacred texts of other religions. I wondered whether it was really necessary to believe in the resurrection. I stopped thinking of God as "He." I fell in love with a photograph of Karim, the Aga Khan, Imam of the Ismaeli sect of Islam, and I read everything I could find about Islam (which was not much) in an Air Force base library. I didn't understand why there was such enmity between Christianity and Islam. I believed for one entire summer that I was born to unite the two religions.

I've always been thankful for the fact that our family tradition was to teach Christianity by doing, not by quoting the Bible. One of my most cherished memories is of the time Daddy came home with an old black man who had been hitchhiking on the highway. He had dinner with us and slept overnight on the couch. In the morning, Mama packed him a lunch, and Daddy drove him to the highway. He was from Georgia or Alabama, someplace down south; he was going to visit his daughter in Seattle. My parents emphasized the importance of charity. Their lessons seem increasingly significant to me now, as I realize how seldom I have truly acted out my own weak faith.

•

My dad retired from the Air Force when I was in middle school, and we entered the civilian world, settling in an African American community in Sacramento, California. Whereas the world I had known was integrated, this new world was strictly divided racially. I did not fit in the black world, where it was considered "white" to be interested in reading, to enjoy studying, to get good grades; or in the white world, where dark skin was a condemnation; or in the brown world, where everyone spoke Spanish. My parents searched for a suitable church, at first going to an A.M.E. church like the ones they had grown up in. But the local A.M.E. church was more about propriety and prosperity than spirituality; it was populated by ladies who wore mink stoles even in ninety-degree California summers, and by teenagers whose highest ambitions were to go to debutante balls and then to Spellman or Morehouse College. Because my family's youngest child had been born with Down Syndrome, my mother had met and become friends with a white woman who fostered Down Syndrome babies. Mrs. Finch was a Lutheran, and belonged to the First English Lutheran church, one of the few integrated churches in the city. Mama started going to services there with her new friend, and eventually she and my sister and brother and I became Lutherans, though Daddy did not.

My first real religious education was in the Lutheran church. I was confirmed there. I was active in Luther League, the church youth group. I worked at the Summer Vacation Camp for children. I worked as a neighborhood canvasser for the church. First English had once been a white church in a white neighborhood, but as the neighborhood changed, it had welcomed its new neighbors and become about 50 percent black. For the first time, I belonged to a church community; I had a pastor I could talk to. And I had Martin Luther, his theses nailed to the door, the priesthood of all believers, grace, and the devil in the outhouse. Though I was never completely convinced that I really believed what I was told I believed when I was confirmed, I felt at home in the Lutheran church.

In 1964, shortly after my high school graduation, a young white Canadian student named Drew spent two weeks as a volunteer "youth missioner" at First English. Drew had just finished his first year at Harvard, and he was an English major, an activist, and the son of a Lutheran pastor in Ontario. We kissed under a tree in front of the church the night before he left. I enrolled that fall at the University of California – Davis, and Drew and I became long-distance sweethearts and penpals. We wrote reams of letters, made many very expensive long-distance telephone calls, and visited back and forth between Davis and Cambridge over the next four years. Our romance dominated this part of my faith journey. Drew was an officer in the international Luther League hierarchy, and his faith led him to spend a year working in the South for the Student Non-Violent Coordinating Committee, then at a community organization called the Urban Training Center in Chicago. I followed at a distance, discovering through Drew the satisfaction of contemplation in action, and of service. I was active occasionally in the campus ministry community at UC – Davis, working on a radical publication that I think may have been censored because of its explicit sexual content. But most of my religious life was involved in my growing commitment to political and social causes. I marched for Civil Rights, for migrant farm workers, and against the war in Vietnam. When I wasn't in class or working at my job in the university library, I was collecting signatures on petitions or carrying a picket sign.

In the summer of 1963 I was placed as a volunteer with a Lutheran church in a Chicago suburb. That was the summer Martin Luther King took the Movement north, so I wrote to the pastor of the Chicago church to ask how many hours in a weekend I would have free to volunteer with the Movement. A few days later, I received a letter from the church, informing me that my services would not be needed. I volunteered instead for a YMCA/YWCA project in Chicago that placed college students in community organizations. At the orientation meeting the first evening, where all of us were assembled from various schools around the country, I was, as usual, one of a handful of African American students in the group. The orientation leader, an African American community organizer who was about ten years older than we were, listened as we introduced ourselves. When my turn came, I said, "I'm Marilyn Nelson, I'm a junior at the University of California–Davis, I'm an English major, and I write poetry." He shook his head and said, "Baby, you gone have a hard time!"

I lived with a group of students — a white guy I knew from Davis, a guy from Kenya, an Afro-Panamanian woman, a white Canadian woman — and worked with them in a community organization which consisted of a solitary man — who sat and chewed cigars in a storefront office on the West Side of the city — and us. He sent us out to survey the neighborhood, to ask what people needed changed in their apartments. When we found an especially horrible apartment building, we sent its owner a letter informing him that our organization would manifest a large demonstration in front of his building unless he made repairs. Then we waited and watched as workmen appeared and made repairs. We also marched for open housing all summer, usually somewhere toward the back of the huge groups led by Dr. King. What a thrill it was to hear him speak!

I graduated from college in 1968. So much was happening in the nation and the world that year. Most of my undergraduate friends joined the Peace Corps, and Drew went to South America for two years on a Lutheran version of the Peace Corps. I was attracted to the Peace Corps, but like many young people in the late 1960s, I believed that the revolution was right around the corner. I felt that it was irresponsible to leave the country at such a volatile time.

Instead, I enrolled in a Ph.D. program in English at the University of Pennsylvania. I held on for one year, dropping out with an M.A. degree.

My connection with the Lutheran Church and with Drew led me to my first full-time job. For one academic year I worked as a lay associate in Lutheran Campus Ministry at Cornell University, with Reverend Lee Snook. One of my colleagues that year was Father Daniel Berrigan, already famous as a radical proponent of peace. The only woman and the only African American on the staff, I was woefully unprepared for the job, especially for offering serious counseling and informal courses on subjects like black power and black theology. But most of my work during that year at Cornell involved counseling male undergraduates about how to meet female undergraduates, and sending them to experienced draft counselors. I still marched for Civil Rights and against the spreading war.

As for changing the church from within: Well, my attempts to divert government grants away from being used to repaint the church basement rooms to instead help starving children in Biafra met with scoffing. While I was popular, I think, with the students, the older members of the church tended to introduce themselves to me after Sunday services by saying, "I don't believe we've met before, Marilyn. I'm a conservative. But I'm glad you're here." I had not realized how deeply a congregation can be politically divided, by both national and international issues and by petty personal ones. At the end of the year I decided to leave Cornell and marry a young German man I had met in grad school the year before. However, my Lutheran connection led to my serving later as a poet on the Hymn Text Committee for the new Lutheran hymnal, and to my and my husband's five years of teaching at St. Olaf College, the Norwegian Lutheran college in Northfield, Minnesota.

•

The man I married was not a believer. My spiritual journey became a subterranean river through our adventurous but troubled marriage, our travels and teaching abroad, and our amicable divorce. And it continued underground through my marrying again, this time to a non-practicing Jew who was as eager to have children as I was. We had two children and agreed not to push them toward either religion, to raise them to have open minds and to feel free to choose their own directions. I took them to a Congregational church whose minister had become one of my good friends, but I did not insist on their having a religious education. They grew up as free of dogmas as I had.

And then, suddenly, I was inexplicably motivated to find again someone I had met as an undergraduate. I've written a book *(Magnificat)* about our relationship, and have written many more poems about my remarkable friend, Jacques.

Our story began with an apparent *coup de foudre* love-at-first-sight meeting when we were undergraduates; the first words we spoke to each other were a vow of unceasing love. But nothing else had ever "happened" between us, except a few shy conversations. And I was already in love with Drew when we met. Shortly after we had graduated from UC–Davis, my young friend surprised me by blurting out his desire. I was shocked, and I laughed. He ran away. And that was the end of that, though I long regretted my laughter and mourned his running away, and I told myself I'd someday find him again. Suddenly, some twenty years later, I woke up one morning with an urgent need to find him. I told my husband our story, and he agreed to help me search. It took several months to find an address. My friend had done graduate studies at Cambridge University, worked in southern Africa, and entered a

Benedictine monastery, which he had left at the end of seven years to live as a hermit. I started writing to him.

Like one possessed, I read books about monasticism, about contemplation, about Christology, about Liberation Theology. One question led to another, book led to book, the first priest I consulted for advice introduced me to a Benedictine community, and I corresponded with one of the monks. I once overheard my young daughter tell one of her friends, "My mom is a monk." I think I was probably out of my mind. But the more I understood about what might make an individual feel called to the religious life, the more I felt I understood something deep and unstated about that boy I had once promised to love forever. It's very hard to explain, but I believe I found him inside of myself before I really found him again.

I started going to Mass. Sometimes the children came with me. We all fell in love with the idea of owning less, of living more simply. I wrote to my friend obsessively, every day for a year. I suppose my letters were a record of my struggle to understand his calling, but they were also a record of my struggle to allow my romanticized memory of our old spark to grow and deepen into a living spiritual friendship, which could in turn lead me to a richer relationship with myself and with the Divine. At the end of one year of writing unanswered letters, I was ready to give up. I wrote a last letter, telling him that I would not write again, but that I felt we were missing out on a pretty wonderful miracle. Shortly after, he sent me a brief telegram. And we have been connected ever since.

I think, by now — though I'm not completely sure — I've completed the transition of the wholly imaginary remembered romance in my head to a friendship rooted in our amazing first meeting and my respect for his calling and his spiritual fatherhood.

The gift of our friendship has changed my life.

He is a Roman Catholic priest and a highly regarded teacher of Christian meditation, but he is no longer a monk, and he has built a hermitage on an island in the Indian Ocean where he lives when he is not traveling to give talks and lead retreats. He's an extremely sociable "hermit."

The first time I visited him at his hermitage, he regaled me with stories of the Desert Fathers, and he told me that he had once identified himself to someone as "Abba Jacob." Now he is usually addressed as "Père Jacques" or "Father Jacques," but in the poems I have written about him and those we have written together, he is "Abba Jacob."

Like other people in his circle of friends, I live in his guesthouse when I visit the hermitage, and I pray the daily office with him in his oratory. We've gone on "dates" to dinners with his Bishop and the Cardinal. He taught his parishioners to sing "Go Down Moses" after I taught it to him and he translated it into Creole.

We've traveled together in the U.S., Europe, Polynesia, and Africa. Acknowledging that our friendship must reach toward something larger than ourselves, we have collaborated on several writing projects, including a sequence of poems in which "Abba Jacob" speaks about what it means to be human, and a series of three picture-books in which "Abba Jacob" is a central character. The first of these to be published, *Snook Alone*, is intended to introduce young readers to the basic concept of contemplative prayer: sitting still in silent longing for the Beloved. I wrote it, but the story is informed by Jacques' solitary retreats on uninhabited islands.

◆

Although I'm slightly embarrassed to reveal that much of my spiritual direction has been determined by my friendships with the men I've been involved with, I suppose most of us find our way by walking with a partner, or by ricocheting off one. In any case, this is where I am: grateful for an extraordinary friendship with a brilliant, funny, wonderful man who is trying very hard to be a good priest; and grateful for the feeling that my early desire to be of service is being fulfilled. I'm not a regular church-goer now, but I do belong to a Congregational church I admire for its way of living its faith. A year ago I participated in the annual "Tree of Life Journey" to Israel/Palestine as a witness for peace. Perhaps this year I will go with church members to visit the sister congregation on the Green Grass Lakota reservation, or on the annual trip to Haiti or South Africa. In the several years of my belonging to this church, I think I have been in church once for the celebration of the Eucharist. I miss liturgy. I miss ritual. But at almost every service I have been to, the congregation's prayers have been delivered from the pulpit by someone from Palestine, or from Green Grass, or from South Africa, or from Harlem, or from the local synagogue, or from the local Islamic Center.

My prayer every day is simply: "Thanks."

Once when I was visiting Jacques' hermitage, we became so involved in a discussion over dinner that we talked for hours, completely forgetting to go to the oratory to pray compline. When I pointed this out and apologized, he said, "We've probably been praying all along, without noticing."

I might call myself a praise-singer as a poet, as in the Xhosa tradition of *griot* and praise-singer. I only know that a large part of my job is celebration.

BLESSING THE BOATS

Abba Jacob said:
Did I ever tell you about the time
I was asked to bless the fishing boats?
I got to the appointed beach at the appointed time,
in my long white tunic, of course, and discovered
the beach had been taken over by a crowd
of Italian tourists, most of them women, and topless.
Luckily — or unluckily for me,
considering the circumstances — they were all
beautiful. One or two of them...
Well, what could I do?
I just walked through them.
They parted before me
like the waves of the Red Sea, silent
and watching. It was almost all I could do
to keep a straight face
and look straight ahead.
I thought such a fancy-dressed audience
deserved a grand gesture,
so I walked right in, shoes and all,
to my chest in the sea.
Inwardly bursting with laughter,
I stroked the nearest prow
and blessed the boats
with the sign of the Cross.
Then I turned and blessed the beach.

I didn't laugh until I got home.
They're probably still
talking about it.

—*Marilyn Nelson*

ANNIE FINCH is the author or editor of numerous books of poetry, including Eve; Calendars; *and the long poems* The Encyclopedia of Scotland *and* Among the Goddesses: An Epic Libretto in Seven Dreams. Calendars *was a finalist for the ForeWord Poetry Book of the Year, and* Eve *has been reissued in the Carnegie Mellon Classic Contemporaries series. Finch's book* Spells: New and Selected Poems *is forthcoming from Wesleyan University Press. Her influential books on poetics include* The Ghost of Meter; An Exaltation of Forms; The Body of Poetry; A Poet's Ear; *and* A Poet's Craft. *She is also the co-translator (with Deborah Lesko Baker) of* The Complete Poetry and Prose of Louise Labé. *Other honors include a senior fellowship at the Black Earth Institute and the 2009 Robert Fitzgerald Award for her work in prosody. She has also completed a number of poetic music, art, theater, and opera collaborations. Finch's opera* Marina, *based on the life of poet Marina Tsvetaeva, was produced in 2003 by American Opera Projects, with music by Deborah Drattell. In 2010, with director Assunta Kent, she founded Poets Theater of Maine. Finch holds degrees from Yale University, the University of Houston, and Stanford University, and she currently directs the Stonecoast M.F.A. program in creative writing at the University of Southern Maine. We interviewed her in her garden in Maine, seated in Adirondack chairs, on a bright October morning.*

Annie Finch

Incantation

I wanted to do what I could to add another spiritual voice to the world, one that honors the earth.

One of the most profound spiritual experiences involving poetry I've had in recent years has been finding friends in an Iranian community and being part of poetry gatherings held largely in Farsi. Poetry represents one of the deepest connections this circle of people can have with each other and with their culture. They really understand poetry as a spiritual experience. An Iranian friend said to me that in this country when people are stressed, they're supposed to go sit alone and meditate. In Iran when you're stressed, you're supposed to go read poetry. It's an efficient way to get back in tune with what matters. I gave a reading a couple of weeks ago, and some of these friends were in the audience. I noticed that the quality of their attention was so much deeper than I'm used to getting at readings. They weren't just listening to the words, they were spiritually listening. It made me want to be a better poet, in the deepest sense. I don't know what it is they have in relation to poetry that we've lost, but I suspect that it's because our culture is so far removed from being an oral culture, and the experience of life is so different in an oral culture. Walter Ong says that if you look at children before they have learned to read, they are alive in a much more immediate way than we are.

I spent my childhood summers in Maine, in a cabin with no electricity. The time there opened space where spirit could well up. It seems to me that people are naturally spiritual beings; most cultures in the world that are not over-stimulated with media and information and consumerism are spiritual cultures. The main gift those summers gave me was simplicity, which allowed a spiritual life to develop that might have had a hard time flourishing otherwise. I had time to be alone, time to be in nature, time to slow down, and I always did a lot of my writing there.

In fourth grade, when I was nine, I started writing poems about nature. I had been hearing poetry all my life. Both my parents liked to read poetry, and some of my siblings would read and recite poetry to me. There were five kids in my family; I'm the only one who has made writing a career. I've often wondered whether somebody had to be the writer, and I was the most likely candidate. There was a lot of talk about literature and many thousands of books in the house, many of them religious books. My father founded the Seminars on Religion at Columbia University and made a lifelong study of different religions. He organized the first conference on Dōgen in the U.S., and he was fascinated by the spiritual teacher Gurdjieff and various cults and gurus. He took me to see Krishnamurti give a series of lectures in New York when I was about twelve; that had a huge impact on me. My father was raised an Episcopalian, but when he began to study philosophy, he decided that he respected all religions and stopped going to church. He frequently talked about the relationships between Christianity and Judaism, and between Eastern and Western religions. Even more than poetry, and aside from philosophy, religion was his favorite topic of conversation.

For years when I was very little, my father read to the family from the texts of a different world religion each week. That stopped when I was six and, after that, there was a spiritual vacuum. Both of my parents were spiritual people, but there was no practice in the house at all. I was very bothered by this. I was jealous of my friends who went to church because they had an accepted outlet in action for their spiritual feelings, and I didn't. My friend Alex went to church — I think maybe it was Methodist — and I would go with her whenever I could; I especially loved going on Easter. I would walk up Snake Hill from my house to another church, a Presbyterian one this time, to sing Christmas carols.

Yet I had no spiritual home of my own. I was looking for a channel, an accepted outlet for spiritual feelings. With all its constant talk about the spirit, my house was a place of perpetual spiritual teasing with no culmination.

My father did not have us baptized. This was important to him; he told us that he believed we should decide when we were older. In a way, this was the only gift of ritual he gave me, my understanding that this mattered deeply enough to him *not* to do it. When I was fourteen, my mother and I began going to Scarsdale Friends Meeting together, no doubt because I was old enough to keep her company then on the long bus ride, and I urged her to go. She didn't drive, and my father wouldn't drive her. He had no interest in Quakerism, though that could have been a natural fit for him intellectually, the way Quakerism combines Christianity with mysticism and a kind of Eastern openness to individual spirituality. My mother had been raised a Quaker and going to meeting with her was the first time I had any sense of belonging to any spiritual tradition.

The Quaker meeting was a small, well-established gathering in an old meeting house; the meeting was held upstairs, and we sat on long benches looking out over the trees. I remember watching my mother's face and learning a lot from her composure. The meeting was quite quiet, and there was very little explicit talk about Christianity. At the end of meeting, the elders who sat on a special bench would signal silently that it was over by shaking each others' hands. I loved the beauty, simplicity, and depth of it all. Soon after, I enrolled at Oakwood, a Quaker boarding school, where I attended required meeting twice a week. I enjoyed that, too, but it was harder because most of the students were not Quakers, so the meeting had less depth. The power of a Quaker meeting can be dependent on the people who happen to be there. I found it off-putting when people would use the meeting to propagate various religions, including Christianity. There was a student who was in a cult, and he would talk for half an hour about his cult, and of course everyone was polite about it, so he went on and on.

I've only recently begun to think of myself again in terms of Quakerism because I have discovered the idea of Quaganism. I think at the moment I may be closer to being a Quagan, a Pagan Quaker, than anything else.

·

In the late 1990s, I moved to Iowa for my first teaching job and found that everyone in Iowa belonged to a church of some kind. If you were liberal, you belonged to the Unitarian church. I started attending the Unitarian church and discovered a wonderful earth spirituality group there. I wrote the poems in *Calendars* about the solstices and equinoxes as rituals for that group, which had a nice mix of spiritual practices — goddess worship, earth honoring, and Wiccan. For years before that, in California, I had traveled individualized paths including shamanic practices, acupuncture, meditation, and energy work. The group in Iowa gave a wider context to these spiritual experiences, and I realized that this deep new level of spirituality, which meant so much to me, was something I could also experience in community and family.

When I was younger, I had an active struggle with Christianity. My book *The Encyclopedia of Scotland* was published in 1982, when I was twenty-three. When I look back at that book (which is one long poem), I see that it was about my trying to deal with the burden of Christianity and to come out the other end. I had no idea what Paganism was, then. I just knew there was a lot of Christian energy, and there was earth power, and I wanted to express the relationship between these in a ritual. The poem was full of earth and animal imagery, and an openness to synchronicity and the immanent spirituality in every element of life. It expressed a sensibility that I didn't have any name for, and that I could not fully conceptualize, except that it had something to do with the experience of belonging to a tribe and living in such a way that art and spirit were part of every aspect of life, not separated out through transcendence. But Christian elements kept coming into that poem, too, in the form of visions and hallucinations that felt poignant and frightening — visions of Jesus as colors and letters, for example. It was almost as if spiritual power had to come out that way because I had no name yet for the other kind. I was struggling to get away from Christianity and to create something else through my art. *The Encyclopedia of Scotland* was written as a ritual performance piece. I got other people involved and performed the piece with music and costumes and banners.

I had always wanted to express spirituality in a way that was communal and public, which is one reason Quakerism didn't quite work for me, especially when I had children and wanted to experience playful richness with them. Though the Quaker experience is shared, in a beautiful way, there is also a distance there. I have my personal experience, and you have yours, and we might look at each other's eyes afterward over coffee, but the connection is minimal and not place-specific. The group in Iowa was goddess-centered and female-centered, and I realized that this is what I had been missing, not only the awareness of nature and the specific embodiment of spirit in nature, but also the awareness of the female aspect of spirituality. Now I understand that the embodiment of spirit in nature and the female aspect naturally belong together. It's so simple and clear to me now, but looking back, I see how many decades it took for me to piece it all together. I didn't have the knowledge or a structure.

Eve was published in 1997. When I put that book together, I collected poems I had written over fifteen years. I wrote the sequence of goddess poems that ties the book together in 1996, just before publishing the book, and because of the way all the poems fit together, I discovered that I had been writing about goddesses for years without even noticing. With *Calendars*, a similar process happened with the seasons and the wheel of the year, because there are poems in that book that are quite old. It was only when the conscious filter arrived that I was able to understand where the energy for these poems had been coming from all along.

Looking back at my struggles with Christianity, I see the real problem was that it didn't provide a structure through which I could appreciate the sacredness of my own life on a daily basis, the way Paganism does, and the way the goddesses do. The polytheism and multiplicity of the sacred are vital to me, and allow me to organize my daily experience in a sacred way. I can look at that bee right there on the marigold, and I can think about the bee goddess of Crete, and how sacred the bee has been for centuries. I can look at the earth right here beneath our feet, and the plants around us, and think of Demeter. Everywhere there's the sacred. I love this. With Christianity, I never had this feeling. I had mystical experiences at times, but they often led to confusion about my body and the physical world, the feeling that I was supposed to transcend my body and that there was something wrong with it. I found this painful, confusing, and disorienting. I did not experience the feeling that everything in nature is sacred, which is so important to me.

A week ago, I was at a temple where I'm part of a women's wisdom circle. The priestess of the temple has decorated it with wonderful images of goddesses, and items evoking the four directions, and amazing powerful objects from nature. I was lighting candles, and in the northwest corner I noticed a picture of Jesus. Encountering this image in the context of all the goddesses, and the Native American symbols, and symbols of nature, for the first time I did not feel threatened by the masculine, Christian principle; it seemed part of the whole, and that was beautiful and very healing for me. But for my entire childhood and young adulthood, I got a clear message that Christianity was all or nothing, and that if I wanted to honor the Christian beliefs, I would have to give up honoring something essential and necessary about the world and myself.

◆

After the time in Iowa, I joined a number of different groups. I have had so much fun raising my children with Pagan rituals and celebrations. We have a solstice tree with a sun on top instead of a Christmas tree, and we color eggs with plant dyes for the goddess Oestra. We celebrate Samhain on Halloween and remember the dead and write them messages. It's a spiritual day, and it's also my birthday; I always felt that being born on Halloween gave me a start as a witch. I have become increasingly comfortable with the word "witch" and the idea of witchcraft, in part through Starhawk and the Reclaiming Collective. I find Starhawk's work inspirational, the way she blends metaphysics, politics, and spirituality into a cohesive Pagan approach to the world. Her classic, *Dreaming the Dark,* is a fantastic book. I especially love how a poetic perspective, with metaphors and correspondences, is key to fitting it all together.

I can't overestimate how much my attraction to Paganism flowered because I felt that this spiritual approach meshed so well with my poetry. There seemed no place for my poetry in Christianity, which I now think was part of the agony of *The Encyclopedia of Scotland.* But when I discovered the earth spirituality group in Iowa, almost immediately I felt fully inspired as a poet on every necessary level: language, imagery, rhythm, and community/audience. There's a practical need in Paganism for good poems, not only for meditation but also for ritual. This often means using rhythm and meter, which I love to do. It felt great to find a spiritual tradition in which I could be useful, so that I could develop both inside and out, so to speak, as I absorbed my experiences on the individual level and worked out a poetic language and rhythm and identity for the wider circle. Like so many others, I have found the goddess mythology to be complex, fascinating, strengthening, and creatively compelling, and I appreciate the way it ties me into so many cultures; whether Hindu, Celtic, Native American, or Yoruba, every single culture has its goddesses.

I became most involved in the nature-based, Goddess-centered branch of Paganism known as Wicca. I was so grateful to Wicca and to the goddess for how happy this was making me that I wanted to make Wicca more visible to more people who might be helped by it also, and to use my writing as a way to do so. I became more explicit about calling myself Wiccan and talking about being a witch. Starting my blog American Witch in 2009 took courage, as I was afraid to use the word witch. I thought I might lose my job or get attacked, because there's still a stigma attached to the word. But I wanted to do what I could to make Wicca more available to other people, to benefit them and to help add another spiritual voice to the world, one that honors the earth and has never had anything to do with violent conversion or domination. Now I am writing a memoir of the same name, *American Witch.*

•

On the literary side of my life, for decades I had experienced a dilemma about the poetess versus the poet. In the thinking I had done about the female poetic tradition, and how it differed from the romantic male poetic tradition, I suspected that there was a spiritual dimension to the question. Christianity allowed Lydia Sigourney, the nineteenth-century poetess, to make the spiritual maneuver in which she was able to take her ego out of the work. These "poetesses" are made fun of for being so religious and corny and bad. The typical view is that they are bad poets because they are religious poets, but I think that to the extent they are religious, they are original and exciting. They did the best they could within a patriarchal religion, but in many ways these poetesses were really witches. They were in tune with the energy of the earth and the energy of daily life, and they had the spiritual capacity to experience both, and the power of the human heart and will to actively change the world through love. That's my definition of being a witch, and of being the kind of poet I want to be.

My next book of poems will be a *Selected Poems* and will include some poems I wrote over a five-year period in the late 1980s. None of those poems had been published until the past few years. They were sitting in a drawer. I called them "the lost poems" and thought they were unpublishable because they were so out of tune with anything that was being published at the time. They were written in iambic meter (later I went on to write in metrical diversity of all kinds). They were quite crazy, without a logical meaning, and this made them scary and intense. When I wrote them, anything in meter could only be published in the most conservative journals, yet given their style and themes there was no place for these poems in those publications. But now their time seems to have come, and people want to publish these poems. It's not just because I have become better known. The aesthetics have changed, and people get what I was trying to do. I think of this work now as the "destruction" poems. I was writing poems that were about the destruction of the patriarchy in myself and in my writing, almost like a purging.

•

I have several altars in my house, places where I embody different aspects of my life and experience. Most of the altars honor the four directions. I try to maintain a sense of the four directions in my garden and in my home. I try to be aware of the balance of the elements — earth, air, fire, water — in any moment or situation. I also might work with colors, minerals, plants, scents, sounds, or any kind of healing energy. Since my life tends to be quite spontaneous, one aspect of witchcraft that suits me is that the practice is flexible. At different times in my life, I've followed varying degrees of formal practice. Sometimes I'll celebrate the wheel of the year — the solstices and the equinoxes and the cross-quarter days halfway between them. I don't always celebrate every single one, but I usually celebrate them, sometimes with my family, sometimes with friends or a spiritual circle, and sometimes alone. A great number of witches are what is known as "solitaries," and this practice works very well alone. Sometimes I celebrate the full moon or the new moon. The women's wisdom circle I'm part of usually meets at the dark of the moon. We open the ceremony by calling the four directions and honoring them, and we call the ancestors. We might do a ritual to raise energy or to help heal something, or we might sing together. At the end we'll close the circle. It's a very simple structure that I can use anytime I want.

One of the most important times I've used this ritual structure was when I had an abortion. I was unable to come to peace with the abortion for a long time. Finally I developed and performed a ritual with my family, which turned out to be exactly what I needed to do to resolve the situation, make peace, and move forward. My book *Among the Goddesses* includes this ritual as an appendix, exactly as we performed it. I'm always trying to be aware of different ways to transform a situation. If a situation feels bad, I look for ways to use my own energy and my own power to improve it. This can come in the form of just thinking, or it could be casting a circle. Often it's a combination of different approaches.

I think many religions that are based in ritual develop out of similar knowledge bases; even religions that have ostensibly different belief systems can include similar folk actions. For example, the gesture of putting your hands together over your chest and perhaps bowing slightly is traditional in Japanese culture and in certain Christian monastic traditions, and many of us in the contemporary U.S. now know it from yoga classes. This is a gesture that can feel like a proper mark of peace and respect to people of any belief, because we all have the same bodies and energy.

As a folk religion that does not hide the fact, witchcraft holds in common with many other religions the basic idea that whatever you believe in "out there" is not as important, in the end, as finding a path motivated simply by human kindness and being fully present in your own ritual actions, which creates a place for the sacred.

•

Folk poetry has been an important influence on my poems. I think that's why I relate so much to Yeats, because of the influence of folk poetry on his work. So many lines in his work resonate for me, including much of his first book. "The Song of the Wandering Aengus" or "The Stolen Child," for example. "The Stolen Child" has a refrain:

Come away o human child!
To the waters and the wild
With a faery, hand in hand,
For the world's more full of weeping than you can understand.

That is like a chant. But the first chants I was influenced by were my own. Some of my earliest memories are of saying words over and over to myself, hypnotizing myself. Since I didn't have any church experience per se, I experienced a vacuum of ritualized language. Maybe that's why I sought it out so much in poetry later on. I was encouraged by Yeats, by Millay, who sometimes has a chanting aspect to her work, and by Langston Hughes, with the bluesy repetitions in his poems. Vachel Lindsay has a lot of good work hidden among the not so good, and his use of chant is quite interesting. Carl Sandburg, too. The whole tradition of American populist poetry from the leftist era in the 1930s drew on folk poetry. I read this work when I was a kid. I did a lot of hunting in used bookstores, and my parents had many old books kicking around. I found poems that were not necessarily fashionable or in print, and I read poetry of all kinds.

I used to feel so split by being drawn to formalism *and* to women's poetry, and being a feminist. I didn't know how to tie it all together. I felt very confused. How could I be interested in all these things? But I was. It was Paganism and the goddess and Wicca that enabled it all to make sense to me. Once I finally figured out that this was my spiritual orientation, and that I was basically a religious poet, or a spiritual poet, everything else clicked into that framework. I could understand how I really was one person.

I recognized myself, just a few years ago, really. I was like Changing Woman, from the Native American legend — the woman who meets herself coming down the road in the opposite direction.

An interesting book by Leonard Shlain, *The Alphabet Versus the Goddess: The Conflict Between Word and Image,* looks at the religions of the world and how the development of literacy brought "the people of the book," the Judeo-Christian-Muslim tradition, out of the right brain into the left brain, into logical thinking. Now partly because of all the media we use, photographs and television and movies, we're moving back into the right brain again, into an age of the image. This is the realm of the goddess and of the unconscious, and it is more, I think, the realm of poetry, especially metrical poetry.

Julian Jaynes talks about how when we're listening to metrical poetry and music, the right brain is more active. With language that's not in meter, the left brain is active. This is part of the spiritual nature of poetry. Poetry has the potential for incantation, which brings us into that timeless realm. This is a potential that could be tapped, a route toward reclaiming the spiritual role for poetry.

•

I see my writing as in service to the muse, and I think of the muse as the goddess. I'm becoming more aware that when the goddess wants me to write something, the way opens to write it. It doesn't matter to me how much I write, but it matters that everything I write is authentically in service to the muse, because otherwise it's static that could be destructive or unhelpful or confusing. At a time when there's so much out there, so many poems, so many books, I'm learning the virtue of trying to be useful to the muse.

I used to think that because I am a woman, I should have a male muse. I tried this for a while, but it didn't work. Maybe it does for some other women, but now I think it's not a coincidence that the muse is traditionally female and a goddess. Poetry seems to come from the part of us that is in touch with the feminine aspects of spirit.

But there is also a divine element that's masculine for me. For a long time, I was not able to accept this idea. I was balancing out my early exposure to Christianity. Even though my father didn't raise me as explicitly Christian, it was always the elephant in the room. When I first talked to my daughter about the goddess, she said, "I believe in the goddess *and* the god." This is of course what Pagans believe. I understood this intellectually, but at first I had a hard time needing both, belief-wise, and I think you have to have *need,* for belief. Now, just recently, in the past year or so, I am finding room for the male divine principle. Janet and Stewart Farrar's book *The Witch's God* has been helpful. This book explores the masculine nature of spirit, including the traditional "green man," which is really wonderful.

·

Quakerism has always represented an important thread in spirituality in the United States. It's been the conscience of the Christian community in this country in many ways, for example the work of the American Friends Service Committee. Quakers have long stood for a deep-thinking and yet responsible mysticism. Not only did they protect slaves in this country, but they stood up for women accused of being witches and took them in. There's nothing explicitly Christian about Quakerism, it turns out, if you go back and look at the tenets. But one thing that was missing in Quakerism, for my taste, was the lack of celebration, in part because of its Puritan roots.

An Indian friend recently sent me a picture of a seasonal religious festival in his homeland, with women dancing in beautifully colored dresses. In America, in what religion can you dance as part of your religious celebration?

When I discovered that there were Pagan Quakers, I was excited, because Quakerism and Paganism have been two sides of the same spiritual need for me — on the one hand the individual connection to spirit, and on the other the communal experience of spirit in the context of nature. I first heard the term Quaganism in 2007. It's very new; I just wrote an essay on Quaganism for the first Quagan anthology. If you Google it, you'll only get about three hits. The goddess-centered acceptance of the physical natures of our bodies and the earth in community — this is, in itself, a sacred thing and cause for worship and celebration. To unite this with the Quaker sense of individual and social responsibility, and to connect their shared mysticism and sense of spirit, feels to me like a complete religion.

There's nothing in the theology of Christianity that requires the proselytizing that has almost been its downfall. The fact that Jesus is the son, not the deity, allows a space for other incarnations of the spirit. The obsession of Christians with conversions and proselytizing has been, it seems, a defense against the knowledge that there might be other manifestations. In Diana Eck's book *The New Religious America*, she throws down this gauntlet: If Christianity could co-exist with other religions, then the United States could become a beacon for tolerance and peace for the entire planet. It's up to Christianity to recognize that it does not have to be the only answer.

There's a controversy among Pagans right now about whether Paganism should try to become a world religion. Buddhism and Hinduism were not world religions to start with, but they were consciously put forward as such by people who wanted to earn that status for academic and other reasons. Many people say that Paganism by its nature shouldn't be pinned down. But Paganism is a religion. It's not just a collection of practices, though it manifests in many different practices; there is a shared belief in the sacredness of the world itself. And it's important to take this belief out into the world.

I also feel that it's important for me to come out as a Pagan and Wiccan because there are so many women in this country, and men too, who are basically practicing Paganism and don't know it, or don't have a name for it. The gender aspect of Paganism is fascinating. The psychological issues so many women have with claiming space — saying this is who we are, deal with us — are playing out on a spiritual level. There are so many women's groups coming together around such practices as yoga, energy, Reiki, and aromatherapy. This is all basically Paganism, the spiritualization of the physical. Yet no one is saying that this is a religion.

People are afraid of Paganism, or they aren't interested. It reminds me of what is happening with women's poetry and women's literature. There's not a lot of energy among women proclaiming that this is who we are, this is what we're doing, we exist. It's time for us to come together and say isn't this fantastic: We're all here together. What seems to me to be missing is the spirit. If the daughters are going to be reconciled to the mothers, I feel that can only happen in light of a greater mother.

The Door

It seemed as if a door came calling,
in a voice as old as carols,
telling lies as old as candles,
in words that were all about
some afternoons, lost on a child,
that could have been simple but
were lost, when I was just a child.

There was a day and then a dream
that I went through, and a cathedral
whose tall choir prayed
a singing message through the nave
until I heard a forest there
(though far outside, the trees were bare)

—*Annie Finch*

*G. C. WALDREP grew up in Virginia and earned undergradu-
ate and doctoral degrees in American history at Harvard and Duke
Universities before receiving an M.F.A. in creative writing from the
University of Iowa. He is the author of four full-length collections
of poems,* Goldbeater's Skin; Disclamor; Archicembalo, *winner
of the Dorset Prize; and most recently, in collaboration with John
Gallaher,* Your Father on the Train of Ghosts. *Waldrep is also the
author of* Southern Workers and the Search for Community, *a
study of the lives of Southern textile workers during the early twentieth century. He is currently an assistant professor of English at
Bucknell University, where he also directs the Bucknell Seminar for
Younger Poets, edits the journal* West Branch, *and serves as Edi-
tor-at-Large for the* Kenyon Review. *Beginning in the mid-1990s,
for nine years Waldrep was a member of the New Order Amish,
and since 2005 he has been a member of the Old Order River
Brethren, a related Anabaptist group. We conducted this interview
over a period of a couple of months, engaging in a dialogue about
how he joined the Amish and the impact of his practice of faith on
his writing and life.*

G. C. Waldrep

Not a Butler to the Soul

We draw existence from non-existence.

Poetry arrived in my life at the same time I was making a serious religious commitment, so for me the two have always been intimately, even essentially, intertwined. I can't imagine writing poetry outside the very large architecture faith affords (although I know, of course, that many — perhaps most — poets do). The question I more often ask myself is not about the relationship between faith and poetry, but rather the relationship between prayer and poetry. They're not the same, by any means, though there is some intrinsic relationship. Sometimes I speculate the two are like adjacent apartments in the same building: when you're in one, you have no direct access to the other, but if you listen closely you can hear sounds — sometimes muffled, sometimes sharp — coming from the other side of the connecting wall. I feel that way about prayer when I am reading or writing poetry and feel that way about poetry when I am praying.

One way to look at writing is as a form of personal, aesthetic, and/or spiritual discipline, as it was for Flannery O'Connor, and as I think it must be for anyone with any faith at all. We draw on the ineffable. In fact, we draw existence from non-existence. We make something out of nothing. Scientists tell us this is impossible, but artists do it every day — especially writers. For thousands of years humankind lumbered along without this or that bit of language, and — now it's here. Abracadabra. It may or may not make a difference, but something has changed, something is truly new. In this, we are little makers.

Everything we do is connected, in Christ as in art; to live otherwise is a violence. But if one believes, with Robert Creeley via Charles Olson, that "form is never more than an extension of content" — better yet Denise Levertov's emendation, "form is never more than a *revelation* of content" — then a living, *experiential* faith is one that will necessarily seek innovation (renewal) in lyric form.

•

I encountered William Faulkner for the first time, on a teacher's recommendation, when I was fourteen. I had the flu and spent the day home with a 101-degree fever; I remember lying on the red velvet bedspread in my parents' bedroom and reading *Absalom, Absalom!* in its entirety. I was enthralled. (It will never make quite that much sense, or not in the same way, again.) *Absalom, Absalom!* not only set forth an experience — a Southern experience — with which I was intimately familiar; it set forth a *texture* of experience that felt true. I had never read anything like it before. From Faulkner I moved on to the other major Southern writers — Eudora Welty, Flannery O'Connor, Robert Penn Warren. Warren was my first serious exposure to poetry.

To those literary encounters I brought a constellation of images and feelings surrounding a childhood in the small-town South on the far side of desegregation. I faintly remember the bomb threats at the schools. I don't remember WHITES ONLY signs on the drinking fountains, but I remember the discolored wall showing quite clearly where those had been. I remember being taught which swimming pools were white and black, which night I couldn't go to the county fair (because that night was traditionally "colored night"). I remember the suspicious death of a classmate who either committed suicide or was murdered in 1984 while dating across the color line.

For elementary school I was sent to a segregation academy (a private school set up by whites as a way of subverting integration), oddly enough by parents who were, if not exactly anti-racist, then at least staunch meritocrats who had no use for the color line per se. The result was that when I transferred into public school in eighth grade I had less of a racial(ized) education than most of my peers. It would have all been very interesting had people's lives and livelihood not hung on the way one did or did not adhere to those disintegrating scripts.

The economy in Halifax County, Virginia, was tobacco farming. The towns — South Boston, chiefly, where I lived — relied on manufacturing, textile mills and furniture plants mainly. All of that's gone now. Vast swaths of acreage planted in tobacco in the 1970s and '80s went out of production when federal subsidies to tobacco ended. The textile mills are shuttered, along with many of the other factories. The entire landscape has changed. Mostly this is a good thing, even if it means the country of my childhood no longer exists, is no longer accessible in any real way.

But this carries us a long way from faith as such. The defining aspects of my childhood were race and class in a small Southern town. Religion, such as it was, was a middle-class cultural ornament. I was raised United Methodist (mainline Protestant). Frankly, this didn't mean much. In that milieu you had to go somewhere on Sunday, or people would talk.

There was a conservative Mennonite group in my neighborhood, however, and as a teenager I socialized some with their young people, even as I made fun of them behind their backs. At the time I didn't drink — my family had a history of alcoholism — and if you were a teenager in that time and place and didn't drink, your social options were limited. An occasional Friday night of Trivial Pursuit with the Mennonites beat staying home or hanging out sober at the Hall Tire parking lot.

The Mennonites had marked me, though, more than I thought.

And in my late teens, after I'd left Virginia, I became involved in shape-note singing (also known as Sacred Harp singing), a Southern vernacular tradition my family had been part of several generations before. I was drawn to the music, both for its own sake and because it helped me to reconnect with my rural Southern roots, which I had to some extent severed when I set off for college. If the music had been about cotton fields and mountains, I suppose I would still have been drawn to it. But it wasn't. It was music with a theological content, and one cannot, I think, keep singing it — whatever one's initial motivation — without that content having some effect. If the music felt true, then perhaps there was some truth in the words, also.

●

I was for the most part a loner as a teenager, a bookworm with a masochistically competitive streak. I was teaching myself Latin and calculus by the time I was fourteen. I steered clear of most of my peers and expected them to steer clear of me. By the time I hit adolescence I knew my primary goal was to get as far, far away as I could from the provincial small-town environment I'd grown up in. That meant Harvard.

I went off to Harvard to study astrophysics, only to run afoul of my secondary education. (I had the math, but virtually no lab experience.) At the end of my first year I switched into history, which had always been an avocation and came more naturally to me. Alongside history I trained in music, in voice and in conducting, specializing in early music. Although my voice was too unreliable to make a professional transition, at one time I hoped to move on in conducting. I dreamed of attending the Schola Cantorum in Basel, Switzerland.

As a teenager, both before and in my early days at Harvard, I had wanted to be a writer — specifically a fiction writer like my Southern heroes. I wrote some poetry, because of Warren's example, but what I really wanted was to be a novelist. In my fourth semester, I got into one of Harvard's competitive undergraduate creative writing workshops in fiction. It didn't go very well. For some reason, I had a terrible time coming up with plot — anything resembling narrative motion. I was too interested in the patterns in the wallpaper. Some of my talented Harvard peers, meanwhile, were already publishing in nationally known journals.

Harvard has many good points, and I'm glad I went, but it was emphatically *not* a good place to experiment, to "find" oneself. You set a course and got out of everyone else's way. After that writing workshop semester, I concluded I really had no creative talent and should focus on my academic studies: pursue graduate school in history and an academic career as a historian. My classical musical connections became attenuated after I left Harvard, so my identity — my sense of a private as well as a public self — became even more intensely bound up in my professionalization as a historian. Walking away from that, eventually, was a good thing, but it was deracinating.

•

The shape-note music, I suppose, started me back toward religious seeking, in my senior year at Harvard. And of course my specialization in early music meant I was singing motets and masses, the early lyrics of the church. (Since Latin was my foreign language, I understood what I was singing, most of the time.) The formal beauty of both musical traditions is still essential to my thinking about both art and faith.

I began reading widely in various religious traditions my senior year and then narrowed myself to Christianity, though with a palpable suspicion of the mainline Protestantism of my youth. Mostly I kept this seeking secret. My roommate knew, because I occasionally left a stray library book where he saw it. (He was an evangelical atheist. I believe he was horrified.)

In the Methodist church of my childhood, I don't recall hearing much Bible preached or studied, beyond certain sections trotted out for the usual occasions (Easter and Christmas). That said, it would have been difficult to grow up in the South — even as late as the early 1980s — without inhaling quite a bit of Scripture, because it was ambient in the culture. I even enrolled in a Bible-and-social-justice class that final year at Harvard because it fulfilled a "moral reasoning" requirement, and I thought (more or less correctly) that it would prove a pretty easy course for me, given my background. That was my first real encounter with the Bible as a text.

When I started reading the Bible more seriously in 1990 and 1991, I was drawn to the parables. The Christian church has provided glosses for all of the parables for going on two millennia now; it's easy to forget how strange they seemed to Jesus's followers at the time. (He had to gloss them Himself at least once.) That revelatory refrain, "He that has ears to hear, let him hear," is relevant. It's not that what Jesus was sharing was too secret or too complex for His disciples to grasp, at least in theory; it's that in order for it to be truly *understood,* they had to apprehend certain truths *through* the material of the parable. The process by which understanding occurred was as important as the object of that understanding.

I came to the brink of making some kind of commitment to Christ in the spring of 1990, then again in 1991 and 1992. I visited various churches in and around Durham, North Carolina, where I was then living. Most did nothing for me. The mainline Protestant churches were still vacuous — there was no *there* there, as Aunt Gertrude so memorably said of Oakland, California — though the people were nice enough. And the churches with more theological content were mostly right-wing. This was during the first Gulf War; I remember visiting a pretty little clapboard chapel out from Durham one Sunday morning and hearing the preacher substitute "the Patriot Missile of righteousness" for "the breastplate of righteousness" in Ephesians 5. (I wondered what he would do when he got to one of the other verses in that chapter, "being shod with the preparation of the gospel of peace." He skipped it entirely, without comment.)

Eventually I found a fairly acculturated Mennonite congregation where I could partake theologically of doctrines that appealed to me without making any cultural changes that might, frankly, jeopardize what social standing I had in the larger world. I had by that point wrestled with the Scriptures and with specific points of Anabaptist doctrine and practice (specifically, cultural nonconformity) for years. I thought I could do what I had to do, if I had to do it. Finding a group where I *didn't* have to do it — change my dress, for instance — was a relief, for a little while.

But one does not invite the Holy Spirit into one's life and expect it to operate on one's own terms, as a sort of butler to the soul. (Not a *tame* lion, as C. S. Lewis famously put it.) I gradually, quietly started making the cultural changes I had long dreaded, not because I wanted to, but because I couldn't bear any longer *not* to make them. In some conservative Anabaptist communities, young people live double lives — behaving one way around their parents or elders, and leading something of a secret life as they explore more "worldly" conduct. I did exactly the opposite — I kept as much as I could secret from my friends and family for as long as I could. I knew I would lose friends and cause a rift in my family. Both of which happened, of course, when I left those acculturated Mennonites and went to the Amish.

•

In 1994 I was living in the North Carolina mountains, house-sitting a cabin my parents owned above the Appalachian Trail, ostensibly working on my dissertation but really struggling through just what shape an organic faith commitment could or should take in my life, *if* I fully believed what I said I believed. This was a special time for me — I rose in the morning and spent my days hiking in the laurel, often taking a Bible with me to read. (I got comparatively little done on the dissertation until the very end of my sojourn there.) I hiked anywhere from three to eight miles a day, sometimes near the Linn Cove Viaduct, sometimes below that, on the Mountains-to-the-Sea trails. My favorite hike was into the Linville Gorge, a few miles south of where I was staying. The question I was really wrestling with was whether I felt the freedom and the courage to affiliate with a more conservative Anabaptist community. As I understood it, this would mean walking away from a career — an academic career — for which I had been preparing myself exclusively over six or seven years. Could I even imagine such a life for myself?

One spring afternoon I was hiking a portion of the Linn Cove Viaduct trail when a few words came to me. I liked them, so I repeated them to myself as I walked — I was toward the end of a long hike and was in something of a hurry to get back to the parking area where I'd left my car before the sun set, so having something to repeat in the head was helpful. A few hundred yards later a few more words came and joined the first, and then a few more. I sprinted up the last incline towards the parking area because by then I had so much in my head that I feared I'd lose it all before I could write anything down. Back at my car I found a scrap of paper and scribbled what I'd come up with. "Oh look, a poem! Huh," I remember thinking, and drove home.

A few days later it happened again. Then the day after that. Then a few days after that. I'm not being disingenuous when I say how surprised I was. I hadn't thought about any sort of creative writing in years, and certainly not poetry. It just came. It was a gift. Is a gift.

◆

In the summer of 1995, I moved to Yanceyville, North Carolina, to a New Order Amish settlement that had been established the previous autumn. I went for what I thought would be an interesting, experimental summer, and then, to everyone's surprise, I stayed.

A new Amish community requires a lot of work. We were always, and rather breathlessly, working together — receiving new families who were moving in (as well as guests who were considering it) from both Amish and non-Amish backgrounds; building or renovating homes and shops; having Sunday meetings and prayer meetings and business meetings. We had regular day jobs, but they were jobs located within the neighborhood and designed (mostly) to bind us more closely within the community, rather than distract or draw us away from it.

At first I worked part-time making trusses at a mini-barn carpentry shop owned by our bishop. (Eventually we had four full-time mini-barn workshops in the community — these were money-spinners, since we were in proximity to the central North Carolina urban areas, and they were also very convenient for plugging in new arrivals to the community, in terms of livelihood.) With help from the brethren I built a bakery next door to the community market, and for three years I ran that. Eventually I was a victim of my own success: I couldn't keep up with the demand, but we had a manpower shortage, so I couldn't hire reliable, consistent help. I sold the bakery (to a community brother who had teenage daughters at home, whom he rather unfortunately volunteered to run it) and went to work at a vinyl window shop owned by another community member. I worked there from 1998 until late 2000.

People often remark that adjusting to horse-and-buggy transportation must have been difficult. "Difficult" for me was adjusting to being in a community setting where you are on call for others' needs 24/7, and in which everyone pretty well knows everyone else's business. As a modern person, I had a great deal invested, psychologically — more than I knew — in certain conceptions of privacy, of private (individual) space versus public (community) space. These were shattered. Minor topics would get traction in the community — gossip, if you will, but not meant as such. Without television, as my bishop once haplessly explained to some tourists, what we watched was "each other." For a little while I was obsessed with this.

Once, watering my garden, a kink in the hose caused it to leap out of my hands — and whack me in the head, knocking me down. It was the sort of accident from which one immediately leaps up to see if anybody else was watching. (The technical term for this is pride.) Fortunately, I lived at the end of a long lane, on the back side of a slope — there was nobody to see. I remember the flash of incredulity I felt the following Sunday when my brother related the episode back to me (with glee). It turned out his teenage daughter was walking along a ridge a half mile away that afternoon and was at the one point on her lane where she could look across a creek bottom, through some trees, and see my house and little garden patch. She just happened to see my altercation with the hose and of course went straight home to tell her family. I felt not only anger — briefly — but a real sense of panic. Wasn't *any* part of my life still my own?

The answer is no, of course. We are bought with a price.

I kept writing poetry in Yanceyville, for a long time as much as a poem or two a day. I also started *reading* contemporary poetry in a serious way. I drove (while I still had a car) or hired a driver (after I got rid of my car) every six weeks or so to the library at the University of North Carolina – Chapel Hill. I checked out twenty to thirty poetry books at a time, starting again with Robert Penn Warren. Sometimes I read a poet because of something I'd encountered in a journal — a poem, or a recommendation by another poet in some interview or article I'd chanced on. Other times I simply browsed the stacks and picked out collections whose cover designs or titles caught my eye.

In the two years leading up to Yanceyville I had reread Flannery O'Connor — the essays, novels, and letters, all of which deal much more explicitly with faith than the stories — and also Thomas Merton's *Seven-Storey Mountain*. I had to make allowances for both O'Connor's and Merton's Roman Catholicism, but they were extremely important in imparting to me the courage of moving forward in both faith and art. O'Connor especially remains a touchstone for me. Anyone who is even halfway serious about faith *or* art should read the essays in her book *Mystery and Manners*.

•

Going into the Amish, I never had anything like the "back-to-the-land" preoccupations I came to associate with most spiritual "seekers" in the 1990s. I didn't have any rose-colored ideas about what "life with the Amish" or "living on the land/off the grid" would be like. Nor was I drawn by cultural nonconformity for its own sake — in fact I had worked long and hard to achieve something like mainstream cultural currency in college and in graduate school, and it was hard to give that up. But I wanted to live in a community setting with like-minded believers, whatever the cost. Living in community is central to Christian belief, for me. One cannot serve oneself communion, or wash one's own feet — or not in the same way, with the same meaning. The Lord's Prayer is rendered in the plural for a reason: "Give *us* this day..."

On the one hand, there were pull factors. I had concluded that New Testament Christianity was valid, and that conservative Anabaptist expressions of the faith were the most scripturally and spiritually persuasive I had encountered. On the other hand, there were also push factors. I had spent several years as a Ph.D. candidate studying human expressions of community under difficult, even exigent circumstances. I was underwhelmed with the guild mentality I experienced among historians — a guild being a professional protocol substituting for true community. I was particularly unimpressed by the anti-war and pro-environmental politics at my university, which were overt but which seemed utterly disconnected from the daily lives that most students and professors were living. I wanted something more consistent, more genuinely organic.

The Amish and related groups do some things very well and some things, perhaps, less well. We aspire to integrate pacifism (we prefer the larger term and concept "nonresistance") and stewardship (which can include environmentalism) into our lives, individually and collectively. We also recognize the essentially countercultural nature of our faith. We do what we do for Scriptural reasons, or at least (we hope) by applying Scriptural principles. We do what we do because we believe in God. We believe Jesus Christ was and is His Son. And we believe the canon of New Testament Scripture is His Word to His people. One can debate the significance and interpretation of particular texts within Scripture — which of course we do, more or less continuously. But these basics are bedrock.

For me, a serious commitment to faith — a living faith, within an orthodox tradition such as conservative Anabaptism — meant that certain questions were settled, if not in my heart, then in the wider sense of how and what the world *is*. Moving within and among those settled questions, as a subjective human intelligence and a sensual being, is the freedom. You could say that the tenets of faith provide something like conceptual constraint, though "constraint" is not the word I would use and certainly not how it feels to me, any more than a physical building is a constraint, if one moves in and around it.

•

Unfortunately, the Yanceyville Amish community broke up over 2000–2001. Intentional community of any sort is difficult, and even with half a millennium of practice, we still fall victim to our weaknesses sometimes. I can't sum up six years of Christian community living in Yanceyville easily or briefly. In fact, when I first "came out" as a poet — into the poetry community — in 2001 (with residencies at Yaddo and MacDowell and a Bread Loaf work-study scholarship), I was working on a series of essays exploring the break-up, primarily for my own sake, to process my emotions in the wake of the community's failure. A publisher (Houghton Mifflin) pursued me for the book that they hoped would result: *Harvard grad joins Amish, tells all!* I turned their offer down, with better sense than I've sometimes had. There is an ethical issue here. The men and women who were my sisters and brothers in the faith at Yanceyville did not make that choice — a living faith is a daily choice — to be walk-ons in some book I might someday write.

I wrote poetry during these years — reams of it. I think working with my hands was very good for the writing, much better, perhaps, than teaching. The chief problem was that we worked *hard,* and frequently I came home too physically exhausted to respond when I felt that flicker of consciousness that meant a poem might be coming. (I typically write at night.)

Another impact, in terms of poetry: the decrease in speed. Like most Amish we hired cars (and drivers) when we needed them, but most of our local transport was by foot, bicycle, or horse and buggy. You learn to slow down and *see* a lot more when you travel in these ways. Good lessons for any would-be writer.

To this day, I don't know why poetry arrived in my life when and as it did. As I've written elsewhere, I thought later of Emily Dickinson, who said her poems were "letter[s] to the World / That never wrote to Me." Crossing over from academia into the Amish was a big step, and I think those early poems were perhaps letters back to a world, or a self, I felt cut off from.

After searching around a bit, I moved in 2003 to Iowa, where there were no congregations of my particular persuasion. In Iowa I attended both Old Order Amish services in Kalona (just south of Iowa City) and Old Order River Brethren services in Dallas Center (west of Des Moines). Since 2005 I've been a member of the Old Order River Brethren, a different constituency within the larger conservative Anabaptist family.

•

As a Ph.D. candidate, my dissertation was concerned with the emotional and spiritual lives of the men and women who made the farm-to-factory transition in the early twentieth-century South. More specifically, I was studying the union moment in Southern textile mills in the 1930s — well known now, but obscure then — and I wanted to know *why.* I wanted to know what it *meant.* Not just while it was happening, but later, after it had failed, disastrously. And meant long after that — years, decades, half a century. Some wounds cast long shadows.

I included many of the stories that moved me in the book that was my revised dissertation, *Southern Workers and the Search for Community.* The ones that haunted me came from two sources: the letters workers wrote to Franklin D. Roosevelt in 1933–36, and the interviews I conducted with several hundred men and women in their seventies, eighties, and nineties in 1993–94.

What struck me was how, in the brief-lived union movement, men and women took terrible, even mortal, risks on the behalf of a collective — an idealized collective. They tried for something better, and they failed. They failed in part because of the incredible array of forces set against them and in part because of limitations inherent in their conception of community itself (such as the pervasive racism). They paid a terrible psychological and spiritual price. The Southern union movement of 1933–36 was a disaster; the region went from being one of the most unionized in the country to being the least.

Over and over again I was invited into old men and women's homes and visited with them for an hour or so before popping the union (or strike) question. Many blanched. Some burst into tears. A few threatened me. Some did not speak or move after I asked the question; I had to show myself out. Nearly all who were willing to talk said it was something they never had spoken about since 1935 or 1936, to anyone, even their children. (Their children, when present, were almost always astonished and devastated by what they heard.)

These days we like to speak about community in the abstract as if it's always a good thing. It is not always a good thing. It can be a terrible thing. It can be a weapon. It can break. You can give yourself to it — to an idea (or ideal) — and experience wonderful benefits. It can also destroy you.

•

What I most disliked in graduate school was a certain commitment to *posture*. There is a war, and we are against it, so we march against it — at the college or downtown, by the courthouse. There we are on the five o'clock news! But some of the same people who were active in the anti-war movement treated one another with stunning psychological violence. One professor, who was known for being particularly manipulative of his graduate students, liked to boast about how he'd "marched with Martin" during the Civil Rights Movement. And of course, as with most moderns our "community" was ad hoc, something that existed, to the extent that it did, only in orchestrated moments (like those marches). Then you went home.

In true community, you don't "go home." The community *is* home. If the community in question is a New Testament community, it is Home. Or as close as we get to that in this life.

It's interesting being back in academia now, after many years, albeit in another field. Some of my present colleagues, whose own identities are rooted in academic work, believe that I live a divided life; i.e. between my faith community and academia. As one put it recently, "It must be hard, living your two different lives side by side." I had to tell her that what was difficult, for me, was this idea that I had two different lives, and the presumption that somehow what she saw of me at the college was equal and opposed to whatever life I must be living in my faith community. She meant to sympathize, but she could not have been more wrong.

Most Americans, I think, live this way, divided, because it is convenient; we find our modern lives intolerable otherwise. Now I am a teacher. No, now I am a consumer. No, now I am a parent, a man of faith, a poet, an investor in off-shore oil drilling, etc. It tears the soul. We compartmentalize our lives to such an extent that even a serious faith commitment can become simply one more compartment. The Anabaptist conception of faith, on the other hand, is encompassing.

Whatever one is doing, one should be doing it with a spiritual aim and value, hopefully in some connection with the life of the body, which is the church. It may seem inconvenient, but our lives are united and made complete in Christ, and in the community and fellowship of fellow Christians.

Of course I know (non-Christian) poets who feel the same way about their art, about the community of work and feeling that poetry convokes. When I am someplace like the artists' colonies of Yaddo or MacDowell, I tend to hear quite a bit about this. But for me, poetry inheres within the whole defined by Christ, His Word, and the church.

•

One key principle that binds conservative Anabaptist communities together is mutual submission — "Submitting yourselves one to another in the fear of God" (Ephesians 5:21) and in the love of Christ. Mutual submission means dropping what you are doing when necessary to help someone else. It's that simple, and it's that demanding. An example: This past fall, the eight-year-old autistic son of one of my brothers in the community here was admitted to Hershey Medical Center, apparently after having eaten a poisonous mushroom. His father tried calling several of our elders but couldn't get anyone, it being the middle of the afternoon. Next he tried me, because, as he later said, he figured I would be at work and available. I was — *and* I happened to know how to get through to two of our elders. So I stopped what I was doing, called the elders, and then set out for Hershey, ninety minutes from where I live.

By the time the elders had arrived — they and I all arrived within fifteen minutes or so of each other — the medical staff was urging a liver transplant as the only way of saving the child's life. We met with the parents and then with the medical staff as a group to discuss other treatment options. The doctors gave up; we later heard that they had scheduled the boy's bed for another patient by morning, since his liver was failing so rapidly. The parents were terrified that their decision (which the elders supported) not to pursue a liver transplant would be interpreted as child abuse, and that they would be jailed. They were also terrified that their child would die.

I stayed there through most of that night, to keep the father company while his wife rested. (Others came in the hours and days that followed.) That night, the father stayed by the son's bed and sang to him, though the boy was only conscious in fits. I remained close, talking with the father when he wanted to talk and keeping quiet when he did not. When the father needed to go to the bathroom or check on his wife, I took up his post by the bedside, stroking the boy's wrist and singing to him. At one point the boy stopped breathing; I signaled for the nurse (as did the machines he was hooked to), but I shook him just a little bit before she got there, and he shuddered back into breath.

This particular story had a happy ending. The point, though, is that our lives are not our own. We not only do these things for one another in Christ; we arrange our lives (or disarrange them) so that we *can* do these things, when necessary. These are choices one makes.

·

It doesn't matter, to the poems, that some of their authors are dead. (I recently wrote to a friend, "Wallace Stevens is dead, only his poems don't know that yet.") Poems talk to one another across time and space in their own idioms, their own zones of exchange. One thing I like about literary journals is how each represents a *conversation* — among poets, yes, but more importantly among poems. I'd like to believe my poems are in conversation with poems and poets of the past. Christopher Smart, of course. T. S. Eliot, Gertrude Stein, Wallace Stevens. Czeslaw Milosz, and Mahmoud Darwish.

One always hopes — at least I always hope — that one's poem has more going for it, more *meaning* as it were, than one initially intended. A good poem's intelligence unspools slowly, sometimes across cultures or generations. One definition of a great poem is a poem whose meaning(s) continue to unspool, across continents and centuries.

The lyric is essentially parabolic. It may evince some level of obvious meaning, some clear reference or subject matter. But it *convokes* a different intelligence, a more subtle array of meaning(s) that may or may not be rooted in time(s) or culture(s). All literature accomplishes this, but lyric poems do so in a more compressed idiom.

All of which is to say that many of my poems remain mysterious to otherwise intelligent, sympathetic readers, and some of them remain mysteries even to me. I work intuitively. I almost never know where a given poem is going — in the act of composition — more than a line or two ahead of where I am, if that. One has to trust the source in these moments. *Meaning* happens later, as a function of interpretation, emotional response, and dream.

Which brings us back to prayer versus poetry. Christian prayer has a specific audience, or Audience. It is possible to write poems that are prayers, poems that are epistles to God. George Herbert did it. Gerard Manley Hopkins did it. Paul Celan did it, addressing the God to whom he lent absence's face. I have never done it — or not in any poem I've cared to share in public — unless the "you" that periodically emerges in some of my work is in fact a stand-in for God.

A poem that has some other audience in mind can't be a prayer as such, but it can partake of that energy, that focus. The directive of prayer is a focused intelligence. The lyric, as an object, is an artifact of focused (even mystical) intelligence, or apprehension. It demands something — *attention,* first and foremost; it is constructed in such a way as to demand this.

So, a poem is an ark. It is a vessel that carries a message across a void. And — this is the crucial difference, I think — carries that message to an audience that will include people who do not know the poet, whom the poet does not know. Perhaps not now. Perhaps not ever.

Prayer is that which conveys a message to God, who is either known or knowing, more or less by definition. Poetry is that which conveys a message to a stranger.

And As They Waited in Their Baskets on the Hillsides It Began to Rain

I meant to write "saved from drowning"
but wrote "drowned from saving"
instead. When I look up from my notebook,
I realize I am writing
once again at the desk made out of the war.

Later, after the lights are turned off,
I hear the jake brakes of passing trucks and litanies
the crickets make. It's as if
at some point, or maybe in some other,
earlier life, they'd all been weavers, artisans of great skill,
but then, somehow, forgot how that all went.

In the fields outside town,
the crickets are trying to piece something
impossibly complex together,
only this time it's going to work, this time
it's going to be about acoustics
and devotion, rather than about covering the body.

It's the war, I tell myself — in the dream —
before letting each fragment drop.

Come down to the water, whisper the cripples
on the tall banks of the levee.
We call what we're doing dancing

because we like that word better than some other words.
It's the sort of thing a god might do,
a god in the shape of a river, in the shape of a bird,
in the shape of a bone tucked inside a scar.

— *G. C. Waldrep*

JOY HARJO is the author of seven volumes of poetry and prose poems, among them How We Became Human: New and Selected Poems; A Map to the Next World; The Woman Who Fell From the Sky, *which received the Oklahoma Book Arts Award; and* She Had Some Horses. *She is the recipient of an American Book Award and the Delmore Schwartz Memorial Award. Her other honors include the American Indian Distinguished Achievement in the Arts Award, the Josephine Miles Poetry Award, the Mountains and Plains Booksellers Award, the William Carlos Williams Award, and fellowships from the Arizona Commission on the Arts, the Witter Bynner Foundation, and the National Endowment for the Arts. An accomplished musician, she plays saxophone and tours with her band, Joy Harjo and the Arrow Dynamics Band. In 2009, she received the Native American Music Award for best female artist. She lives in New Mexico. We corresponded with Joy Harjo over several months' time, during which she was also completing a new collection of reflective essays,* Soul Talk, Song Language: Conversations with Joy Harjo

Joy Harjo

Beyond Time and Place

When we write, we can find ourselves beyond time.

Language is a key to knowing any culture. In the world, it is an anomaly to speak only one language. America is one of the very few places where this is so.

I didn't speak the Mvskoke language growing up. My father's mother died when he was relatively young. My mother's mother grew up speaking some Cherokee, but that too was discouraged. It was difficult for people to maintain their language when it was forbidden.

North Tulsa, where I grew up, is in the Creek (or Mvskoke) Nation. After we were forcibly removed from our homelands, around 1836, Tulsa was the site of an early Creek settlement, and it's still considered the Creek Nation. I grew up in mixed neighborhoods: Creek, Cherokee, Seminole, and non-Indian.

I am learning the Mvskoke language now, song by song.

I am learning the language through singing, by writing songs in Mvskoke and learning them in Mvskoke. My latest album, "Red Dream, A Trail Beyond Tears," includes many of them. It is difficult to learn to speak a language when you cannot practice it every day, but not impossible. Each new word, phrase, or concept opens up to a different reality. When I hear the word *vnvketckv* I see dignity, I see survivors of a several-hundred-mile walk, I hear the sun being acknowledged as a person, I feel kindness. It's very similar to the Hawaiian word *aloha*. Both are embracing words.

What is most resonant is that sense of connection between all beings. All beings have their own dignity, their own humanness. And the philosophy of *vnvketckv* remains at the center of what it means to be a Mvskoke person — that is, always keep your path in the direction of kindness.

•

My mother loved music. I grew up with her singing and songwriting. She loved rhythm and rhyme, and William Blake was one of her favorite poets. She was born with a caul over her face and had a strong sense of knowing.

If my father had followed his traditional line, he most likely would have been a healer. I always saw that gift in him. He was a great dancer. He was damaged by losing his mother when he was young, and by never quite finding his place as a Creek Indian man in Oklahoma during very racist years. Oklahoma prides itself on its Indian heritage, but it remains quite racist. My father died when he was fifty-three. He had asbestosis from doing sheet metal work and working on brake linings. His lungs gave out. Lungs carry grief. He's still around me, though not so much as of late.

When we write, perform, heal, or are otherwise in that creative space, we can find ourselves beyond time. N. Scott Momaday has a beautiful passage about his grandmother Ko-san appearing to him in that space where he speaks about the power of words, about the calling into being. My earliest memories have nothing to do with Oklahoma. In the time between birth and speech, I lived primarily somewhere between the natural world and the dream world. I would travel to other times where I was not a child. And it was not Oklahoma. I knew the earth as a living being.

Often I feel beyond any of the definitions ascribed to me as a person who is political, a feminist, indigenous, and so on. It is my spirit who is writing, speaking, singing, playing saxophone, and acting. My spirit is acting through a time and a place, a skin and a history. And I am identified with the time, place, skin, and history even as these feel small and far away. I am absolutely in the world — the struggle, the concerns, the celebration, and the mourning. I am entranced by the diversity of experience on earth, even as I feel — how do I say this? — beyond all that, when I am in the dreaming/visionary place.

◆

I stay clear of membership in any organized religion. From my study of history, theology, and metaphysics, especially from the perspective of an indigenous person in this country, I understand that organized religion is responsible for dismantling and destroying indigenous cultures all over the western hemisphere. This is still happening within our tribal nations. Factions from organized religions are behind nearly every armed conflict presently going on in the world. Most churches are corporate structures whose aim is to grow the congregation, to make money.

As I say this I can feel my grandfather Henry Marsey Harjo standing near me. He was a Creek Indian Baptist minister and someone I love very much, though he had passed from this world before I was born. He grew up in an orphanage staffed and run by Christian missionaries near Eufaula, Oklahoma, in the Creek Nation at the turn of the last century. He loved to ponder the spiritual world. He loved to speak of insights gained while studying biblical scripture. He was a full-blood Creek Indian who was active in tribal government and his community, in a time of many changes. He found his spiritual expression in Christian religion, and found and sought love there. I understand that many people do, despite the history. I have felt compassion or *vn-vketckv* in a few churches.

In my mid-thirties, I began to sense my grandfather Henry Marsey Harjo around me. He was interested in my writing and the spirituality of it. There we merged, but we disagree about Christianity. He is still a presence in my life, and I love him dearly.

◆

I started going to a Bible church on my own when I was around seven. I was lured by the church people who stood outside of the school and gave us candy and invited us to vacation Bible school. Church was a refuge from my stepfather's psychological and physical abuse. I loved the songs, poetry, and thinking about God, but from early on I was not in agreement with many of the doctrines and beliefs espoused by the church. They used the Bible to prove racist beliefs, to justify misogyny, and to judge others. We were not to question, and I had many questions. I was the only child who attended the church with no parents, and I was Indian. It was a very uncomfortable situation, but not as uncomfortable as being home with my stepfather.

When I was in high school, my stepfather came up with a plan to send me to a fundamentalist Christian school. Neither my mother nor my stepfather was a fundamentalist Christian. Sending me to the school was a punishment invented by my stepfather, who knew that I had walked out of church at thirteen. He didn't know why; he just knew that I had abruptly stopped attending. When he came up with the plan to send me to the church school, I found an alternative. My mother took me to the Bureau of Indian Affairs office and signed me up for the Institute of American Indian Arts (IAIA) in New Mexico.

The IAIA saved my life. Being there was one of the first times I felt at home. New Mexico was for me a place of refuge and inspiration. The roots of cultural creative synthesis were born for me there. We were indigenous students from communities all over the country, from Alaska to Florida, who came to that school and were asking important questions about cultural regeneration and experimenting in form. For instance, in my art, how could Jimi Hendrix, the stomp dance, Thomas Hardy, and the Bhagavad Gītā all fit together?

It was the place — the mountains, desert, and light — that coalesced and inspired.

I remember saying to a friend of mine that I would "never get on a stage" when she said she was signing up for drama class and asked me to sign up with her. I did sign up anyway, and became a member of an innovative drama and dance troupe. Our teacher, Rolland Meinholtz, had a great interest in Greek drama and saw many correlations between Greek drama and what would become the principles of American Indian drama. We took several hours of dance a week, learned stagecraft, and rehearsed hours into the night. We were incorporating dance into the plays. It was quite thrilling. José Limón came out from New York City to see what we were doing, and we had support from the actor/comedian Jonathan Winters, who was part Indian. We took the show on tour and performed in the theater under the Space Needle in Seattle.

I am returning to theater now in my life. The Public Theater in New York just accepted my one-woman show (in collaboration with a musician), *Wings of Night Sky, Wings of Morning Light*, and is commissioning another. In a play, I can include music and dance. For native peoples, just as my teacher Meinholtz found, theater is ceremonial. My play is very ceremonial.

•

New Mexico is where I first claimed myself within a place. I was there as what became known as the "American Indian literary renaissance" became a moving force, beginning with N. Scott Momaday's Pulitzer Prize–winning *House Made of Dawn*. I was a student at the University of New Mexico in the early 1970s when the multicultural arts movements swept the country. I was in the presence of major Chicano/Chicana, indigenous, working-class, feminist, African American, Asian American poets, artists, and musicians. I'm convinced that the spiritual presence of the land was behind the emergence of the movement(s). We are of the earth, the flowers, and the desert — the forces and spirits who move within, above, about, and around it. In New Mexico, where the population of the state is relatively small (close to two million), the land and sky are an obvious presence.

I met Simon Ortiz, the Acoma Pueblo poet, in those years. We had a daughter together. Through Simon I met Leslie Marmon Silko. I didn't start writing poetry until I was in my mid-twenties, around the time my daughter Rainy was born, which is also around the time I started learning the Navajo language for my university language requirement.

I had always loved poetry and read it on my own. We were not encouraged to read poetry in the Tulsa public schools. Most of the teachers were afraid of it. At Indian school, there was a natural love of language and poetry among the students. After I met Simon, the first "real" poet I had known, and the first native poet, and after meeting Leslie Silko, I decided to take poetry workshops. I changed my major from pre-med with a minor in dance to creative writing. I began to see myself as a poet by my senior year. We were all part of a political awareness that emerged with our art in the midst of the indigenous rights movements. As native people, we basically had been disappeared by America and the American story, and we were writing ourselves back in, in the "enemy's language."

•

I had always wanted to travel to the South Pacific. I finally made it to Hawaii in 1990 and gave a performance at the University of Hawaii–Manoa campus. I will never forget it. A chanter composed a chant in honor of the event. I felt as if I had come home. After I heard the chanter sing, I was changed. The way I heard poetry and the possibilities of poetry changed, just as they had when I realized that most poetry in the world was not written down, not in books, but was oral. The poetry of the Mvskoke Nation is carried in the songs.

The chanter was talk-singing a poetry I had been hungry for my whole life. The ancestors are addressed, as are the plants and the rains. I could literally see the waving of life in the chant. I wanted my poems to be like that.

Incantation and chant call something into being. They make a ceremonial field of meaning. Much of world poetry is incantation and chant. The poem that first made me truly want to become a poet was sung and performed by a healer in Southeast Asia. As he sang and performed the poem he became what he was singing/speaking, and even as he sang and spoke, his words healed his client. When in the early 1970s I saw that on a television program, the idea of what it meant to be a poet shifted utterly for me.

I moved to Hawaii in 1998 and became an outrigger canoe paddler and racer. While I lived in Hawaii (I moved back to the mainland in 2009), I went to many Hawaiian cultural events. Theirs are similar in basic beliefs and understanding to my tribal beliefs; in fact, we have a story at our tribal ceremonial grounds that connects us to Polynesians. It is said that canoes from Hawaii came ashore and that we are also their descendants. Current anthropological research backs this up.

Hawaii is about 2,500 miles from any other major body of land. As Haunani-Kay Trask has said, "We are not Americans." And it's true, Hawaii is Hawaiian, despite American citizenship forced on them in the takeover by the American government. It is a very different place, though it has been militarized and Americanized. I was far from the mainland, and far from Indians. Of course, there are many Indian people in Hawaii, most brought there by the military, but this was not Indian country, as the mainland is. I had to find my bearing. I was no longer part of a known cultural stream; I was at the edge, even invisible. Eventually I became more and more one with the land, the ocean, and the people, and was seen less and less as an outsider.

The first years I moved to the island I was perceived as unreachable, too far away from the usual sources of performances, speaking gigs, and other work. I was in a place that exists for most in the imagination, and

I faced a crisis of place within myself. Though I had lived for almost a year in Los Angeles before I moved to Hawaii, there was a road from California to New Mexico. To be so far away in another realm ruled by the ocean shifted creative place for me. I had to find myself in another context. Still the spirit of the art, or that which is creating within me, ultimately exists beyond place. I learned that the source of creative power comes from within. Without is also within.

Hawaii continues to live utterly and beautifully within me. I miss the island of O'ahu and am often there in my spirit and dreams, and when I can actually be there physically. What I learned there is ocean. The ocean surrounds the island and has an immense physical and spiritual presence. It was always in my eyes and my ears, and in the sound waves of the Hawaiian language.

•

When I first added music to poetry, I encountered much opposition. I grew up in educational institutions in which "literary" meant solely written work. Books meant education. But for much of world history, most literature existed (and exists) before books. And music and poetry have gone arm in arm.

The saxophone always sounded to me like a human voice, a voice of tears and laughter, of falling in love, of singing while on the edge of danger.

I went against the usual convention of a "girl and guitar" by beginning with a saxophone as an accompaniment. I didn't start playing until I was nearly forty. I picked up a tenor sax and had someone write me out the G blues scale. And then I gathered a kind of dub poetry band, Joy Harjo and Poetic Justice. The music taught me. The saxophone taught me how to sing. Now I play ukulele, guitar, and native flutes, and I'm learning bass. I have to see them all as one large being.

I've come to understand that music is pure spirit. Words are a little clumsier because they carry the weight of history and laws, and have been so misused.

·

Some moments I sense that I am in alignment with those who have perfected their art when they were living. I am working alongside them. And some days I feel utterly alone and back in the muck. That is the human condition. No matter where we are in the process, it's important to keep going in the best possible manner.

Our most beloved spiritual teachers are those who have been tested the most in this world. Many suffered debilitating health problems, alcoholism or other addictions, or severe accidents or events which they navigated to survive and inspire. If we omit judgment or shame from any experience and use the experience to gain insight and assist others, then it can turn what appears to be absolutely destructive and disastrous to an experience that is healing and regenerative.

I've always kept my spiritual practice private and close to myself. I will share that I do a sunrise and sunset ceremony. I greet the day, even if I'm a little later than actual sunrise, and give thanks. Sunset is a time to let go, to ask forgiveness.

The sun is a person. We either ignore the sun, or we acknowledge the sun and make our own personal relationship with the sun. At the least, we owe gratitude for the light and heat, for the illumination of our days. As a child I didn't need words to understand this. I just did. The relationship with the sun as a being is essential to human understanding in my tribal philosophy, as it is in ways of being all over the globe. Colonization and globalized religions cut our connection. The sun became a set of equations, an energy source, or a distant star. When you know the sun as a being, the dynamic changes. There can be a conversation. We need to honor the sun for the gifts. The sun likes to be sung to.

What is common to all indigenous peoples is a belief that we are all relatives, all being. All is sacred. I have been given glimpses of what some call the "everlasting." I have seen this place in a newborn's eyes, in sunrise, in dusk, the darkest night, and the face of a flower — here and in dreaming. The everlasting is who we truly are, where we truly belong. It is the stuff of poetry, music, and dance, of all arts. In this place, we are one person, one poem, one story, and one song.

EAGLE SONG

To pray, you open your whole self
To sky, to earth, to sun, to moon
To one whole voice that is you.
And know that there is more
That you can't see, can't hear
Can't know, except in moments
Steadily growing
and in languages that aren't always sound
But other circles of motion
Like eagle that Sunday morning
Over Salt River
Circled in blue sky, in wind
Swept our hearts clean with sacred wings
We see you see ourselves
And know that we must take
The utmost care and kindness
In all things
Breathe in knowing we are made of all of this
And breathe, knowing we are truly blessed because we were born
and die soon within a true circle of motion.
Like eagle, rounding out the morning inside us
We pray that it will be done
In beauty, in beauty

—*Joy Harjo*

ELEANOR WILNER has published seven collections of poetry,
including Tourist in Hell; The Girl with Bees in Her Hair;
Reversing the Spell: New and Selected Poems; *and* Otherwise.
Her other works include a verse translation of Euripides's Medea
and a book on visionary imagination, Gathering the Winds. *Her*
work has appeared in more than forty anthologies; she has been
the recipient of numerous awards, including fellowships from the
MacArthur Foundation and the National Endowment for the Arts,
the Juniper Prize, and three Pushcart Prizes. She has taught most
recently at the University of Chicago, Northwestern University, and
Smith College, and she is currently on the faculty of the M.F.A.
Program for Writers at Warren Wilson College. She lives in Phila-
delphia. We corresponded with Wilner over the course of several
months, and in response to our questions she explored the impetus
behind much of her poetry and the role of belief, as it can most
widely be defined.

Eleanor Wilner

Natives of the Earth

Protest, too, is a form of praise.

The two most significant moments of my childhood were not individual, but cultural, the moments when my life intersected with events that tore away the meanings I'd been taught: the opening of the concentration camps, and the bombing of Hiroshima and Nagasaki. *Life* magazine brought those images into our home, and they became, for me, indelible. Those atrocities were unforgettable because indigestible, because they left no one with clean hands; and because they not only did not fit any of the precepts or assumptions with which I had been raised, they shattered the child's comfortable world forever. And the larger world was, from then on, inseparable from my inner life.

Like some of my friends who are news junkies, I need to know what is happening "out there" because it feels personal. Perhaps this comes of growing up before the me-first cult had fully taken hold and from coming of age in the 1960s, though it may be especially from being a young child during World War II. That war was taken quite seriously by Americans. The draft took most people's sons and lovers and fathers, and the war was felt up close, whereas our distant wars are now just that: distant from our thoughts and news focus, fought by a small percentage of our citizens from what is largely a written-off underclass, and only television spectacles for most of us.

But aside from history and the crimes of a "managed savagery," there is a larger existence that transcends human atrocity and the follies of history, the great and unthinkably brilliant and complex web of life, what Charles Darwin called "the tangled bank," in which we have our unlikely existence, and of which our awareness gives us some understanding. And yes, being a part of that — rather than, as our childhood religions have it, apart from it — that is very much something I feel, and never so feelingly as when I write poetry and seem to touch those vibrant strings, or springs, of connection.

◆

Protest, too, is a form of praise. As is lament. And because our media lie to us around the clock, and we are filled with false cheer and manufactured fears, I suspect that too much of our own witness is forced to counter lies and falsehoods, and is bent by the very forces it attempts to counteract. The years from Reagan through Bush, with their continuous expansion of violence matched by the concentration of wealth, along with a vicious campaign of disinformation, have darkened our days and the chances of the common life. My own recent poems could not help but respond to that, and they may be too reactive. I don't know where one draws the line between speaking out and becoming a chameleon darkened by the shadows on the branch to which it clings. I do know that I don't feel as if the choice of what to write is entirely my own, simply because of the way the poems come. But even the darkest poems, at least to my mind, can't help but contain the light or at least the awareness of its absence. I think here of my poem for Federico Garcia Lorca, "Up Against It," which begins with the assassination of Lorca and ends with his — and poetry's — legacy of renewal and light.

In all its chiaroscuro, I see poetry as inevitably engaged with the larger world. Many of my poems are in some sense "political," having to do with the power arrangements of society and the world. It is a trick of the Right to call their pronouncements "patriotic" and those of dissenters "political." I have long been aware of and deeply disturbed by the bias against politically engaged poetry in America, which relates to the "me" culture, the over-emphasis on the personal, as if oneself and one's family were not embedded in and influenced, even heavily controlled, by the cultural matrix in which they find themselves. "The Marlboro man thinks for himself." Perhaps we are too narcissistic and self-involved a culture to encourage a communal kind of seeing, and certainly, our poetry since the mid-twentieth century has privileged the personal and sometimes confessional lyric. Yet this has been changing, while the world has begun to bleed into our poetry as a result of current history and cracks (or fissures) in the armor of America's "invulnerability" and "exceptionalism." I don't believe in "rendering unto Caesar what is Caesar's," since the media and the false myths being propagated so widely and effectively demand response — imaginative, mythic response that is informed and impelled by reality. Facts by themselves seem helpless against the emotional power of falsifying myths. My favorite quote about writing is from Toni Morrison, one of our great revisionist mythographers: "Make it political as hell, and make it irrevocably beautiful."

·

I began writing poems in my mid-twenties after closing the last volume of Proust, who was obviously a kind of catalyst. I had no plan to write poetry; the poems simply began to arrive. I never took a writing course, and I published my first book late, in my early forties, partly because the Great Dead were my teachers, and by comparison, well, you know. Instinctively, too, I think I was protecting myself from fashion, and from the belittlement of the wrong kind of men. I think, in retrospect, I was wiser than I knew.

My mother died when I was nineteen (so long ago), and my father, a self-made man, was contradictory. My family was pretty complicated, but I figured my way out of there long ago. As to being a woman, I went my own way, and kept my poems to myself, and wrote as I wished. I was lucky in my mentor, Professor Richard Macksey at Johns Hopkins, who was crucial in helping me go my own way. In general, I was lucky. I did notice that the few women poets who got press in those days were suicides, and frankly, I thought that revealed something about the men who did the reputation-making, not about poets or women poets. I dislike and have often denounced the Romantic myth of the unhealthy, suffering poet. I think the imagination represents the health in us, and that any creative activity is a form of health and a symptom of it.

My parents' tradition was Jewish, but neither especially religious nor even "ethnic," as it was for friends I met in college and later from New York and the East. I was raised in the Midwest on pork roast, fish on Friday, and the Sunday joint. Jews were quite assimilated, our Temple was "reform," and the family went only on High Holy Days (twice a year, and as I recall, there was little piety in those events and lots of emphasis by the congregation on clothes). At the time, except for my paternal grandmother, religion seemed not especially significant, other than in social circles, which were drawn by ancestry and religion. Christians tended to circle their wagons and exclude Jews, and German Jews looked down on Russian Jews, and so it went. My mother's religion was strictly one of kindness, an ethical position based on human interaction and a generous, loving nature. My father kept some residual guilt, but his interests were elsewhere. I was raised, I should say, as a skeptic. What I retained from Judaism, or attribute to it, is from history rather than doctrine or observance: a distrust of institutions and government, a dislike of tribalism, an overdeveloped sense of the absurd, a hopeless desire that "justice shall come down like rain," sympathy for the underdog, and the notion that it is possible to argue any point, with anyone, even with God. "Therefore choose life" is the one credo I've kept, though, like all oracular directives, how best to do that remains undisclosed.

•

I think that I define "personal experience" more broadly than some of my compatriots. I once redefined Eliot's notion of the impersonal in poetry as the "transpersonal," meaning that there were emotions and events too powerful (or general) to be only personal. But that "only" means that they are also deeply personal. Each consciousness, obviously, is an idiosyncratic intersection between the individual and larger world, both present and past. The very language we use embodies the history of invasions and migrations, scholars and pig-farmers, Shakespeare and "that raving slut who keeps the till." The further inside one goes, the more one finds everybody. And personal experience involves everywhere you've been, what you've read, who you've known, what plays you've seen, the music you've heard, the sounds of night on your street, the millions of years that produced your DNA and present form: Who knows how far back we go? Or how far out we can see?

What is most urgent to the imagination, as in natural history, is what must change in order for us to continue in a changed world. Many of us, contemporary writers and historians, are called by what has been erased or left out of traditional stories, by those who didn't speak, the ones who suffered history rather than the winners who wrote it. For me, this impulse comes partly of being a woman and one of the anonymous, who are, after all, most people. Behind us stands a great literary silence, and out of it these voices come, to break that silence, and with it, the old narratives, altering history with the missing accounts of it. So that many old glories are seen in a new and glaring light.

I have no personal memory, I once read in Osip Mandelstam, *only cultural memory.* I felt exonerated by these words, because my experience as a poet was exactly that. By personal, I mean (and suppose that he meant) strictly autobiographical material, what one remembers from childhood and so on. By cultural memory, I mean the rich lore of a culture's past, classical epics and myths, and biblical myths, and how they transform through time.

I often refer to cultural memory, into which personal memory is assimilated when I'm writing, as the Dreamtime of the West. "Dreamtime" is from a usage of the aboriginal Australians, the "songlines" that connect them to their land, and I like the way this word suggests the depth at which we carry what we think of as mythology or cultural memory, how far back it goes. I suppose I choose the term as a way of identifying ourselves as natives of Earth.

·

For me what is most potent in the Bible is its poetry, the brilliant luck of having the King James translation, and the fact that the poetry was based on the concrete language of Hebrew and the use of parallel syntax as form in its construction. Some of our best poetry (starting with Whitman) descends from its cadences. I have taught the Bible as literature and in its historical place, and that is how I see it. The two books that speak to me, timelessly, are Ecclesiastes and the Book of Job (without the false ending tacked on by priestly editors).

The Bible is a foundation text in our society, remains America's number-one bestseller, and is found in the drawer of every hotel in America (though Joseph Brodsky tried to start a movement among poets to remove the Gideon Bible from every drawer, and replace it with a book of poetry!). Seriously, though, the Bible's stories and its theology continue to shape the thinking, or lack of thinking, in America. In short, it is, as Faulkner said, the lumber in the lumber room; believe it, or not — it is the material out there for reconstruction, or deconstruction, for which the times cry out. And because its women are by and large silent (Sarah laughs, Rachel weeps), and because what they never said changes the story, they speak to me, or through me. Reading Melville, I discovered the Shekhinah — the merciful, immanent, feminine aspect of God that was expunged from the Bible as the priestly editors assembled the texts from various versions. Melville invoked the Shekhinah in *Moby-Dick* when he named a ship *Rachel,* the ship whose captain, combing the waves for his lost son, rescued Ishmael from the sea and from Ahab's wrath at the book's close.

These are figures of cultural memory, and the tribal partiality and teleology of the Bible's structure, and its rather terrifying and self-justifying sense of righteousness and speaking for God (as if one could!), and the outdated ideas about nature and women — these are the things that are, for me, most in need of un-sanctioning.

When a figure from the deep past speaks in the present tense, then this timeless space opens up, and the result is that, as she speaks, not only is the past made present, but the past is changed by her entrance into another era.

I am in the habit of saying, when people wonder at the *chutzpah* of revising biblical stories, that they should imagine the *chutzpah* it took to write them in the first place. The plain truth is that we know that a book like Genesis tells us nothing about the origins of nature and our species, but a great deal about the people who wrote this account. It seems to me, by the same reasoning, that the mythical realm — which opens when we re-enter its symbolic gardens and wastelands, and which lets us see through the transpersonal eyes of figures who have accompanied us through time — would tell us much that we, at this radically different moment in time, need to know about ourselves. That includes how we may be justifying current crimes and dangerously magnifying ourselves by the use of atavistic myths whose tribal glorification, ethnocentrism, and anthropocentrism have become untenable. The poems I have written about the women in the Bible come, obviously, out of female as well as contemporary experience, and women, by and large, have lived a different history — since history is really only a version, one that we seem condemned to repeat, not because we don't know it, but because it's the one we do know, the one the history books treat with such veneration, as if the more people a ruler kills, the bigger his share of history, the more important his exploits.

I knew, for instance, in my poem about Sarah that she would say "no" to the Voice that ordered her to kill her son, but the other things she said were nothing I had anticipated; it was she, a transpersonal figure, who had lived those many centuries through the human generations who read the Bible, who could state the reason to revise myths. When she is leaving the tent of Abraham to seek reconciliation with Hagar and Ishmael, she gives Isaac the choice to come with her. He is scared, he wants assurances; he wants to know "what will happen if we go?" And Sarah says: "I don't know. " And then: "But it is written what will happen if you stay."

That is why we must look back into myths to watch them change from certainty to doubt, from determinism to openness; that is what I mean about how we repeat the history that we know, replaying the self-serving narrative that is already written. I have to tell you, though, that I now feel my poem is still too much in thrall to the old version; I learned this from a young woman, a rabbinical student who, in her response to the poem, also used the myth to free us from its historical limitations, but who was so very much freer: "Oh," she said, "but Sarah would have heard a different voice." Of course.

•

Would I describe myself as an atheist? Yes and no. Theism means belief in a god or gods, and so atheism would suggest the rejection of that kind of construction, which is to say, the notion of a god as a person, in short a kind of divine projection of a figure who is something like ourselves and who cares what we do or think or want. To me this is a personification of what is beyond us, which is arrogant and altogether too satisfying. It seems to be part of what comes from the childhood of the race. Does this mean I believe that nothing is holy? No. Do I believe in worship? Yes. I agree with David Foster Wallace, who, in his famous commencement speech at Kenyon College, said the following:

> You get to decide what to worship. Because here's something
> else that's weird but true: In the day-to-day trenches of adult
> life, there is actually no such thing as atheism. There is no
> such thing as not worshipping. Everybody worships. The only
> choice we get is what to worship. And the compelling reason
> for maybe choosing some sort of god or spiritual-type of thing
> to worship — be it JC or Allah, be it YHWH or the Wiccan

Mother Goddess, or the Four Noble Truths, or some inviolable
set of ethical principles — is that pretty much anything else
you worship will eat you alive.

He goes on to say that if you worship money and things, you'll never
have enough; if you worship sexual allure and beauty, you'll always feel
ugly, and fear age; if you worship power, you'll fear weakness, and grow
paranoid; if you worship intellect, you'll feel stupid, and a fraud, and so
on. All of these he calls "the default setting."

On one level, we all know this stuff already. It's been codified
as myths, proverbs, clichés, epigrams, parables; the skeleton of
every great story. The whole trick is keeping the truth up front
in daily consciousness.

This is why I write poetry, to keep that "truth up front," to pay attention to what otherwise goes unnoticed as we go on default setting.

.

What, then, is the difference between a poem and a prayer? It depends
on what is meant by prayer. There is prayer and prayer *(pace* Gertrude
Stein). If it's the sort of prayer that is a kind of plea bargain, and as-
sumes an Auditor who is capable of answering the prayer, or the pleader
wants something material to ensue as a result, then it is nothing like a
poem. But insofar as the poet must relinquish a certain kind of control,
and attain a kind of self-forgetfulness; must, as the ancients had it, call
in the Goddess, the Muse, the power of the imagination — that which
must be invited and cannot be commanded — in that sense, in which
prayer involves a humbling and earnest entreaty for vision, and a creative
deepening of perception toward a kind of ease of being, then okay, the
difference begins to fade.

I am remembering William Blake's phrase: "Jesus Christ, the divine
human imagination." I like that he blurred the difference, moving us to-

ward relying on the imagination's "renewable energy," without (one day) needing such figures from the old dispensation and mystery cults of an older world. I do think the mythic imagination of our time is relocating the sacred in the living and dying world, so perhaps that is a religious statement, though it involves subversion of the anthropocentric religions from the childhood of the race, and it means that we must relinquish the egotistical idea that nature takes us personally and begin to take nature personally. I think that is going on among the young, especially the more thoughtful young.

•

I believe in the revelatory power of visionary imagination, and I think that this is different from what has historically been called "vision" in the sense, first, that it depends on language, which is to say that the vision unfolds as we write — attention and creation being somehow simultaneous. And unlike what I think vision means in reference to religious vision, in poetry there is no confusion between the literal and the imagined. When one has what has traditionally been called a religious vision, it has a hallucinatory quality and seems impossible to tell from actuality. Or at least this is what I gather from the descriptions of those who have had what they experience as visions.

I do not confuse with actuality what the imagination unfolds before my eyes as I write; I know it as an imagined landscape that brings a world with it, has a kind of complex and symbolic truth value, and is revelatory in certain non-literal ways. I learn from such poems after they are written, and feel them often as admonitory, and always as offering a kind of knowledge — not of things metaphysical, but insights pertaining to both our past and our current situation. These are rather mysterious faculties, which we can describe better than explain, and I sometimes worry that too close a scrutiny will only bank the fires that heat the crucible of imagination.

•

For me, the poem is never just about experience, it *is* an experience; we can't know where a poem is going, and should be surprised (and even enlightened) by what it reveals. The whole point of getting out of the way, and inviting the imagination, is that you have a chance of discovery, of the imaginative freedom to create what you didn't consciously already know, or didn't know you knew, or couldn't see until you'd found the metaphoric instruments to transform this into vision. As many writers through the ages have reported, it's this relinquishment of will, this non-attachment to the ego that makes possible entrance into a kind of otherness, a shift in perspective that brings fresh insight. Reading the work of others requires the same discipline: to get out of the way in order to try and take the work on its own terms.

I suppose that the constant litany in writing workshops to "write what you know" inevitably brings up what such an instruction ignores about the poetic process itself: its mystery. I love Constance Merritt's lines:

Write what you know. And go on knowing only what
we know? And never know the lakeness of the lake?

Rainer Maria Rilke wrote: "The great poetry begins in elegy and ends in praise." I am feeling, and powerfully, that last phrase. My age, no doubt. Frankly, I have always had trouble knowing what to make of my good fortune in a world so full of suffering.

But I am sensing a shift in my own vision after closing my most recent book of poems, *Tourist in Hell.* I have just written a new poem which is almost nuts with jubilation, though (admittedly) much of it is written from the point of view of a frog, awakening from winter somnolence to the sounds of spring.

I read somewhere that Tchaikovsky called the breaking up of the ice on the bay outside Saint Petersburg, "the thunder of the spring." I have heard that thunder before, and I am hearing it again, but this time differently.

HIGH NOON AT LOS ALAMOS

To turn a stone
with its white squirming
underneath, to pry the disc
from the sun's eclipse — white heat
coiling in the blinded eye: to these malign
necessities we come
from the dim time of dinosaurs
who crawled like breathing lava
from the earth's cracked crust, and swung
their tiny heads above the lumbering tons
of flesh, brains no bigger than a fist
clenched to resist the white flash
in the sky the day the sun-flares
pared them down to relics for museums,
turned glaciers back, seared Sinai's
meadows black — the ferns withered, the swamps
were melted down to molten mud, the cells
uncoupled, recombined, and madly
multiplied, huge trees toppled to the ground,
the slow life there abandoned hope,
a caterpillar stiffened in the grass.
Two apes, caught in the act of coupling,
made a mutant child
who woke to sunlight wondering, his mother
torn by the huge new head
that forced the narrow birth canal.
As if compelled to repetition

and to unearth again
white fire at the heart of matter — fire
we sought and fire we spoke,
our thoughts, however elegant, were fire
from first to last — like sentries set to watch
at Argos for the signal fire
passed peak to peak from Troy
to Nagasaki, triumphant echo of the burning
city walls and prologue to the murders
yet to come — we scan the sky
for that bright flash,
our eyes stared white from watching
for the signal fire that ends
the epic — a cursed line
with its caesura, a pause
to signal peace, or a rehearsal
for the silence.

— *Eleanor Wilner*

JULIUS LESTER was born in 1939 and grew up in the Midwest and the South, the son of a Methodist minister. Drawn to Judaism after discovering as a child that his maternal great-grandfather was a German Jew who emigrated to America in the 1850s and married a former slave, in 1982 he converted, an experience that he describes in his memoir Lovesong: Becoming a Jew. *For thirteen years, Lester served as the lay religious leader of Beth El Synagogue in St. Johnsbury, Vermont. A photographer and musician as well as author, he has written more than forty books and been a finalist for the National Book Award, the National Book Critics Circle Award, and the National Jewish Book Award. His works include* To Be a Slave, *winner of the Newbery Honor Award and the Lewis Carroll Shelf Award;* This Strange New Feeling *and* Tales of Uncle Remus, *both winners of the Coretta Scott King Award, which recognizes outstanding books for youth readers about the African American experience; and* John Henry, *winner of a Caldecott Honor and the Boston Globe–Horn Book Award. For thirty-two years he taught at the University of Massachusetts–Amherst in the Afro-American Studies Department, in addition to teaching English, History, and Judaic Studies. He lives in western Massachusetts, where we interviewed him at his home.*

Julius Lester

A Convert's Story

One practices faith at the very moment when you really don't believe anything.

Ritual is a place in which I can have an impersonal relationship with God. I know people talk about having a personal relationship with God. I wonder sometimes if people who talk about having a personal relationship with God really want that. I'm not sure God is someone to have too personal a relationship with. I like the impersonal space that ritual gives me, because in the impersonal space ego and a lot of personal stuff can fall away. When I say impersonal, I don't mean it necessarily has to be cold or distant, but I worry about an attitude of over-familiarity creeping into worship, which smacks of a kind of hubris. In a ritual space I connect to the fear of God. I know that people don't like to talk about the fear of God, but I think we lose something then in relationship to God, the attitude of distance, respect, and *no, I am not on your level.*

I remember many years ago when I had to be clear with students that I am Professor Lester. I recognize that students today grow up calling their parents by their first names, so they aren't being impudent by calling me by my first name. This is how they're used to relating to adults. Yet I think they lose something when they do that. And I think we lose something by personalizing the ritual space. I remember when my oldest daughter was eleven, she said to me that I didn't treat her as an equal. I said, "I'm not your equal, I'm your father." That whole sense of authority, that I have a certain authority because of what I have done and because of my age, is important. That should be respected. If we don't do it on the human plane, we don't do it on the religious plane. We need the impersonal space, and we're losing this in America.

◆

I don't think one can be a preacher's child and not be influenced, either in a positive or negative way. I had an older brother, who was nine years my senior, and he reacted against it completely. He would come to church drunk and do all kinds of things. I went the other way. My father was the kind of person who was on very friendly terms with God. God was like a member of the family almost. God talk was just very ordinary in our house.

When I was fourteen, we moved from Kansas to Tennessee, and I didn't want to go. I remember my father taking me out in the back yard. We went for a little walk, and he said, "You don't know what God has in store for you." That opened things up for me and settled it. He was quite right. Those years of living in the South made a huge difference in my life. If I had had a different father, I don't think I would be as God-obsessed as I am.

Growing up in that atmosphere, with the social pressures that are on you, marks you. You do have "standing" in the community that other kids do not have, and you can get away with certain things that other kids can't, but you also have responsibilities. I never resented it that much. It was just what was given. I really admired my father, so that certainly made a difference. He was a man of great dignity. People relied on him, especially in the 1940s. He would go to court for people, and people would be paroled in his custody. Black ministers had that kind of standing in the community then. My father's standing in the community was such that if we were in a grocery store, and he saw a child who was not obeying his mother, he would go over and speak to the child or spank the child, and this was totally acceptable. Now he would be busted; they would arrest him. But then parents would thank him.

My father died in 1979. When we came back from the funeral, my mother asked me if I would clean out my father's study. I realized afterward that was a cruel thing for her to ask me to do at that time. I went in and opened his desk drawer. Inside there were these handwritten obituaries he had written over the years, and I could see the handwriting get more and more shaky the older he got. Suddenly I was in the ceiling of the room looking down at this old black man trying to make sense of his life and to write his obituary. That's where my novel *Do Lord Remember Me* started.

A few years before he died, my father said, "Why don't you write a book about me?" I just dismissed it. I thought, he's a minister, he hasn't done anything. Then after he died, it was as if quite literally he inhabited me. This was a frightening experience in some ways. I had to write the book to save myself. I don't think he would have left me in peace if I had not written the book, which tells a story about the role of the black minister in the South in the days before the Civil Rights movement, the line they had to walk. One of the things about growing up as I did is that because my father was a minister, we were not dependent on white people for our economic welfare. We were probably the only ones in the community who were free in a way, because of that. So that was the story I wanted to communicate, how the black minister embodied and carried history at that time. It was a story that hadn't really been told.

•

The year when I studied for conversion was a pretty frightening year. It came out of my father's death, which was probably the most devastating event of my life. There was an incredible void in my life. I had no idea that he occupied so much space, archetypically. I don't know that we were that close — my father wasn't a person you got that close to — but archetypically he was just huge. Six months after his death I had a vision of dancing with a yarmulke on my head. That was a mystical experience in terms of its transformative power. I knew I had to become Jewish, but I had no idea what that meant. The image I remember is being in the midst of this darkness, and I knew that I could not go back, but I had no idea how to go forward. It was scary. I didn't have any personal support. I was very alone. Faith is not something that one has; faith is something that one practices at the very moment in your life when you really don't believe anything, and you're in the worst kind of despair. I think the element of faith certainly comes into relationship with what we think God wants of us, but it's something of a guessing game.

I went to a bat mitzvah at the synagogue in Amherst prior to my conversion, and the music meant so much to me. I remember sitting there and feeling so sad that I would never be able to sing that music. I was drawn to the music for years before I converted. At the synagogue in Northampton that I attended, the rabbi would hear me singing in the congregation, and he said to me one day, "When are we going to get you on the *bimah?*" His invitation got me started leading parts of services. It was a process of knowing that this was something I was put here to do and that I could do it. There was no doubt in my mind about that. Then I began getting invitations from synagogues to go around and talk about my journey. Through the conference on Judaism in rural New England, I started leading services at the synagogue in Montpelier. Then the synagogue in St. Johnsbury asked me to come once a month. It had never crossed my mind to become a lay leader. This was not in my life plan, but I said yes.

Much of my life has been sitting at home waiting for the phone to ring. I'm not an aggressive person, and I don't go out and beat the path to make something happen, because I don't know how to do that. I'll be sitting at home and the phone will ring and people will ask me to do something. God spoke to Moses through the burning bush; with me it's the telephone.

Knowing that my great-grandfather was Jewish put a very important question in my life. If I had had a different great-grandfather, I would have been a different person. So the question was: What is this man's relationship to me, and what is my relationship to him? As a child, I did not conceive that this would mean ending up becoming Jewish. But if he were not one of my ancestors, I wouldn't be here. One of the difficult things about becoming Jewish was reconciling that I was black, but I was becoming Jewish. Having a great-grandfather who was Jewish helped, because it was part of the family history. I said to my mother once, "I'm just bringing the family full circle." This helped me get over a big chasm that I felt, trying to reconcile being black and being Jewish. But Judaism has given me and continues to give me a place to stand and face the universe. It's made a huge difference.

Judaism gave me a way to be in relationship with God that was comfortable. My understanding of things like prayer and sin changed with becoming Jewish. But I think I understand less about God than I ever did. I like the concept in Judaism of *chatat*, which is translated as sin and means "to miss the mark." In Judaism, sin doesn't have a big moral overlay. It's accepted that of course you're going to miss the mark. What's important is taking responsibility for having missed the mark. That was a whole shift in emphasis for me, which I really responded to. Judaism seemed to me more accepting of my humanity. And then in Judaism the fact that we pray in song and in silence, that's heaven to me. Prayer in Judaism is built so much around praise and not supplication. That was one of the things I had been looking for in a religion. Having a religion that makes this central keeps me in touch with the wonder and the awe. Part of my personal journey was coming to a religious sense of awe, the wonder that I'm alive, and all this is here, too.

One example of this is the dietary laws. People talk about the dietary laws in terms of "Well, they didn't have refrigeration back then," and so on. But in Judaism we see the table as being a substitute for the temple in Jerusalem. So following the dietary laws is a way of making you more conscious about what you eat and a way of bringing the sacred into daily life. We all eat. Is this going to be an act of just filling my body with food or is there going to be something sacred about it? Having a kosher home gives me the instrument by which I am aware that I'm Jewish. Any time I go into the kitchen to do something, I have to stop and think, is this dairy or is this meat? Keeping the dietary laws is a very powerful way of expressing that one is Jewish.

Judaism has a series of blessings that one is supposed to do on seeing lightning, which reflects the consciousness that such things are manifestations of God. The morning service talks about how each day God makes a decision to create the world anew. I see Judaism as being a religion of consciousness. Judaism wants us to be as conscious as we can be of all these things we take for granted. I also see Judaism as a religion of relationship. The prayers and the blessings keep us in relationship to the divine.

So the ordinary ceases to be ordinary. One can become overwhelmed by the wonder. Abraham Heschel talks about this better than anybody. That's what I had been looking for in a religion.

I did not find this in Christianity. I tried. Thomas Merton was a huge influence on me. I went on retreat to Gethsemane (the Abbey where Merton lived), but Jesus just never made sense to me. God made sense to me, but the figure of Jesus and the centrality of sin and Jesus dying to save me from my sins didn't work for me. I liked a lot of my sins. I didn't want to be saved from my sins. I'll take responsibility for my sins. I don't want anybody taking them away.

◆

So much of church and synagogue is social. In some traditional synagogues, the cantor faces the ark and not the congregation. I love it when I go to one of these synagogues, and they ask me to lead part of the service, when I can turn my back on the congregation. Then I can pray. People need that social contact, and they want to see the prayer leader. But I don't go to synagogue for social contact. Synagogue is the place where there is the ritual and the prayer book, and I can make a connection once again with God. I don't want to socialize (even though that's almost heresy).

This is a very exciting time for Judaism because you have these entities called Conservative, Reform, Orthodox, and Reconstructionist. Yet

I think we're living in what some people call a post-rabbinic era. Rabbinic Judaism does not have the authority that it had years ago. People don't relate to rabbis in the same way, especially in America. You have the growth of the *chavurah* movement, people getting together voluntarily to have services and study Torah without rabbis. You have a growing number of unaffiliated synagogues that are not part of any movement, but are synchronistic in combining elements of all the movements. I define myself as re-conserv-odox. I mean that very seriously because I really like a lot of the Reform and Reconstructionist philosophy and theology, but I don't like their liturgy. I'm drawn to the traditional liturgy of the Orthodox and Conservative. That's why I don't fit in any of the movements, and I don't think that most American Jews do. Most American Jews pick and choose and combine elements from the different movements. So for that reason I find this an exciting time to be a Jew. I think new paradigms are going to evolve over the coming decades.

A lot of people think the future of Judaism is in Israel. I don't; I think the future of Judaism is in America. Americans are very individualistic. We see ourselves and our experience as being the ultimate authority. Judaism, by contrast, is not a democracy. It always shocks people when I say this, but there is nothing democratic about Judaism. In Judaism you have an all-powerful God at the top who lays down what is to be and what is not to be. Your personal experience has no bearing whatsoever. Americans don't like that too much. American Jews are faced with combining their individualism and sense of democracy and fairness and egalitarianism with a religion for which all this is new. I think that a whole new expression of Judaism is going to evolve.

In Israel you're either orthodox or you're secular. There isn't this ferment that we have in America. I know that all the rabbis would disagree with me, but that's why I'm not a rabbi and prefer to be a lay leader. I don't want to have an obligation to carry on that rabbinic tradition, which I have learned from and respect and love and admire. But archetypes wear out, or at least certain expressions of them wear out. The synagogue where I was a lay leader in Vermont is not affiliated. I gave a sermon a few years ago at the High Holidays that dealt with the fact that this little synagogue in St. Johnsbury, Vermont, was really on the cutting edge of Judaism, because it was trying to be a place where all Jews would be comfortable and was not affiliated with any one movement. This synagogue is trying to create its own brand of Judaism.

♦

In the 1960s I was caught for a while between the political and the spiritual, trying to mediate between them. I finally reached the conclusion that I had to go to what I considered to be the spiritual side or the individual path. The primary form this took was the realization that the only thing that I have control over is me. I spent a month in North Vietnam in 1967. I really came to like the country and the people.

I remember the day a few years later that President Nixon ordered the mining of Haiphong harbor. I was very upset, and I wanted to do something. I realized in rapid order: I really hate the water, and I haven't been swimming in thirty years. If I could swim, I wouldn't know what to do with a mine if I found it. What can I do?

The answer that came to me was: I can make a promise that I will try to treat everybody I come into contact with every day as if they're human beings. The only thing I can control is myself and the people I come in contact with. This is the only thing I have power over. That was a big turning point, in terms of the importance of the power of an individual. One of the insights that came out of the thinking of the movement was that individuals don't have power unless they are in groups and are organized. That's certainly a legitimate mode, which I don't argue against whatsoever, but I don't underestimate the power of a single individual acting with integrity and with soul in the context of his or her life.

I do believe that social change is possible. There's not much doubt about that. I grew up under segregation, and we don't have segregation anymore. What happens to people who get involved in causes and in movements — I see this with feminism, I see it with Jewish nationalism and all kinds of other things — is that the idea becomes more important than the people. Because they're willing to sacrifice themselves for an ideal, then they become willing to sacrifice others for the ideal. I always felt that the ideal was being in service to people, not people in service to the ideal. I think that's part of what happened in the 1960s. Eric Hoffer, in *The True Believer*, identified and described a kind of phenomenon that is still with us, of people who get so wrapped up in a cause that they become blind to what they are doing to human beings.

My feeling in 1960 was that real social change took place one heart at a time. In my shortsightedness, I did not see that if you change laws, you change behavior, and that eventually changes hearts. Now there's a generation of white young people who grew up with much more aware-ness of racism than we ever did, and that's a significant change. I didn't see that if the law forces people to change their behavior, this is another way to change the heart. Two or three generations later, the hearts will be changed.

◆

There's no question that my writing is part of what you might call my ministry. People say to me that I do so many different things, but to me they are not that different. They are all expressions of the same thing. Writing is a way of praying, and so is teaching. I just love to teach, and teaching is a way of praying. To put it another way, the ideal life is to do those things through which you express Being with a capital B and be paid for it. I'm very lucky and very blessed to be able to do what I do and get paid for it.

One of the writers who influenced me where fiction is concerned is Edward Lewis Wallant, who wrote *The Pawnbroker*. One of the things I learned from Wallant was his compassion for all of his characters. He never took sides against a character, and that is what I have tried to do in fiction, to show the character so that you empathize with the charac-ter — not to approve, not to like, but to say, "Ah, yes, okay." I think that you have to love your characters, and I don't think there are many contemporary writers who really love their characters. If you love them, then you're able to show them in their full humanity. This includes the things that are not so likable about them, but that are part of their humanity.

It's easier to write about despair and hopelessness and to see the emptiness. What's difficult is to see that most people do their best to live their lives with courage and dignity. Hey, maybe they only succeed for five minutes in their entire lives, but that five minutes is probably a redemptive five minutes. So I like to look at ordinary people in ordinary situations, to show the courage in ordinary lives. That's been a constant theme in my work since my second book, *To Be a Slave*. But this is a lot harder to do, and I think you have to love people, to love their humanity, to do this.

I write for children because I enjoy the audience. I enjoy that with children I can tell a story. So much of modern literature is not involved in telling stories. Popular fiction, which is looked down upon, is involved in telling stories, but literature is not. I think telling stories is fundamental to being a human being. You come home from work and somebody says, "How was your day?" and you tell them a story. With so much of contemporary fiction, there's a concern with form, so that sometimes you read a book and you have to piece together the story for yourself. Children are the perfect audience. They still like to hear stories. I ended up writing many more books for children than I ever thought I would. Writing for children is much harder than writing for adults, but I want children to have books that are carefully crafted, books in which the language sings. I want to bring them into the world of the imagination that is possible through literature. I want them to have books that are as fine as the books that adults have access to.

•

My energy and intention is almost always being given to whatever it is I'm writing. I'm always writing inside myself, whether I'm sitting down at work or not. So relationships in my life can suffer because the energy is not infinite. The biggest pain for me has been in terms of my children — not having given them the kind of attention that they deserved. I think they understand that now, better than they did in the past. I think of a story about Thomas Mann, who is one of my minor gods. He had to have absolute silence, so his wife's job when he was writing was to keep the children absolutely quiet. She would sit in a room with them in quiet until he finished writing. One of his children committed suicide. I was not as bad as Thomas Mann, but I came close sometimes.

If you live with a writer, you have to accept that there's a part of that person that simply does not belong to you. And it isn't personal. In another context, I'd say that's the part that belongs to God. I think there's a certain amount of ruthlessness that's required to be a writer, as well as a certain amount of arrogance. If I was going to be nice, I'd say self-confidence, but I think it's really arrogance.

From the time I was a teenager, it never occurred to me that I would not get published. It never crossed my mind that people would not read what I had written. This is just sheer arrogance coming from somebody who had never published anything, but that was the kind of confidence I had. The fact that I had that kind of confidence was a sign to me that this is what God wanted me to do. One of my favorite stories is about Vidal Sassoon. When he was seven years old, he ran his hands through his mother's hair and knew that's what he wanted to do with his life. God is so weird, but that's also God's way. That's what you were put here to do, Vidal, to deal with women's hair.

I think we're the moralists; I don't think God is a moralist. He enjoys all these things, all the things we're called to do. There's no moral judgment.

I first wrote about Moses in an essay in a Jewish magazine, which was when I came out, as it were, as a Jew. I wrote about Moses as the first person in history, it seemed to me, who had an identity crisis. I'm still exploring the issue that because you're born something doesn't mean that's who you are. Who you are is a matter of inner listening and self-definition. I'm fascinated by identity. I think it's the essential question of our lives. It's an ongoing process. In the title of my memoir, *Lovesong: Becoming a Jew*, I meant *becoming* in both senses, in terms of my immediate conversion and of the ongoing process of becoming a Jew.

The questions of identity change, especially as one gets older. A whole new set of issues has come up, now that I am in my sixties. In many ways, getting older intensifies life because of your awareness that most of yours is behind you. Each day becomes enormously important. When you're thirty, you've got years. But I redefine myself now in terms of being aware of what's important. What are my priorities? *Who am I* becomes a whole different question. It's a very exciting question.

My hope is that I get to experience old age. I want to experience it all and answer the questions at each phase. The *courage to be* has to do with, as I used to put it to the congregation sometimes: Whose opinion matters most to you? The *courage to be* comes from living in a way that God's opinion is the one that matters the most. What your relatives, what your colleagues, what your friends think of you is secondary to what you think God thinks of you, and acting on that. With age, there comes more freedom to do this. You've been through a lot, and you've been tested. A lot of things drop away, in terms of whose opinion matters. It's very freeing.

Excerpt from

WHEN THE BEGINNING BEGAN:
STORIES ABOUT GOD, THE CREATURES, AND US

The angels had witnessed the battle down on the world and were confused.

"What was that all about?" Aviva asked.

"And who was that who came out of the water?" Gabriel wanted to know.

"I'm not sure," Michael answered.

"And who was that with skin like darkness riding the horse of fire?" Aviva asked.

"I think that was God," Jennifer put in.

Moe shook his head. "Couldn't have been. God looks like ribbons of light."

"What if," Sara began, wonder filling her voice, "what if God can look like anything or anyone? What if God can change whenever he wants and be whatever he wants?"

"Are you serious?" Satan returned, shocked.

"I am."

"Do you mean God can be a he, a she, or an it?" Gabriel asked.

"I think so," Sara told him.

"Do you realize what this means?" Satan asked.

"It means we can never be sure when we're seeing God," answered Alexander.

"That's right!" Satan agreed. "We can't ever be sure when we're talking to God and when we aren't."

"I'm not sure I like that," Jennifer offered. "I want to know who I'm talking to and I *really* want to know when I'm talking to God."

They were silent for a moment. Finally Sara said softly, "Maybe it just means we should talk to everyone as if it was God."

—Julius Lester

CHRISTIAN WIMAN was born in 1966 and raised in West Texas. He graduated from Washington and Lee University and has taught at Northwestern University, Stanford University, Lynchburg College, and the Prague School of Economics. Since 2003, he has been editor of America's oldest magazine of verse, Poetry. *His first book of poems,* The Long Home, *won the Nicholas Roerich Prize, and his most recent book,* Every Riven Thing, *was named by* The New Yorker *as one of the best poetry books of 2010 and awarded the Ambassador Book Award from the English Speaking Union. He has also published a wide-ranging book of contemplative essays,* Ambition and Survival: Becoming a Poet, *which includes an account of Wiman's experience with a rare form of cancer and his reflections on how a person and an artist contends with the immediate possibility of death. His poems, criticism, and personal essays have appeared widely, including in* The Atlantic Monthly, Harper's, The New York Times Book Review, *and* The New Yorker. *His awards include a Lannan residency fellowship, a Pushcart Prize, a Whiting Writers Award, and a Stegner fellowship. We interviewed Wiman in Chicago, where he lives.*

Christian Wiman

Nimble Believing

The dormant life of language can lead us, if not to God, at least to the possibility of God.

Some of my writings — poems and prose — express a deep ambivalence about Christianity and about the possibility of genuine faith. I've had someone ask me if I'm an "atheist Christian," whatever that might mean. I do think Christianity has to be reinvented, reimagined, that its whole nature is contingency and change; Christ himself seems to demand this, and to exemplify it. "No truth but the way to truth," as Paul Tillich said. Or, if you want to go back further, Pascal: "If you are searching for God, then you have found him." But the truth is: I feel an enormous relief and release when I call myself a Christian in public, perhaps because in private I so often doubt myself, and because in public I'm often silent in moments when I shouldn't be. Sheer pride is part of that; contemporary Christianity in this country is dominated by the religious right, and who wouldn't want to separate himself from that rhetoric of absolute assurance, as well as the anger and (often) outright hatefulness. But all that means nothing. The real reason I hesitate to call myself a Christian is because I so often fail to live up to the name, the real name and what it means and requires of us: that we be loving, selfless, that we put other people's needs before our own.

•

I grew up in a conservative Baptist rural church where the Bible was read literally and a very formidable hell awaited anyone who was not born again. I now go to a liberal Protestant urban church so open and determinedly undoctrinaire that even the walls are woozy. I'm not sure which is better, really. Secularism has penetrated conservative churches in shallow ways. When I go to church with my mother at her enormous mega-church in Texas, the preacher usually refers to some advertisement or element of pop culture to make his points, and the music is a throbbing awful uplifting analogue to contemporary "Indie" music. But secularism has entered the very soul of liberal churches, where you can sometimes go months without hearing the name of Christ. I often think that theologians like Karl Barth and Dietrich Bonhoeffer were right to call for a "religionless Christianity," a return to first principles and a deinstitutionalized divinity. They were talking about remaking the church, though, not doing away with it. (And of course they were deeply influenced by the fact that the churches in Germany were complicit with the rise of Nazism.) When I do away with church — and I've gone long periods without attending — my spiritual practice inevitably becomes purely interior, and that inevitably becomes despairing. Christ is always stronger in our brother's heart than in our own, Bonhoeffer said. Which is precisely why we need community, need other believers, need a social element to our belief.

•

I am drawn to mysticism, and mystics, and weird ways to God. Poetry is one of these; not always, but sometimes. And sound, the internal music of the language, the pure physical existence of the word — this seems to be the route I take out of unconsciousness, into reality, toward God. Obviously I believe, all of postmodernism notwithstanding, that words have some reach into, some purchase on, reality. And I would go even further: The dormant life of language, when stirred by poetry, awakens and releases the dormant life in us, and that current can carry us, if not to God, at least to the possibility of God. The last step is fully conscious, artless, selfless, and silent.

•

I had a conversation with a poet recently about the word "mysticism." She objected to its use altogether, as for her it merely pointed to a state she'd never experienced and didn't really believe in; the word had the acid of abstraction about it and killed the very world it supposedly kindled. Another poet — another poet whose work I admire, I should add — told me that he was a pure materialist and believed that any "supernatural" experience, including the visitations of poetry, could be explained physically, neurologically, chemically. I kept thinking of a line from the Polish writer Anna Kamienska's notebooks: "Pietak thanked God for every poem. He scribbled his thanks on the margins of his drafts. And he was an atheist."

It seems to me that to believe in pure materialism is, for now at least, a kind of faith no more solid or provable than faith in God. We don't know where inspiration comes from — and I don't simply mean the kind of inspiration wherein you come across the word you've been long searching for or when a poem finally falls into place; no, I mean the self-obliterating, soul-creating kind of experience when a poem is purely given, when you know in your bones you had nothing to do with it, and — this is the real test! — can take no pride in it. This seems to me a mystical experience, the most powerful one that I'm aware of (though I feel quite sure that some saints and other focused souls attain a much more blessed obliteration than this, one utterly selfless and given over to love). But I also think that this creative experience has ways of happening in "ordinary" life as well. It can happen between two people, it can happen between a person and nature, it can happen between a person and his own elusive psyche. It can happen whenever that membrane between our selves and everything that is not our selves thins, and we become what we are not, or — more accurately — what we more truly are. People seem to expect God to come in a whirlwind, not in a real wind. But it's his presence in reality that is so mysterious, and insistent.

The whole notion of sacred experience, the sense that there are holy moments in this life that should be honored and consecrated as such, is being systematically eliminated by contemporary culture. I see poetry and poets as a bulwark against this tendency, this metallic materialism that, so far as I have seen, is never present without inconsolable despair.

◆

Simone Weil created a whole language of accessible loss. That is, she gave a shape and form and feeling to the things that we had lost, in order that they might *be* lost and not simply specters haunting us. For years, like most people in my generation of artists, I was not just ill at ease in the world but positively desperate, though for what I couldn't say — until I read Weil. "We must believe in the real god in every way," she writes, "except that he does not exist, because we have not yet reached the state wherein he might exist." Enigmatic, apophatic, heart-piercingly clear right down to its ultimate obscurity — sentences like this one gave me a way to think of God as both absent and anywhere, grace as both gone and given. What has stayed with me in Weil's work is the distilled sense of creative destitution, the energy that can come out of absence. I do miss a sense of abundance in her work, though, of joy that spills out of and also enlarges reality. In Christian terms, she's all cross, no resurrection. But then, sometimes things *are* all cross.

◆

I remain uneasy with the equation of poetry with religious experience, not because I don't feel the connection — it's often the only reason I write — but because my own experience of poetry is (terminally?) contaminated by my life in the world — by pride, mostly, the need to be known, to have the self acknowledged, the poem *claimed* rather than released as the free gift of grace that it was. I would say that this is just a personal failing, except that I've never met a poet who transcends it.

Our minds are constantly trying to bring God down to our level, rather than letting him lift us into levels of which we were not previously capable. This is as true in life as it is in art. Thus we love within the lines that experience has drawn for us, we create out of impulses that are familiar and, if we are honest with ourselves, exhausted. What might it mean to be drawn into meanings that, in some profound and necessary sense, shatter us? This is what it means to love. This is what it *should* mean to write one more poem. The inner and outer urgency of it, the mysterious and confused agency of it: all love abhors habit, and poetry is a species of love.

•

It is strange to discover that so much of one's belief is pinned to a document one finds so often estranging. I read the Bible fitfully, restlessly, and I can virtually never find my way to that state of mind that Augustine says we must attain, wherein we assent before we know in order that we may know. It is pride, I guess. Christ's one clear injunction with regard to entering the "kingdom of Heaven" (which I take to mean the kingdom of Earth in its revealed splendor) is that we must become like little children, and I remember as a child listening to Bible stories with rapt, unmediated wonder. Moses parting the Red Sea; Jesus risen and walking with the disciples unrecognized, talking with them, eating with them, right *there* (as he always is). These were utterly familiar, familial even, and they occupied the same dimension as stories about my relatives: the uncle who would get so mad that he would punch a recalcitrant cow in the face and break his hand, the brilliant but silent aunt who at the first sound of summer thunder made for the fields and the most open place she could find, lifting her hands for the lightning that never came.

But no more. Now much of the Bible seems exactly what it in fact is: a document written by men (the pronoun is crucial), with all of their immediate anxieties and needs and inadequacies. I don't think of it as a "sacred" book, though sacred spaces can open when reading it. That is to say, the sacredness is contingent upon the reader's engagement and openness, her willingness to listen and be changed. It is a quality activated by consciousness and by a heart at risk, rather than something latent in the text. Pick up the Bible without this openness, without this sense of one's very self being at risk, at stake, and it is as mute and impenetrable as a rock — and as likely to be hurled. But I guess I'm just updating Augustine now.

I should say, too, that community is essential here; the Bible, like Christianity itself, is not really about individual illumination. You need to be a part of a community of believers, no matter how spiritually ragged and intellectually irascible that community may be. Its meanings — again, like Christianity — are disclosed within relationships it enables, and deepens, and sustains. I *have* experienced this at times, but it's been a while.

◆

"Can you build a vocabulary of faith out of a rhetoric first
made of dread and then stand behind this new language? Is
faith created by a shift in rhetoric, one that can be consciously
constructed, or must there be a shattering experience, one that
trashes the old words for things?"

— *Fanny Howe*

There must be a shattering experience. Words are tied ineluctably to the world. Language has its bloodlines, through history and through our own beating and immediate hearts. "To change your language," writes the poet Derek Walcott, "you must change your life," though that still smacks of the will. Humans — especially artists — love to imagine that they might will themselves into new dispositions of self and soul. Otherwise it's all waiting, all readiness for a change that may never come. But that is in fact the condition of the contemporary artist — the condition of anyone, in fact.

No artist ever changes from the inside. One cannot build a vocabulary of faith out of a rhetoric of dread unless and until life and experience have made that rhetoric of dread unrhetorical, so to speak: given it urgency and voice beyond volition. And yes, sometimes the work is for nothing and should be stopped. You work your way as far as you can in one direction, and then life — God — either changes you or not. The mistake young artists make is in thinking they can *will* such changes, or float their little boats of words near them without being burned, and burned beyond the capacity to learn from it:

> O should a child be left unwarned
> That any song in which he mourned
> Would be as if he prophesied?
> It were unworthy of the tongue
> To let the half of life alone
> And play the good without the ill.
> And yet 'twould seem that what is sung
> In happy sadness by the young
> Fate has no choice but to fulfill.
>
> — *Robert Frost*

◆

I once believed in some notion of a pure ambition, which I defined as an ambition for the work rather than for oneself, but I'm not sure I believe in that anymore. If a poet's ambition were truly for the work and nothing else, he would write under a pseudonym, which would not only preserve that pure space of making but free him from the distractions of trying to forge a name for himself in the world. No, all ambition has the reek of disease about it, the relentless smell of the self — except for that terrible, blissful feeling at the heart of creation itself, when all thought of your name is obliterated and all you want is the poem to be the means wherein something of reality, perhaps even something of eternity, realizes itself. That is noble ambition. But everything that comes after, the need for approval, publication, self-promotion: Isn't this what usually goes under the name of "ambition"? The effort is to make ourselves more real to ourselves, to feel that we *have* selves, though the deepest moments of creation tell us that, in some fundamental way, we don't. (What could be more desperate, more anxiously vain, than the ever-increasing tendency to Google oneself?) So long as your ambition is to stamp your existence upon existence, your nature on nature, then your ambition is corrupt and you are pursuing a ghost.

•

Here's a quote from Susan Howe's very beautiful book *That This:*

> Nietzsche says that for Heraclitus all contradictions run into harmony, even if they are invisible to the human eye. Lyric is transparent — as hard to see as black or glare ice. The paved roadway underneath is our search for aesthetic truth. Poetry, false in the tricks of its music, draws harmony from necessity and random play. In this aggressive age of science, sound-colored secrets, unperceivable in themselves, can act as proof against our fear of emptiness.

This seems to me a description of what poetry — lyric poetry — can do and why we read and need it. It is also a beautiful — and, I think, accurate — description of what an experience of God can be and do in our lives. Instead of the paved roadway being our search for *aesthetic* truth, though — of what value would that be, finally? Can there even be aesthetic truth without some other, more ultimate truth as precedent? — the road is our search for spiritual truth. This is why a poet's technical decisions are moral decisions, why matters of form and sound have existential meaning and consequences. It's also why poetry is so important in the world, even if few people read it. Its truth is irreducible, inexhaustible, and atomic; its existence is as natural and necessary as a stand of old-growth trees so far in the Arctic that only an oil company would ever see it. And just like those threatened trees, its reality ramifies into the lives of people for whom it remains utterly irrelevant and/ or obscure. The same may be said for other arcane ways of facing God. "Sorrows have been passed," as Susan Howe concludes in that passage above, "and unknown continents approached."

•

People expend so much energy worrying about the ways in which technology is changing our relation to the written word, even changing consciousness itself. I'm tired of the noise around this issue, even though I have at times contributed to it. Poetry will survive. It may even thrive, as it seems to be doing recently in America despite all the dire predictions. (When you consider the coverage of, and audience for, contemporary "serious" music, poetry seems to be doing quite well.) But its effect will always be one poem at a time, one consciousness at a time, one ineluctably human hunger — which isn't going anywhere, this hunger, this need to *be* — at a time.

•

Abundance and destitution are two facets of the one face of God, and to be spiritually alive is to recall one when we are standing squarely in the midst of the other. For a long time, though, I could only write out of absence and despair. I was in thrall to Modernism, which seemed to me (wrongly, I now think) one long cry of splendid misery. Certain writers — Abraham Joshua Heschel, Thomas Merton, Jürgen Moltmann, Dietrich Bonhoeffer, Paul Tillich — helped me to articulate the limits of my intellectual and artistic situation, but it was people and life that drove me beyond those limits, love and faith that let me see, for the first time, the love and faith latent in the absence I had come to idolize.

◆

I think of Dickinson and the ongoing argument about whether she was a "believer" or not. There is ample evidence for both sides, which is no doubt why both sides entirely miss the point. Roger Lundin has a wonderful book about Dickinson in which he describes her relation to God as one of "nimble believing": God was her chief obsession, and though she could never stand still in belief, nor could she stop moving toward him. It's the difference between belief and faith, perhaps. Belief has objects, faith does not. That you cannot define the nature of, or commit to, your "ultimate concern," to use Paul Tillich's phrase, does not invalidate that concern. Quite the opposite: With regard to God, a certain intellectual uncertainty confirms spiritual authenticity. It's striking to me how clearly Dickinson's nimble believing, her inability to stand still, mirrors her poetic practice of not "finishing" some poems in the way we expect: not choosing between a list of words, say, or having alternatives available in the finished version. She was very true to her experience of truth being both immutable and imperceptible.

Of course there's a fine line between what is nimble believing and what is spiritual and intellectual indolence, between the mind that is torn between internalized dogmas and the mind that doesn't even know what dogma is. There's no gainsaying Dickinson's intellect or devotion, but it ought to be readily obvious, too, that few people are as strong as she was, and also obvious how much she suffered from *not* being able to settle on the particulars of belief.

◆

There's a kind of pure current of being running right through the work of the poet Osip Mandelstam, which is why his tragic poems are touched with joy, his joyful poems laced with pain. I love particularly the later poems when he attains — or is overwhelmed by — a seething, almost savage, Stravinskyan sort of music that is always testing, and teeming out of, its own angularities. Like this:

> And I was alive in the blizzard of the blossoming pear,
> Myself I stood in the storm of the bird-cherry tree.
> It was all leaflife and starshower, unerring, self-
> shattering power,
> And it was all aimed at me.
>
> What is this dire delight flowering fleeing always earth?
> What is being? What is truth?
>
> Blossoms rupture and rapture the air,
> All hover and hammer,
> Time intensified and time intolerable, sweetness
> raveling rot.
> It is now. It is not.
>
> *(4 May 1937)*

This is one of Mandelstam's last poems, in my own translation. It may *be* his last poem, in fact, though we can't be sure, as there were a couple of other poems written on that day. At any rate, shortly after writing this he was finally sent off to Siberia by Stalin, who was obsessed with and tormented by Mandelstam's spiritual vitality and the threat that it represented. (Threat to what? Total control. People who say that poetry has no power have an oversimplified notion of what power is. Even now some little lyric poem is eating acidly into the fat heart of money.) The last anyone saw of Mandelstam he was picking through a garbage heap for food at a transit camp. When this poem was written — or not written, actually, as Mandelstam composed in his head; better to say: when this poem was visited upon him — Mandelstam was fully aware of the fate that awaited him. Imagine being able to make such a statement at such a time. What does it mean to understand abundance and destitution as two facets of the one face of God, to experience one always in the context of the other? This poem is as good an answer as I can think of.

•

In the end the very things that have led us to God are the things that we must sacrifice. The capacities that we have developed and refined, and that have enabled us to perceive some endlessly creative absence at the center of this life, some vitality in the void, some vitality *of* the void — in the end these gifts must be given entirely away, that we may be light enough for this last passage:

> No more thy meaning seek, thine anguish plead.
> But, leaving straining thought, and stammering word,
> Across the barren azure pass to God;
> Shooting the void in silence, like a bird, —
> A bird that shuts his wings for better speed!
>
> — *Frederick Godard Tuckerman*

Every Riven Thing

God goes, belonging to every riven thing he's made
sing his being simply by being
the thing it is:
stone and tree and sky,
man who sees and sings and wonders why

God goes. Belonging, to every riven thing he's made,
means a storm of peace.
Think of the atoms inside the stone.
Think of the man who sits alone
trying to will himself into the stillness where

God goes belonging. To every riven thing he's made
there is given one shade
shaped exactly to the thing itself:
under the tree a darker tree;
under the man the only man to see

God goes belonging to every riven thing. He's made
the things that bring him near,
made the mind that makes him go.
A part of what man knows,
apart from what man knows,

God goes belonging to every riven thing he's made.

— *Christian Wiman*

DUNYA MIKHAIL worked as the literary editor for the Baghdad Observer. *Facing increasing harassment from Iraqi authorities for her writings and editorial work, she fled Iraq in 1995 and after about a year in Jordan came to the United States in 1996. She has published five books in Arabic and two in English. Her first book in English,* The War Works Hard *(translated by Elizabeth Winslow), was a finalist for the 2006 Griffin Prize and was named one of the twenty-five best books of 2005 by the New York Public Library. That book also won the PEN Translation Award. This was the first contemporary poetry book by an Iraqi woman to be published in the United States. Her most recent book,* Diary of a Wave Outside the Sea, *is a multi-genre, bilingual book in two sections, depicting her life before and after she left Iraq to live in the United States. This book won the 2010 Arab American Book Award from the Arab American National Museum. She currently lives in Michigan and works as an Arabic resource coordinator for the Dearborn public school system. We corresponded with Mikhail about the ways in which poetry can be a haven in a time of war and exile.*

Dunya Mikhail

Homelands

What's lost and gained in translation becomes the poem's life.

Poetry is my homeland and my religion. The first emotional connection I could make with my new place, when I moved to America, was the moment I went back to writing. It was about a year or so after my arrival. I think it was the poem titled "I was in a hurry" that I wrote first, here. It starts with the words "Yesterday I lost a country." I noticed then that wherever I was (even on an airplane over cities I knew or did not know), just being with poetry, I felt at home. There is that sense of belonging unconditionally. You witness your two special lands (the old one — Iraq — and the new one — America) fighting each other. It's only in poetry you can yell at them both to stop that fighting. They may not stop despite your good poetical yelling, but where else can you give life to that voice that takes no side?

When I think back to my childhood, I have memories still with me of my neighborhood friends playing outside, and the bag of wishes for which I lost most of my pocket money. In the bag there were folded papers; you picked one, opened it, and you got the animal toy written on the piece of paper, or you got nothing if you found the paper blank. I remember sleeping on the roof in summertime with my grandmother. She used to tell me Aesop's fables, which fascinated me. I asked her for a book of those fables, for I wanted to read them myself and see pictures, but she kept telling me that she didn't have the book. They were just stories told from generation to generation. I remember the *razqi* flowers (small white flowers with the best fragrance ever) we had in our garden. I remember the war — the loud sounds of explosions and sirens, and the electricity going off with every siren. The windows of our classroom shook following the scary siren, but the teacher kept on with her teaching. The war became the norm. I remember getting lost one day on my way walking home from elementary school. The first person who tried to help me find my way asked me, "Are you Muslim or Christian?" I said, "I don't know." I really didn't know.

My mother is a Catholic who never misses Sunday Mass, but I went to church with my father only two times a year, on Christmas and Easter. I didn't, however, learn that I was Christian until my communion time, when I was nine. During my teenage years I read the Bible and the Quran. I was reading everything that I could read out of curiosity and just for the love of reading. What I loved in the Bible was its stories, the symbols and the signs I found full of poetry. What I loved in the Quran was the musicality of its language. When I was in college, I worked on writing a new religious book that took the best of those two books and created a third. But that writing was not good enough to put in the one suitcase I took with me when I left Iraq.

We had "religion" as a school subject during the secondary school years. We, the minority Christian students, had the option to stay or leave during this class, which was meant to teach the Muslims about the Quran. I was the only Christian student who chose to stay during most of those Islamic religion hours (I was a nerd, as they call it here in American schools). I remember the teacher saying that there was only one God and that God had neither father nor son. That of course contradicted what I had learned from the church and the prayers I been taught. She also talked about the "people of the book," referring to the non-Muslims, and said that the good ones among those will go to a cool place that's not hell, but will never go to paradise. And then she looked at me (remembering that I stayed in class) and added that Issa (Jesus) and his mother the Virgin Mary are mentioned in the Quran with great respect. But they, she explained, are a prophet and a mother of a prophet and not a son of God and a mother of God. Despite the questions I had, I didn't raise my hand. I was afraid that I didn't have the right to take up the time with my questions. But I was happy when the teacher didn't exclude me when the students, by turns, were asked to read from the Quran's verses.

•

Before I left Iraq, I felt that I was in exile. My dream was to be in real exile and not in a fake one. I would even sing "Exile sweet exile!" But after I arrived in the United States, I started to sense home in a deeper and clearer way. The good memories started to climb over the bad ones. The Iraqi songs and the familiarity of the music evoked emotions and brought me into a semiotic experience of certain signs or codes. A word can occupy only one space in a language. In the same way, a human being can only occupy one space at a time. But just as a word has more than one connotation, a human being in exile lives two existences, for the exiled becomes a body that bears, in addition to its own meaning, the meaning of another place. Exile becomes, for the exiled person, a word with two codes, the second code added to the exile's memory of the original place. The understanding of place becomes dual: First, its real substance as a space, and second, its connotation to the other place. Thus, "here" becomes an occasion to think of "there." This here/there duality in exile is similar to the structure/function of language. The words make sense or don't make sense to us because of their prior semantic existence. However, until the new geographical space that the exile comes to know becomes (if ever) a place with meaning, an experience of survival needs to be achieved, somewhere between life and death.

The Internet makes the exile closer to home. You can open a window of your homeland to see what's going on, expand it or reduce it, save it or cancel it for a moment. But you can never delete it. You communicate with some of your friends back home, although you feel that something is changed probably forever:

I am sorry I left you among the ruins.
I am sorry I left without saying good-bye.
I apologize to my new home, for carrying the ruins with me.
I apologize for not being able to be in two places at once.
I apologize to the war for avoiding its nightmares by turning my
    face to the wall.
I apologize to the sirens for preferring the sound of music and
    the rhythm of water fountains.
I apologize for running to lose weight instead of running to
    escape explosions.
I have left my friends, too busy for their sufferings.

I often have dreams about returning home. Sometimes I am regretful, or frustrated, or afraid of being trapped. Sometimes I am eager to surprise my friends with my return.

◆

The alarm clock wakes me early in the morning for work. The red, yellow, and brown leaves of Michigan's fall crunch under the feet of children on their way to school. I have to arrive before them. I have to be prepared, ready the classroom, and receive them at the door. Most of them have Arab backgrounds, and they know how to speak Arabic but cannot read or write it. We open the textbook from right to left and some of them say, "This is a backward language." The classroom is always a chaotic din of loud voices where rules are broken and erasers leave marks on papers. I don't know how to be strict with teenagers. My classroom looks like an invaded country.

Some twenty years before becoming a teacher in Michigan, I was in a high school in Baghdad with the other girls reciting the national anthem in front of the Iraqi flag: "A homeland that spreads its wings to the horizon and wears the glory of civilization as a scarf..." My teacher blamed everything on the colonizer. When I asked who that was, she said, "Obviously, Britain."

In biology class, my teacher taught us about amoebas. "An amoeba has an eye and a foot," she said, "but it doesn't have a real form. You can draw it any way you like." So I discovered poetry is an amoeba: It has an eye for witnessing, a foot for leaving traces, and a flexible form.

During my elementary school years, I kept a notebook for copying songs and poems. My first real poem (or at least my first writing that I thought of as a poem) was written when I was on a ship on the Tigris River with family and relatives. It was something about the waves of the sea, how one wave reaches its end and at the same moment another one just starts off for shore. My cousin, who was standing there with me, made a paper boat from that poem and threw it into the river. We enjoyed watching it drift away. In secondary school, I started to think of myself as a poet. I was giving some of my poems as gifts to friends for birthdays and other occasions. I wrote a novel during that teenage time but later recognized that it belonged to stuff to be thrown away. The character in my novel faced life challenges but was ambitious and clever. It was a boring novel, though. With poetry, I feel I am in love. With prose, I feel I am in a marriage.

My real experience with poetry started during my college years. I had my first book published and was popular among the students. That's when I started to give poetry readings and to get media attention and reviews. We did not have M.F.A. programs in Iraq, but the informal meetings between young poets and their feedback for each other was like an informal M.F.A. During that time, the 1980s of the Iraq–Iran war, there was a trend for what they called "mobilizing poetry," which was encouraged and rewarded by the government. It was meant to encourage the soldiers to die that senseless death. But we who had other ideas and wrote "non-mobilizing" poetry were respected by the readers.

•

The voice of "God" in the first half of my memoir *Diary of a Wave Outside the Sea* was an attempt to imagine giving the world a second chance, a better chance:

Where were you when I established the sea
and painted the sky beside it (I don't want airplanes).

Where were you when I established your shadow
and carved my teardrop on it
so that rivers of wax flowed in the city?
The candle's shadow is trembling!

Where were you when I established a flower
and asked you to pick it for me?

Where were you when I established the universe?

In the beginning, there was only a shapeless, single-celled
        amoeba.
I breathed my astonishment into it,
so that mighty and conflicting things flourished.
The air circled around the cell,
pressing it into an unparalleled slightness.
I saw that this was good,
and stars sparkled with my joy.

I gave the birds to the air and the beasts to the land.
Then I took a handful of dust
and soaked it with my tears.

I was stricken with boredom,

so I mixed the fire and air and water and earth,
and here I am smelling the odor of the debris.
I ran leaving behind me a city
with steam rising from it.

I don't know why I chose to write in the voice of God, but maybe this was one response to living in Iraq and witnessing all that violence and injustice:

But I turned back
despite the voice saying,
"Any who turn back will become a pillar of salt."

I ran away
though my feet remained in place;
and in my mouth was a strange taste
and a mysterious feeling
of dissolving into the water.

Oh... How did it remain alone,

this city, full of oil and grief?

Maybe it was my attempt to make the voice of poetry (symbolizing all the beauty of the world) louder than the sound of the war. Adopting God's voice and writing about God's actions probably came from my need to have the power to stop all that violence, and thus recreate a new, more peaceful world.

◆

The first half of *Diary of a Wave Outside the Sea* is more interior and deals with the impacts of war on the soul. In the war, the killed one dies physically and the killer dies morally. They become equally dead.

This portion of the book was written and published in Iraq before I left the country. My writing then was full of symbols, mythology, and metaphor due to the censorship by the Iraqi government. I had to use layers of meanings (like an onion) to hide the true meaning from the censors. I used mythology (the god Zeus, for example) to refer to a dictator who was extremely cruel with his people: "Some human skeletons stumbled on the way to him and he used them to play music, squeezing songs out of their hollow figures."

During the Iraq–Iran war (1980–88), almost every day the Iraqi TV channel showed war generals being rewarded (for killing) with star-shaped medals put by "the leader" on their chests. You could not say this directly in the Iraqi media unless you were ready to lose your life (and I was not ready), but I said it this way (which still put me in trouble):

In his spare time Zeus kept himself busy cutting the stars from the sky and sticking them onto chests and shoulders. He busied himself with this hobby so much that eventually the sky lost all of its stars.

The Censorship Department in Iraq was a building with actual employees. Their job was to approve or deny writers who wanted to publish their books. They monitored "public morals" and decided what was "appropriate" or "inappropriate" for you to read or write. Even if they approved your book, you, as a serious writer, felt annoyed to have a censor instead of an editor. One of them interrogated me about the text of *Diary of a Wave Outside the Sea*. I answered him that it was not my task to explain.

And they blew trumpets to make the clouds rise.
And the clouds rose.
Then why do they keep blowing the trumpets?

They went out — trailing coffins
searched for a place to rest.
They complained and cried out,
"Why did we come to this world
just to fall under the sword
and have our children become prey?"
They rose to the clouds.
They rose.

The importance of censorship in the Arab world tells us how much the governments fear the writers, and how much the published word has a leading role in the public life of people there. It can even cost one's life. In the best-case scenarios, they push you into exile.

The second half of the *Diary* was written after I left Iraq, and this half of the book is different: it's a direct narrative that is realistic. In the second part, I name things by their actual names. A friend from Baghdad said to me, "Your writing was better before!"

.

As a woman I needed a *mahram*, a male relative, to chaperone me in order to leave the country. I hated that law. My family was liberal. My father wanted to send me to study in America when I graduated from high school, but I was prevented from doing this. The Iraqi law did not allow it. Women were not allowed to leave the country for study at a time of war. But my real suffering was not as woman but as a writer who could not write freely, and as a human being who was witnessing social injustice. I witnessed the way my father died, and how writers were imprisoned or killed for saying the truth. We witnessed soldiers going to war by force and dying that senseless death.

Before I left Iraq, I was working for the *Baghdad Observer*. My writings for the paper were usually reviews of books or interviews with artists and writers. I had to be careful in my choice of words. We would, for example, have to change the phrase "the invasion of Kuwait" into "the annexation of Kuwait." The *Observer* was laid out like all Iraqi newspapers: On the front page, there was the president's picture and his activities with a reminder in the corner to "write with no fear or hesitation whether the government liked it or not." We knew this was just for decoration. We did not have computers then but typing machines and white ink for correcting the errors. We would place our finished articles in a reed basket that hung from a long rope and dangle the basket down to the floor below so the editors could type, cut, and paste the articles using what my students nowadays use: scissors and glue.

I left the country because of poetry, but poetry, in return, saved my life. That's not metaphorical. I could leave the country only because it was written in my passport that "the current profession of the passport bearer is poet." A friend of mine used his influence at the passport office so they changed my profession from "journalist" to "poet." I needed a leave of absence as a journalist and that could have taken forever, while a poet does not need a leave of absence from anything. In Jordan, where I lived for a year before moving to the United States, I worked as a journalist for the *Al-Mashriq* newspaper. I wrote a weekly column titled "Scribbles" where I could express opinions a little more freely.

＊

I write from right to left in Arabic, and then I try it from left to right. But sometimes I find myself writing some phrases or sentences in English inside the Arabic writing. English has made me more sensitive toward Arabic and more thoughtful. What's lost and gained in translation, however, becomes the poem's life. And how much of the work is translatable or untranslatable becomes one of the writer's concerns.

I feel more comfortable coordinating translation with a native speaker of English. I like translating into Arabic more than translating from it.

Kafka says that all language is but a poor translation. The matter of having my Arabic poetry turned into other language(s) is a predicament. Translations are always accused of being "bad" or "betraying" because they make up a whole new being no matter how much suffering and effort is traced in this process. But it's a predicament for me not because the translation may be bad (on the contrary, I have been lucky with the translation of my poetry), but because I don't feel anymore that I have finished a poem, since I always need it to be translated. If I translate it myself, I have the tendency to change it in my own way. It's easier to translate others' work than to translate your own work; it's easier to be "faithful" than to be a "traitor."

•

The war for me is always the same one. It's that familiar visitor that comes with gifts, such as a basket full of bones, or a broken picture taken from under the ruins, or a wet handkerchief. It likes to travel to various countries, but it especially likes to reside in Iraq, the country of palm trees over two rivers. Sometimes when you are so upset or have a strong feeling, you turn to irony when you write. My poems, although they have one style, vary in their ways of coming to life. "The War Works Hard" and some other poems came to my mind as ideas, and I only had to write them down in one sitting. Other poems take years and require me to go back to them over and over until they stand on their own. Other poems are born dead. All those details of the war that I witnessed in person for fifteen years (from age fifteen to thirty), and then witnessed after that from a distance, came to me like pieces of one film and then took on capsule form in "The War Works Hard." Doctors know a lot about disease and witness a lot of problems, but all they do is give you a small piece of paper with a prescription. Poets do the same. But doctors can heal you; poets can only give you X-rays so that you see your wound.

One of the war's advantages is that it makes you appreciate every minute of peace. My personal story, however, was affected by the public story. My marriage to my fiancé was delayed some ten years because when he escaped the war, I did not know if he was dead or alive. He sent me letters to Baghdad, but I had left. He didn't know where I was until he saw a poem of mine published in a London-based newspaper. He traced my whereabouts through that poem titled "The Exodus of Friends" and sent me a letter from Australia. He is now here in the U.S., and we have a daughter.

These days, if you send an email and you don't get an answer within a few minutes, you think the person is dead.

When I came to the U.S., I found Michigan too cold, but I discovered the cozy corners of the bookstores' cafes. I used to drink tea with mint in Iraq, but I found that the mocha here was also good. I found the people spoiled and kind. The moment I became an American citizen was emotional for me. That hyphen between Iraqi and American looks like a subtraction mark, but it's actually a great addition.

If I ever return to Iraq, will I see what I know? Will I know what I see? I'm not sure. In the beginning of the second part of *Diary of a Wave Outside the Sea* I write:

> As I left I knew I was forgetting something: It bothered me to leave it behind but I was determined not to look back, like Orpheus leaving the underworld. I would not look back at such a city: beautiful and ugly, lovely and hateful, strong and fragile, hot and cold, cruel and tender, intimate and indifferent. I left with that one condition: to not look back.

At the end of the book, I wrote about my daughter:

> Larsa scatters the old pictures and mixes them with the new ones. She mixes pictures of snowballs in Michigan with pictures of a round city with two rivers, palm trees, poetry, wars, a

thousand and one nights. Inside that city was our home, inside the home was our garden not separated from the neighbors even by a wall, and inside that garden was a *razqi* flower I will never smell again.

But poetry is my religion. And my homeland.

The War Works Hard

How magnificent the war is!
How eager
and efficient!
Early in the morning,
it wakes up the sirens
and dispatches ambulances
to various places,
swings corpses through the air,
rolls stretchers to the wounded,
summons rain
from the eyes of mothers,
digs into the earth
dislodging many things
from under the ruins ...
Some are lifeless and glistening,
others are pale and still throbbing ...
It produces the most questions
in the minds of children,
entertains the gods
by shooting fireworks and missiles
into the sky,
sows mines in the fields
and reaps punctures and blisters,
urges families to emigrate,
stands beside the clergymen
as they curse the devil
(poor devil, he remains
with one hand in the searing fire) ...

The war continues working, day and night.
It inspires tyrants
to deliver long speeches,
awards medals to generals
and themes to poets.
It contributes to the industry
of artificial limbs,
provides food for flies,
adds pages to the history books,
achieves equality
between killer and killed,
teaches lovers to write letters,
accustoms young women to waiting,
fills the newspapers
with articles and pictures,
builds new houses
for the orphans,
invigorates the coffin makers,
gives grave diggers
a pat on the back
and paints a smile on the leader's face.
The war works with unparalleled diligence!
Yet no one gives it
a word of praise.

— *Dunya Mikhail*

GREGORY ORR is the author of ten collections of poetry, most recently How Beautiful the Beloved *and* Concerning the Book That is the Body of the Beloved. *His other volumes of poetry include* The Caged Owl: New and Selected Poems; Orpheus and Eurydice; City of Salt *(a finalist for the Los Angeles Times Book Prize);* We Must Make a Kingdom of It; The Red House; *and* Burning the Empty Nests. *A lyric sequence,* The City of Poetry, *will appear in 2012 in Sarabande Books' Quarternote Chapbook Series. His works of prose include the memoir* The Blessing *and* Poetry as Survival. *He has received an award in literature from the American Academy of Arts and Letters, a Guggenheim fellowship, two National Endowment for the Arts fellowships, and a Rockefeller fellowship at the Institute for the Study of Culture and Violence. He teaches at the University of Virginia, where he founded the M.F.A. program in writing in 1982 and served from 1978 to 2003 as poetry editor of* The Virginia Quarterly Review. *We interviewed Gregory Orr at Goddard College in Vermont, at a picnic table on an autumn morning.*

Gregory Orr

The Given

The spiritual is here in the palpable, physical world around us.

The sense that there was no meaning in human life was not something I arrived at intellectually. It crashed into me experientially. When I was twelve years old, growing up in upstate New York, I killed a younger brother in a hunting accident. That of course was a completely horrendous, terrifying experience. And two years later, my mother died suddenly.

My brother's death happened very early in the morning, at dawn, and I spent the rest of the day hiding in my room. There were two crucial events for me that day connected to meaning. One was that my mother came into the room for a short time. She didn't talk much, ever, but that day she said, "This was an accident." I was still just sobbing and trying to hide. And then she said, "Something very much like this happened to your father when he was your age." She never said anything more about this, never expanded on that cryptic, alarming statement. Twenty years later I learned that when he was a kid my father had killed his best friend with a rifle. They had smuggled the rifle out of the house with some paper plates to shoot, as if they were shooting at clay pigeons, and only my father came back from the field. But at the time I didn't know what my mother meant by what she said.

My father was a country doctor, and his nurse came into the room later that awful day with some soup that she had made and brought to the house. This was the second significant utterance connected to meaning. She said to me that my brother Peter was already in Heaven. "He's with Jesus," she said. "He's sitting down to eat with Jesus in Heaven." When she said that, it was all over for me. I lost what faith I had. He's not in Heaven, I thought; there's no such place. When the gun went off, my brother was there, lying lifeless at my feet, and that was the last time I saw him. And I could still see him there, couldn't *not* see him there whenever I closed my eyes that day, so I would try to keep them open. But if I kept them open, I would see the ambulance coming to the house, or I would see the world in its unchanged, ongoing ordinariness and that was equally unbearable. I couldn't keep my eyes open; I couldn't close them.

I was raised in the Dutch Reformed Church. Our little church had stained-glass windows showing Jesus sitting at a table with the disciples. I'd like to think it was something celebratory, like the Wedding at Cana, but the Dutch Reformed Church is a little grimmer than that. They *did* have stained glass windows, though, and that's a pretty impressive phenomenon of beauty in a country life, to see this radiance turned into bright-hued pictures and the pictures resonating into stories. Maybe that was the nurse's reference for my brother sitting at the table with Jesus, but her words were what I would call extremely premature consolation, and they had the opposite of their intended effect. If this was the best my world had to offer in the way of meaning, after an experience which I could already feel was destroying my life, then there was no meaning. I had the nurse's offer that everything that happened was all part of God's plan, and everything was fine; in fact, according to her, Peter was happy. Or I had my mother saying it was an accident, which was equally terrifying. My mother was telling me that I lived in a random world where this could happen, and her remark about my father killing his friend suggested another terror: a world of sinister, inexplicable repetitions. I was shocked that either of those worlds was real. Until then, I had believed I lived in a safe world where we were a family.

What I experienced at twelve with my brother's death was reinforced by my mother's sudden death only two years later. After Peter's death,

I'd clung to the unspeakable hope that maybe someday I could tell her how sorry I was about Peter's death, but that had not happened by the time she died. After her death, the project was to hang on in a world that didn't have any meaning, a world where I had destroyed all the meanings I might live by.

The deaths of people we love are among the greatest challenges to meaning that we experience as individuals. If, in addition to the loss itself, you feel responsible for the deaths, as I did, clearly with my brother, but also with my mother, then it's an even greater challenge. Unfortunately for me, those events happened during early adolescence, just as I was struggling to bring a sense of self together so as to formulate a coherent ego, and these losses kept shattering me.

◆

By definition, trauma is something destructive and chaotic and pattern-less that overwhelms the self. I've noticed that many traumatized people, including myself, take the experience of trauma and turn it into what I would call anecdote — into a brief, shaped narrative that unnerves any-one with whom you share it. The self-contained story just floats there in its terror. The greater terror of trauma, of course, is when it remains silent, when it can't be turned into words and articulated. There is tri-umph, then, in turning trauma into language, maybe into an anecdote, yet there is a tendency in anecdote to create a little bubble.

When I wrote *The Blessing*, I began, as any memoirist must, to move from anecdote to an unfolding narrative in time. To write a memoir, I had to link up isolated, crisis memories in order to construct a coherent narrative with a time line. In the process, I realized that this remembered event happened before that one, and that another event occurred before this happened, and I saw that if this happened before, then it might have affected what came after. This narrative-construction was a new way of thinking, and it forced new understandings of my experience.

For example, in the first version of the memoir I wrote about my life, my father was the hero, because that was the story I was comfortable with. I admired him; he was all I had left after my mother died. But the more I wrote, the more I remembered. I gradually began to realize that my father had been seriously addicted to amphetamines, basically since medical school, a drug that encourages impulsivity and recklessness and mercurial behavior. That changed some of the ways I understood my childhood, changed my understanding of some events, suggested to me how certain events were set up or made more likely to occur by events that came before. I had always resisted narrative as a form of meaning, I guess because temperamentally I'm a lyric poet, and, left to our own preferred strategies, we lyric poets tend to conceptualize meaning around crisis moments. Memoir urged me to understand my life as narrative as well as crisis.

·

When I was sixteen I discovered writing poetry. A high school librarian, a wonderful woman, introduced us to all kinds of writing and encouraged us. The first time I wrote a poem, I knew this was it. As one might predict, that first poem was a poem of escape. That's one legitimate function of lyric poetry, to imagine an ecstatic moment, a release from the heaviness of the world. One of my favorite poems is Keats's "Ode to a Nightingale." What is that poem about but a longing to be where beauty exists, with the bird high up in the tree, rather than down here in the shadows where we suffer and die? Keats's brother had already died in his arms, and Keats knew he would probably die soon. Of course you don't have to be dying in order to appreciate the release of ecstasy.

The high school librarian, Mrs. Irving, wrote on my poem, "You continue to astonish me." I thought, okay, that's a reason to live. I was completely lonely and isolated and despairing. Hers was a gesture of love and approval, and this went a long way toward confirming the joy of making poems and the excitement of my discovery.

Over time it became clear to me that an even deeper existential function of the lyric was to express what you felt inside, and try to give form to that — to turn the world into words, and then to make those words cohere into something. This to me is the making of meaning. When I say I tend to think of poems as "making" meanings rather than discovering them, it's a signal that I was coming from a rather desperate place in which each poem becomes what Frost calls "a momentary stay against confusion." I also think of Emily Dickinson, another existential high-wire act. She has a wonderful poem that goes:

I stepped from Plank to Plank
A slow and cautious way
The Stars about my Head I felt
About my Feet the Sea.

I knew not but the next
Would be my final inch —
This gave me that precarious Gait
Some call Experience.

She's sketched a bleak situation, and one doesn't for a moment doubt that were she to fall off the planks, she would plummet. For much of my life, I felt that way as I stepped from poem to poem.

•

By a series of strange events, I became involved in social activism. CORE, the Congress of Racial Equality, was holding a meeting in a city not too far from the small village where we lived. I got involved and in 1965, when I was eighteen, went as a volunteer to Mississippi for the summer. That resulted in the enormous misadventures of being arrested and beaten by the police in Jackson, Mississippi. I was overwhelmed by the experiences I was having, and when I was released from jail, I decided that I had had enough and would head back north. On that journey home, I was kidnapped at gunpoint on a highway between Selma and Montgomery, the same place where the Selma–Montgomery March had taken place three months earlier, and the same stretch of highway where Violet Liuzzo had been murdered. I was taken into custody again, my life was threatened, and I was held in solitary for a week in a little jail in a small town. Essentially, they were trying to find out if anybody knew where I was so that they could decide what to do with me. The people who kidnapped me were not good people. One of them murdered another civil rights worker, Jonathan Daniels, later that summer, in that same little village. Daniels was shotgunned in broad daylight in the town square by one of the same people who kidnapped me off the highway. The man was called "a special unpaid deputy," but he was really just a vigilante, a friend of the sheriff's in a lawless town. Of course he was not convicted. He was found not guilty by reason of self-defense, by an all-white, local jury.

I managed to get out of that jail. When I came back from the South, I was pretty confused, and was convinced that social and political activism were not going to be my path to meaning. I had thought activism might be an easier path than poetry. I had been entertaining an adolescent male heroic dream of giving oneself for a noble cause. Goodman, Schwerner, and Cheney had been killed the summer before I went south, and I was impressed by the way that one could become a martyr and inspire people. This is unfortunately what also causes young men to join the Army. Male adolescents live with totally contradictory assumptions — that they are immortal and nothing can harm them, and that it would be absolutely fabulous to die for a great cause. The one is pure delusion, and the other is pure idealism. The contradiction is probably locked in the history of testosterone. If we ever get to the bottom of this, we should come up with a hormonal antidote.

When I came back from Mississippi, I was pretty disturbed, shattered really. I came very close to suicide that summer. The high school librarian who had encouraged me to write invited me to visit, at her cabin in the Adirondacks. She took me to a place called Bolton's Land-ing, where a sculptor named David Smith had lived. He had died earlier that spring in a highway accident. We went to his place, a little house and a big shed where he'd made abstract sculptures, and there was a huge field with easily two hundred pieces of his sculpture arrayed in it. Extraordinary field. I had never seen abstract sculpture. I didn't know what to make of it. I don't mean to say I was a country bumpkin, but I certainly wasn't ready, at the age of eighteen, for the concept of abstract sculpture; I had no conceptual terms for or experiential understanding of abstract art, but I knew these were beautiful and that they created meaning. We walked together in the field without talking, and it amazed me to see these creations of human imagination and human hands just standing there, one after the other, radiant with mysterious significance. They said to me, "Okay. You make art." For me the form would be poetry, but I knew the question was settled, that this was what I was going to do with my life.

After my experience of Peter's death and what happened the day of his death, I concluded that this is the only world. This is the world we're given, and the terms of our being in it as individuals are birth and death. But I was desperate for meaning, for some space for the spiritual, some space for greater or transpersonal significance. The person named David Smith was dead, but his sculpture was still there. He had created something that went beyond his mortal allotment, and continued to give to the world, to radiate meaning and beauty. I thought, "That's a pretty good bargain. I'll take that offer. I'll work toward that as an artist." I didn't see at the time that there was a spiritual hope hidden inside the artistic project, and even if I had I wouldn't have accepted it at the time, because my despair was too deep. In retrospect, thinking back to that day, I can say that I was holding out some hope to myself, but I was also thwarting myself, successfully resisting something in me that believed in things beyond the secular.

•

In my twenties and thirties, even in my forties, "spiritual" was not a term I was comfortable with. I was too afraid of people laughing at me, or maybe even of laughing at myself. My religious life was traumatically terminated at the age of twelve. By religion I mean those notions that naïve religion offers as consolation. Nor does most religious terminology guide me forward. Certainly, the other-world, post-death world of conventional Christian thought is not persuasive to me. On the other hand, poets' attempts to articulate spiritual meaning I often find very compelling. The French poet Paul Eluard said, "There *is* another world, but it is in this one."

Yes. A recent, brief poem of mine goes:

River inside the river.
World within the world.

All we have is words

To reveal the rose
That the rose obscures.

I understand this to mean that the spiritual is here in the palpable, physical world around us, the world of people and things. And that it's the task of language and imagination to unveil the spiritual.

There is a phrase that has grounded and guided my two most recent collections of poems: "the Book that is the resurrection of the body of the beloved, which is the world." Whenever I write out that phrase, I capitalize the word Book, but not because it refers to the Bible or any other sacred scripture. The Book I'm imagining is secular/spiritual, if there can be such a thing. It's a giant anthology of poems and songs that's been gathering itself since human consciousness could be recorded in language. We individuals go to this humongous, self-gathering anthology, into which songs and poems constantly stream, to search for the particular poems and songs that will sustain us. So Book gets capital-ized, but the term "beloved" does not. The beloved is with a small "b," because this refers to humans. I, of course, am haunted by two particular beloveds, my brother and my mother.

I have faith that when the emotional, imaginative, and spiritual life is activated inside a person, when one becomes fully human, feeling and caring deeply, this represents a resurrection of some kind. This happens for me often when I read poems or hear songs. The feeling of being moved represents a resurrection. Every time meaning or feeling flows into your experience, that's resurrection. I choose to believe that this has something to do with the beloved.

One of the perils of being human, and of lyric poetry, is narcissism, the solipsistic sense that the self is all there is. Likewise, one of the perils of trauma is extreme isolation of the damaged self. To me, the beloved is that figure that exists independent of the self, that figure that calls us into relationship with the world and saves us from what I consider the emotional, spiritual, and psychological error of solipsism and narcissism. The beloved calls us out into connection with the world, into reciprocal relation with the world.

Sappho has a poem, Fragment 16, in which she has a line: "whatever one loves most is beautiful." I go to that line, that fragment, when I want to remind myself that the beloved is "whatever one loves most" and that the recognition and acknowledgment of the beloved floods the individual life with meaning. Notice Sappho says "whatever" — she doesn't limit it to being a person, and I think that's crucial. The beloved can be a person, a place, a creature. For example, the passage in the eighteenth-century poet Christopher Smart's "Jubilate Agno" ("Praise to the Lamb"), where he devotes seventy lines to celebrate his cat. This visionary poem was written in a madhouse and anyone reading those lines knows that "my cat Jeoffry" is Smart's "beloved" — that entity that sustains his anguished being. And Sappho makes clear that each person chooses or has his or her own beloved (or beloveds) — that it's a choosing/longing of the particular, individual heart.

I keep returning to Sappho's line. One of the terms we poets use in our considerable effort to avoid religious and spiritual terminology is "beautiful." Of course no one can define the word, or everybody defines it differently, and yet we believe in it. Beauty is an article of faith among poets. I think many of us are trying to sidestep religion, and beauty is a word we use to do that.

·

I published my *New and Selected Poems* in 2002. I was thinking about that book just this morning, especially the section of new poems, and it struck me that they represented a wall I had encountered in my life. The poems in the new section are quite varied, they go in different directions, but I see many of the dense, imagistic ones as tunnels trying to burrow underneath that wall. I also wrote ten villanelles then — a highly formal kind of poem, very uncharacteristic of my work — and I saw that those villanelles were rigid ladders that I used to try to climb over the wall, but they didn't reach its top. The upshot of that set of poems was that, spiritually speaking, I wasn't going to be able to tunnel under or climb over the wall. I want to resist the temptation here to disparage that phase of my writing — I was doing the best that I could. But the fact was, the wall was the central imaginative fact for me at that time, and it was a fact that the poems I wrote couldn't alter.

The Blessing was also published that year. A lot of material that had been inside me for a long time came out in the memoir. Writing a memoir is an amazing experience of drilling down through layers of stories, many of which one has told oneself for years, and yet they are not true — or they are only provisionally or anecdotally true. To connect up all the moments in your life into what the police call a timeline is a very strange experience, because it's archeological. Once you've uncovered one layer of civilization or culture, you need to dig down to another, and then another — story hidden below story. It's not revelatory, because it's hard labor. You wouldn't call an archaeological dig a revelatory experience, would you? But the results are revelatory.

That same year I also published a book called *Poetry as Survival*, a prose book about the personal lyric and how it helps people to live. How the lyric is a universal and essential cultural gift that encourages individuals to engage passions and confusions and traumas in their lives — to engage them and, by turning those experiences into words and then shaping those words — to master what threatens to overwhelm them. It may be that the two prose books exhausted a direction for me and that the poems in the selected's "New" section couldn't quite get past into a new place.

It's a truism that everything you do is preparation for what happens next. On the other hand, there is no point in saying, "And then I broke through the wall." I didn't. That would not be true. The wall vanished, or I woke up on the other side of the wall. I don't regret anything I have ever learned or read or written, but all these things put together didn't take me to the other side of the wall. This is a fact that it has taken me a little while to come to terms with, because I'm basically a secular person, but the best term I can come up with is "grace."

Whatever was going on, I woke up one January morning in 2003 with a phrase in my head: "the Book that is the resurrection of the body of the beloved, which is the world." A voice in my head spoke this phrase with great clarity and authority. I didn't speak it. Of course, we hear a voice speak to us constantly; we hear "Radio Free Brain" chattering inside us all the time. This was a different voice, one that spoke with enormous certainty. Somehow I understood completely what this fairly cryptic phrase meant. I wrote it down, and then poems started saying themselves to me. And I wrote them down. I risk my professional reputation as a poet saying this, but the voice would pause, and I would know that that poem was over, and then it would start again. I think there were probably thirty pieces spoken to me that morning. I just listened and wrote them down. I was quite intrigued, to put it mildly. The next morning there were more, again with my having just a sense of recording them. This went on for several months.

I've spent my life figuring out what methods help me to bring language to the page, and then what skills I can bring to bear on the language to turn what's there into the most successful poem possible. By the time I was in my mid-fifties, I was completely undaunted by the idea of revising a single poem three or four hundred times. The work of revision, which some people experience as tedium (especially young people, or certainly myself at a younger age), was as much a pleasure as the original impetus to the poem. What was the original impetus to most poems? As is true for most poets, for me this is usually a phrase. We call it "the given." A phrase comes into your head and sets the mind and imagination into intuiting the form of a poem. You have to catch up to that intuited form before it disappears. You have to find the words for it, even though only the first words may be given. Then comes the work of infinite revisions, when I'm pursuing some dream of a beautiful, lucid calm.

What happened that morning in 2003 was completely different. I had never written in this way before. The poems presented themselves. "Here. This is it. These are the words. Write this down." Pause. "Write this down." The thirty poems that came to me that first morning all explored different facets of the initial phrase "the Book that is the resurrection of the body of the beloved, which is the world." By the end of four months of this, I was beginning to fear being overwhelmed by the material. I had mostly written it out by hand, and it was getting to be quite a pile. So I typed them up, and then I tried to be as professional a poet as I could be, with my forty years of experience. I'm a disciplined critic of my own work. I did my best to decide what was interesting and what wasn't, as a linguistic, imaginative experience. Many of the poems, or utterances, seemed insignificant. They had meaning, but they didn't have interest. It became a matter of what might be of interest to other people, what might communicate some of the excitement that I was feeling receiving the poems. But it was more than excitement. With these poems, it was as if I had woken up on the other side of the wall, in all new territory.

•

I'm not entirely sure what the wall in my life was. The image of the wall has just come to me in the course of this conversation, so I haven't worked it out. But I wouldn't be surprised if the wall was the last stand of my doubt and despair, of my resistance to meaning coming into my life. I ran across these lines somewhere: "Israel cries out to the Lord, 'When will You redeem me?'" And the Lord answers, "Not until you have sunk to the lowest depths. Only then will I redeem you." There's a psychological or spiritual truth in this. One can't begin recovery until one has reached the purest moment of despair. That's the turning point. The wall was that pure last stand of doubt for me. And then there was a door through that wall, which I can't explain.

I have complete faith in what I've written since the experience of the voice speaking to me. I don't know whether the poems interest other people or not. It doesn't matter to me. I certainly know that many of my professional friends, other poet friends, are alarmed by my new poems. They don't know what to make of them.

I remember having a discussion with a friend thirty years ago about where poetry comes from. He said, "I write poems to discover meaning." That of course is a pretty standard statement. I said, "I write poems to make meaning." He said, "What do you mean?" I said, "I believe existence is meaningless, and we have to create meaning in order to sustain ourselves." At the time this was true to my experience. Through acts of will and discipline and imagination, I tried to make meaning, but it wasn't enough to get to the other side of the existential wall I kept encountering. Now from the other side of that wall, I can think back on my life, when such a grim statement as "life is meaningless" was true for me. I can see that I had to create meaning, and love, and secure environments for myself, and that the most exciting form of meaning I could create was poetry.

William Blake is one of my heroes:

I shall not cease from mental fight
Nor shall my sword sleep in my hand
till we have built Jerusalem
in England's green and pleasant land.

He's registering the Industrial Revolution in this poem, but those "dark Satanic mills" are also the vast destructive forces in the world that would turn against the life of the human spirit. Jerusalem is not a physical city; it's a visionary city that he feels we must build. This is where visionary poetry and the spiritual meet and fuse, for me, and are identical. What would Jerusalem be? I have no idea, but we always have to build Jerusalem. I don't believe it's ever been built or ever will be built, but I know of no more worthy project than to try to add a few bricks. I think when we poets put our poems into the Book, just slip them into this giant anthology on the off-chance that someone who needs them might find them there someday — I think we're doing our part in building that city.

Death is a mystery. We're fascinated by it or appalled by it. After hearing the voice in 2003, my preoccupation with death suddenly seemed ludicrous to me. It's not that people don't think about it or shouldn't think about it, but I realized that I really ought to be thinking about being alive and speaking about being alive. I respect that speaking about death in poetry is an indirect way of speaking about life, but the indirectness of this just struck me as suddenly ludicrous. Rilke cultivated what I would call a cult of death. Some of his poems about death and what a blessed state it is seem ridiculous.

I wrote about death constantly in my earlier work. But I'm alive. I used to say that the lyric poet is given the responsibility to talk about two of the big human mysteries, sex and death, or love and loss. I had always used poetry to talk about love and death, though more often than not about death and loss. But now I'd rather talk about life.

(UNTITLED)

This is what was bequeathed us:
This earth the beloved left
And, leaving,
Left to us.

No other world
But this one:
Willows and the river
And the factory
With its black smokestacks.

No other shore, only this bank
On which the living gather.

No meaning but what we find here.
No purpose but what we make.

That, and the beloved's clear instructions:
Turn me into song; sing me awake.

— Gregory Orr

ACKNOWLEDGMENTS

We want to thank the first readers of this manuscript for invaluable suggestions about the shape of the book as a whole: Hildred Crill, Jocelyn Earnest, Katie Farris, Joy Roulier Sawyer, Susan Sinnott, and Jim Sparrell. We are grateful to Pattie M. Wells, who gave us assistance with transcribing, and to the editors of the magazines in which some of these interviews first appeared, including *The Sun* (Li-Young Lee), *Poets and Writers* "Direct Quote" online (Grace Paley), and *Agni* online (Jane Hirshfield). Stuart Hancock, editor of the *Mars Hill Review*, deserves particular thanks for starting us on this series and for featuring the interviews with Carolyn Forché and Julius Lester. Special thanks, as well, to Christian Wiman for featuring excerpts from the book in *Poetry*. Jeffrey Levine, our publisher, and Jim Schley, our editor, brought a passion and vision to this project that meant more than we can express. Our deepest gratitude goes to the writers we interviewed, who patiently responded to repeated rounds of questions and articulated their thoughts so eloquently. Their generosity made this book possible.

The following featured poems, listed in order of appearance in this book, have been previously published. Permission for inclusion here has been granted as noted.

OTHER BOOKS FROM TUPELO PRESS

Fasting for Ramadan: Notes from a Spiritual Practice, Kazim Ali
This Lamentable City, Polina Barskova,
    edited and introduced by Ilya Kaminsky
Circle's Apprentice, Dan Beachy-Quick
Cloisters, Kristin Bock
Stone Lyre: Poems of René Char, translated by Nancy Naomi Carlson
Severance Songs, Joshua Corey
Atlas Hour, Carol Ann Davis
Sanderlings, Geri Doran
The Flight Cage, Rebecca Dunham
Other Fugitives & Other Strangers, Rigoberto González
The Us, Joan Houlihan
Nothing Can Make Me Do This, David Huddle
Manoleria, Daniel Khalastchi
Phyla of Joy, Karen An-hwei Lee
Lucky Fish, Aimee Nezhukumatathil
Intimate: An American Family Photo Album, Paisley Rekdal
The Beginning of the Fields, Angela Shaw
Cream of Kohlrabi: Stories, Floyd Skloot
The Forest of Sure Things, Megan Snyder-Camp
Traffic with Macbeth, Larissa Szporluk
Archicembalo, G. C. Waldrep
Dogged Hearts, Ellen Doré Watson
Monkey Lightning, Martha Zweig

See our complete backlist at www.tupelopress.org

CPSIA information can be obtained at www.ICGtesting.com
Printed in the USA
BVOW01s0147060514

352247BV00002B/9/P